FRACTURED
not broken
a Memoir

by

Kelly Schaefer

with

M. WEIDENBENNER

Published by Kelly Schaefer LLC with R. Publishing, LLC.
Cover design by Cathy Helms of Avalon Graphics.
Many of the photos are courtesy of *The Herald*, Jasper, Indiana, and David Pierini, photographer and friend.
Editing by Vie Herlocker.
Pineapple icon by Christopher T. Howlett through The Noun Project

ISBN: 978-0-9863362-2-5

Endorsements

"Life has its tragic moments of defeat, setbacks, and fracturing for everyone. No one can escape events of emotional, sometimes physical pain. Kelly's story proves, however, that individual momentum, personal progress, and genuine achievement can still be attained. Her courage and optimism are uplifting. Open these pages and experience the joy of ultimate victory."

Dr. Dennis E. Hensley, author
Jesus in All Four Seasons

"Oh, how I relate to these pages! This book has been a true encouragement to me. Thank you Kelly for sharing your story – the loss and the unexpected joy – so that each reader can be uplifted knowing there is a full, rich life available to those who lean in to our Lord Jesus. Mike and I look forward to joining you and Shawn on the heavenly dance floor one day!"

Renée Bondi
Still, I Will Praise

"Rarely if ever do we choose our crosses in life. We often have the choice, however, of embracing life's challenges or allowing them to defeat us. Adversity has a way of bringing out the best or the worst in us. Life is changed, in such moments, but not ended. This is a real life story of heroic virtue—especially of courage, humility and generosity—a triumph of faith, hope, and love. Though there are many characters involved, as told through the main character, Kelly, this story involves the very essence of the human spirit, family and community. To know Kelly and her journey of miracles is to know that *with God all things are possible.*"

Most Reverend Charles C. Thompson
Bishop of Evansville

"I was so moved by the courageous journey of Kelly in *Fractured, not Broken* that I made a list of people I want to share it with. It would be an enormously helpful book for anyone facing overwhelming difficulties, but especially for anyone who has a loved one who is a quadriplegic. I know I will never look at another person in a wheelchair the same way after reading Kelly's story. This is a book I will read more than once."

Patricia Bradley
Gone Without a Trace

(David Pierini/*The Herald*)

(Me and my brother, Jason)

Chapter One

One day can make your life; one day can ruin your life.
All life is is four or five big days that change everything.
Riding in Cars with Boys

July 10, 1999

I don't remember what Eric or I wore that day, or what we ate that morning, but I remember feeling invincible, freer than a kite in the wind, flying high in love, and looking forward to a new life in Arizona. We were young lovers, college kids with the world at our fingertips, seizing opportunities that would take us places we'd never been, confident we'd have fun on our way.

But then everything changed.

For a long time after that day, I wished I'd died. How naive I was to

believe I was untouchable, that my *cake* life would go on forever.
Nothing was forever.

It was a dark night, dark in the way most traumatic stories start. The summer air was as hot as my passion for Eric, my boyfriend of almost three years. He was vacationing with me and my family—Mom, my stepdad, Andy, and my brothers Jason, Ryan, Ted, and Tyler—on a dude ranch in Durango, Colorado, riding horses, hiking, and shooting archery.

It was our last day of vacation. Tomorrow we'd fly back to Indiana. I hated endings. Even in my favorite TV shows, I dreaded the end of the season knowing I'd have to wait until fall to see the characters again.

I didn't want our fun to end because school would start again, and since Eric and I were transferring from Indiana University to the University of Arizona, I'd be far from my family and friends in southern Indiana.

For our last-night event, a group of us decided to drive into Durango to attend the local fair. Before heading into town, Eric and I waited for the others in the parking lot at the ranch. Eric circled me in his arms, his breath warm against my face, and his lips near mine. "I love you and what's ahead of us. No matter what happened in the past, we're forever, Kelly." He set his hands on my waist and lifted me *cheerleader style* until my eyes were level with his.

"Get a room," Jason, my seventeen-year-old brother, said as he approached.

Eric laughed and set me on the ground.

Several of the other young ranchers gathered with us. Stephanie, a ranch hand, wanted to celebrate her twentieth birthday, so she'd invited many of the other ranch hands and guests to go.

She pulled up in her small purple truck. "Hop in the bed."

I moved toward the truck, but Eric held me back. "Let's wait and go with John in his car. It's safer."

John was a ranch hand, too, a college guy, who worked at the dude ranch for the summer. We didn't know him before vacationing there, but we had become friends during the week.

"I'm not going," Jason said. "I don't want to hold you back from the bars."

Most in the group were twenty-one, but those who weren't had fake IDs.

"We're not going to the bars," Eric said. "Come with us."

Jason finally agreed.

John waved a few of us over to his brown Taurus. Jason, Eric, and I climbed in the back seat. JoAnne and Brian, two other ranch hands, sat in the front seat with John.

He pulled out onto the highway following Stephanie's truck. Eleven kids sat in the open bed of her purple Toyota, their hair and T-shirts flapping in the wind. The summer air smelled of pine trees from the nearby forest.

John talked to JoAnne and Brian in the front seat, while the three of us in the back seat had our own conversation.

"Out of all the schools to transfer to," Jason said to Eric, "why did you choose to play for Arizona? It's too far. I'll never get to go. And the cheerleaders are hotter there."

I heaved my elbow into Jason's side. "How do you know?"

Eric laughed and squeezed my hand then reached around me and slugged Jason. "We'll have to arrange for you to come as a *prospect*."

Jason laughed and his eyes got big. "That would be awesome. When?"

Months before, Jason had visited us at IU and Eric had told a few girls that Jason was an IU basketball prospect, which was a total lie. The girls flirted with him all night, and Jason wore a grin for days.

"Maybe you could come after your football season is over," Eric said.

Up ahead, the dark sky glowed from Durango's city lights. Our car climbed and twisted with the road.

Then in an instant—in the time it took me to inhale—a pair of headlights, one dim light and one bright one, crossed the centerline, and grazed the back end of Stephanie's truck. Her truck swerved. Bodies spilled onto the road like watermelon off a produce truck.

I held my breath. The headlights careened toward us.

Closer. Closer.

Someone screamed. Others told me later the screams were mine.

The last thing I remembered was the curve in the road and the headlights—especially the dim one.

Then everything went black. The curtain closed. The Kelly Ann Craig I'd been for nineteen years had a scene change.

Earlier That Same Day
Durango, Colorado

On that bright summer Saturday, in the distance of the plush San Juan National Forest, Willy Short woke from a deep sleep. The house was quiet except for cars zooming by and a neighbor's muffled radio sounding in the distance.

Zach Ridgewall, Willy's roommate, must have gone out. Willy sighed and enjoyed the quiet of Zach's absence. He stepped over dirty clothes and into the bathroom and caught sight of his black eye in the mirror. *Damn you, Ridgewall. It looks worse today.*

He threw on a pair of shorts and a T-shirt and went outside to have a smoke.

Shortly after, around 11:30, Zach pulled into the driveway in a white truck. He entered the kitchen where Willy was making breakfast, and threw the keys on the countertop.

"Whose truck you driving?"

"Boss's. He let me borrow it since mine died." Zach opened the fridge, pulled out a can of beer, and popped the top.

"That's cool." Willy flipped the egg in the frying pan. "Hey, can we do laundry at your old lady's?"

"Yeah, she won't care."

The two men spent the rest of the day doing laundry, watching TV, and getting haircuts. During that time, Zach drank four mudslides, a combination of Kahlua and vodka, and several more beers. In the early evening, Zach stopped at a local bar along the Animas River on College Avenue to pick up more alcohol.

Willy watched Zach head into the crowded bar, his gait slightly off-balanced. Willy shifted to the driver's seat.

Zach returned to the truck and opened the driver's side door. "What are you doing? I'm driving."

"I need to drive."

"Get out of the effing driver's seat, or I'll put you in the passenger seat myself."

Willy remembered his black eye from Zach's drunken temper two days prior and didn't doubt that Zach would throw him around. He moved over.

It was approximately 8:30 p.m.

The two men returned to their place where Zach drank more beer. At about 9:15, Zach reached for the truck keys. "I need to return the boss's truck. We can sleep there for the night. That way we'll have a ride to work in the morning."

"You shouldn't drive."

"We're going and I'm driving," Zach said, and lumbered out the front door.

Willy considered taking the keys from Zach, but didn't want to spark his temper. Willy needed to keep Zach under control, but when he peeled out of the driveway, Willy knew he was in trouble. He buckled his seatbelt.

As Zach wove down Florida Road, Willy glanced at the speedometer, which neared the seventy-miles-an-hour mark. "The speed limit is only forty-five here, man."

"Shut the f— up."

Willy flinched. The mountainous road ascended and twisted. How had he thought he could keep Zach under control? "You better slow down. This is my life too."

"Shut your effing trap."

The truck crossed the double yellow line. Headlights glared. Willy's body went rigid. "Look out!"

Zach veered across the center at the top of the curve, clipping the back corner of a small truck.

Willy yelled and shrank down into the seat, and a second later, his body juddered forward when the truck smashed into the front corner of another vehicle. He grunted as the seatbelt seized his chest and shoulder.

Sounds of metal against metal grinded, then a hissing noise

permeated the damp air.

Several seconds later, an eerie silence fell. Nothing moved. No one spoke. A strong odor wafted around them. Gasoline? Oil? Transmission fluid?

Willy moaned and cussed. People in the road shouted. A girl's high-pitched wail cut through the air.

"Oh, my God." someone cried.

"You asshole. Look what you did!" another person shouted from the road.

Zach groaned, his body pinned inside the door. "Shut the hell up!" he barked back to his victims.

Someone cried a pain-filled sob.

Another person knelt at the side of the road and prayed.

Willy couldn't move. He was frozen in a real life nightmare.

(The Durango Herald)

Chapter Two

You never know what's coming around the corner of your life;
the best you can do is what you're doing.
Margo Philpott, the nurse

Margo rolled down her passenger window and inhaled the woody scent of the Ponderosa Forest while her husband drove along the dark highway toward Durango. Summer's humid air pressed into the wrinkles of her cotton shirt. She turned in her seat to talk to her husband and her two teenage sons in the back seat. "Where should we go for Christmas break this year?" Every year since her boys were in middle school they planned their Christmas break skiing in the mountains.

"I don't want to ski this year," her oldest son said. "I want to learn how to board instead."

Margo listened and sighed. She was confident he'd learn, too. That was the beauty of youth. Kids had no fear, unlike her. She'd stick with what she knew—skiing the same way she had since she was in her twenties.

As they approached Durango's city limits down in the valley, the highway weaved and dipped until suddenly the cars ahead slowed to a crawl. Red brake lights flashed, illuminating the dark road. Margo's husband pumped the brakes until the car stopped, and after a few minutes of not going anywhere, he put the car in Park. "Wonder what the holdup is?"

Margo stuck her head out of her window. Voices in the distance shouted, but she couldn't see past the bend in the road.

A man, two cars up, stepped out of his car and stood on the shoulder of the road staring up ahead.

Two teenagers walked toward him. "There's been an accident! We need blankets and a doctor!"

"I'm a nurse," Margo called out her window. "What happened?"

Before she had time to open her door, the two teenagers ran to her and practically lifted her out of the car.

"We need you," one breathless teen said. "There's been a bad accident. Kids are splattered all over the highway."

"It's bad," the other kid said.

"What happened?" Margo followed them, her flip-flops snapping as she ran up the hill.

"A truck crossed the center line and grazed a truck and hit a car," one teen said.

"I'm an OB nurse. I deliver babies," Margo said. "I'm not sure how I can help, but I'll try." She prayed, *Dear God, show me what to do. Guide me.* Her mind shifted into nurse-mode, preparing to triage the victims.

At the top of the hill, kids groans filled the air. Bodies were splayed over the ground, silhouetted against the headlights of a car someone had parked at an angle to shower light on the accident scene. A smashed truck faced the mangled car.

The air smelled of metal, rubber, and petroleum products. A radiator hissed slow and constant, like the sound of potatoes boiling over the sides of a pot. Fluid leaked from the car onto the hot pavement causing steamy fog to float around the scene.

A young man knelt in the shoulder of the road, head bowed, hands folded in prayer.

Margo approached the first victim, a girl who sat on the side of the road, rocking and holding her arm, which was bent at the wrong angle. "Keep your arm close to your body, like this." Margo guided her.

The girl nodded, grimaced, and pulled her arm in close to her body.

"An ambulance is coming." Margo patted the girl's leg and hurried to the next victim. The girl could respond. Her life wasn't in immediate danger.

Another guy held his bloodied leg. Girls cried. Margo checked them out. If they could move and talk, she continued to the next patient. She quickly examined at least six kids, all without life-threatening injuries, and proceeded to the more serious victims.

One young man sat outside the wrecked car's door, dazed. Blood spurted from an open gash at his ear down to his neck. Had he torn his temporal artery? "I'm bleeding," he said, as if surprised.

Another young man, who sat beside the bleeding one, had taken his T-shirt off to help.

Margo knelt beside them and addressed the bare-chested man. "Hold your shirt over his wound. Apply pressure here," she demonstrated. "Can you do that until the ambulance arrives?"

The man nodded.

"Press firmly." She gazed into the car beside the bleeding man. Two teens were in the back seat—knee-to-knee—one girl, one boy. The girl, who hung half in the car and half out, whimpered and cried for help.

Margo knelt at her side, placed a hand on her arm, and checked her pulse. It was slow, but she could talk and breathe. "Help is on its way."

"I'm tingling," the girl said.

"Try not to move. Be still. We'll get you to an emergency room soon."

Margo hated to leave the girl, but needed to triage the others. She rushed to the other side of the car.

"Hey, get me the hell out of here!" A man hollered from the smashed truck, his words slurred. He was pinned behind the truck's door, but since he could breathe, Margo knew he didn't need immediate help. She continued to the car.

"Shut up you asshole," someone said to the truck driver. "Look what you did."

Margo approached the driver's side of the car where an older man yanked at the dented door, working to get it open. Finally, with an eerie groan, the door fell off its hinges and revealed the driver's body. Margo knelt at his side.

The steering wheel had imbedded in his chest, and blood oozed at the place of impact. The young man raked in shallow breaths.

She took his warm hand and held it. *What if this were my son? This is someone's child.* A lump rose in her throat. "Help is on its way," she said, but she doubted anyone could save his life.

Time slowed. She wanted to breathe for him, to make everything better. Tears filled her eyes as she watched him struggle. All she could give him were words. "I'm here. Help is on its way. Hang on. We're getting you help right now." One second felt like eternity. *Breathe. Keep breathing.* She comforted him, reassured him, while fighting tears and praying for God to help him. When his gasping subsided, she slowly lowered his hand. Tears trickled down her cheek.

Margo moved to the back seat—to the other boy. She bent her body into the mangled metal and reached in to him. His body lay limp, his head in the middle of the crunched seat, his face nicked and bloodied, his hands curling in at the wrists, balling into tight fists, toward his body, then away from his body—posturing—a sign of brain trauma. She bit her lip and placed her fingers on his neck, checking for a pulse, feeling the slow, erratic beats. "Can you hear me?"

Nothing.

The boy looked about the same age as her oldest son—a senior in high school. Except, this boy was fair-haired and built like a football player. She moved her lips close to his ear. "Help is on its way."

But where was the help? How long did it take to get there? These kids needed medical attention. *Now.*

There was nothing more she could do. She let out a helpless cry and looked out over the car. She saw the silhouette of her husband handing his cell phone to someone, her son wrapping his jacket around another kid.

The scene was surreal. Minutes ago, in the comfort of her own car with her family, everything had been calm and familiar, but now mayhem surrounded her. A feeble whimper came from the front seat, beneath the dash. Margo's eyes flashed forward at movement. How could a body even fit under there? She left the boy in the back and hurried to the front to help the girl who cried, hunched over, one hand holding her abdomen and the other covering her face. Blood oozed between her fingers and dripped onto her shirt.

Margo's heartbeat raced. Even though she'd been trained to save lives, this was impossible. She had no medical supplies and no assistance. "Help is on its way."

Finally, sirens sounded in the distance. Their shrill warning sliced through the air. Flashing lights from a police car sped toward them.

Margo almost cried as relief washed over her.

Chapter Three

Then it hits you so much harder than you ever thought it would.
Matchbox Twenty

Nine minutes after he was dispatched, Officer Perry sped along the shoulder of the road on Durango's highway and arrived at the accident scene. His flashing lights dimmed from the steam rising from the hot pavement. He parked his car next to a white truck and jumped out with his clipboard. Looking around, he realized he was the first responder.

The mass of bodies scattered in the dusk stopped him cold. A man cussed, girls cried, a radiator hissed, and loud groans permeated the scene.

A woman wearing a T-shirt and flip-flops rushed up to him. "I'm a nurse. I've triaged the kids. There are several severely injured in this car." She explained the rest of her triage findings.

Officer Perry radioed them in, requesting the JAWS extraction team. "There's a whole load of bodies here. Send at least five ambulances."

"They're on their way," the dispatcher answered. "They should arrive any minute."

A young man approached the officer. "Sir, can I tell you what happened?"

Officer Perry handed the man a pen and the clipboard. "Write your name here. Can you draw a picture of the scene and get the names, addresses, and phone numbers of all the people who were in each vehicle? Can you do that for me?"

The young man nodded, taking the clipboard from the officer.

Perry returned to his cruiser to grab another clipboard when the fire trucks and the EMTs arrived. Perry proceeded to the white truck. The driver was still behind the wheel, cocooned in the door.

"Hey, help me out of here."

"Are you hurt?" Perry asked.

"Screw you. What the hell do you think?" The truck driver had alcohol on his breath and empty beer cans in the bed of the truck.

"What's your name?"

"Zach Ridgewall. Now get me the hell out of here."

Perry ignored him and moved to the other side of the truck to where a passenger sat bent over, holding his bloodied head.

"You guys been drinking?" Perry asked.

The passenger, a man maybe in his twenties, rocked back and forth. He nodded. "Some, but I haven't as much as him." He pointed to the driver. "I tried to take his keys away, but he wouldn't give them to me."

Perry asked his name and scribbled it onto his clipboard.

Dan Imming, an EMT, sped to the scene in his ambulance. Sirens blared. He weaved in and out of traffic. Even though he'd worked as a tech for ten years, his adrenaline still energized his senses, putting them on hyperalert. He approached the scene. Everything slowed around him. Like a computer, Dan's movements became controlled and purposeful. He diagnosed and executed an action plan based on his triage findings.

Injured kids huddled on the shoulder of the road, but at first glance, their lives weren't at risk. They had lacerations, hematomas, and possible broken bones. The worst injuries would be in the crushed car.

Officer Perry greeted Dan and briefed him on the accident. They worked the same shift and their paths crossed often with accidents and domestic violence.

Through discipline and training, Dan began to make order of the mess. He combed every minute detail, recognizing broken bones and other injuries he was trained to see. Every second mattered.

A woman's voice sounded. "We need an ambulance over here."

Dan went to the woman who stood waving next to the crushed car. "I'm a nurse. I've triaged the patients." She gave him her summation of the injured, sounding out of breath.

Dan nodded and thanked her. Steve, Dan's partner, was already on a two-way radio with Mercy Medical Center. The two men quickly assessed the victims, relayed the injuries and requested equipment. Four more ambulances and the JAWS extraction team arrived. Dan moved to the shoulder of the road and stood on a large boulder that towered above the scene where he could orchestrate the actions of the arriving EMTs and shout orders. To one, he said, "You get the girl hanging out of the car there. Get her on a board."

He turned to the JAWS team. "We need two people cut out of the car. The driver and the kid in the back seat."

The truck driver bellowed, "Hey! You need to get me out of here, too!"

The man sitting next to the car with a neck wound called back to him. "Shut up, you asshole."

The JAWS crew positioned their lights and their trucks began the loud, roaring extraction.

Dan pointed and ordered the EMTs to place bodies on boards. The nurse stayed with the kid in the back seat who seemed to have sustained head trauma. The tech placed him on a board and loaded him into an ambulance. There weren't enough ambulances for the injured. The techs loaded thirteen victims into the ambulances and sped to Mercy Medical.

The man with the neck wound sagged against the car, his friend still applying pressure to the wound. The T-shirt was thoroughly saturated with blood. Dan shouted to the last EMT. "Get this guy with the neck wound on a board! Hook him to an IV. Stat!"

The tech, with help from the fire chief, lifted the young man onto a long board, fastened bandages around his neck, and strapped him down. "What's your name?" the tech asked as he took the victim's vitals.

"Eric."

"Can you wiggle your toes, Eric?"

He did.

They lifted him to the ambulance and inserted two IV lines attached to bags.

Meanwhile, the JAWS tech freed the truck driver and Officer Perry read him his rights and cuffed him. But by that time, most of the ambulances had left.

Dan nodded to Perry. "Load him in my truck with the neck wound victim. He can sit on the bench."

Perry assisted the drunk driver and loaded him into the same ambulance with Eric. Perry sat the drunk on the bench, exited the vehicle, and turned to Dan. "I'll meet you at Mercy."

Dan nodded.

Perry closed the ambulance doors, leaving Dan with both patients.

Dan called to the fire chief, who was the only man left to drive the ambulance. "Let's go." He stood over Eric and grew concerned by his ashen skin. The kid had lost too much blood. They needed to clamp the artery. Soon. The bleeding wouldn't stop.

The drunk driver cussed. Dan turned to the drunk. "Knock it off."

Eric thrashed his body side to side. "Shut up."

Dan gripped Eric's shoulders tightly. "Ignore him."

Eric busted out of the restraints and flew off the gurney. He pressed his large body up against Dan and pinned him to the wall of the ambulance. "Get that asshole out of here!"

The truck driver remained seated. "What's the big freakin' deal?"

"You need to lie down—now," Dan said to Eric forcefully. "I need to keep firm pressure on your wound or you'll bleed to death." Eric's reaction was typical of someone in shock, but Dan knew the man would collapse any moment from the extreme loss of blood. "Ignore him and lie back down," he ordered again.

Eric slowly backed off and laid back on the gurney.

"We're on our way to the ER," Dan told Eric, refastening his chest restraints. Dan shoved his hands back over the bandages applying pressure to the gushing wound.

Chapter Four

Strong women don't play victim, they don't make themselves look pitiful, and they don't point fingers. They stand and deal.
Mandy Hale

My mom, Brenda Krempp, could have written that quote if she was a writer. She isn't, but she's a courageous woman.

Once when I was a little girl, Dad stepped on her face. It only happened once, but a girl remembers things like that. I didn't know what to do. Mom was crying, so I offered her a granola bar.

I don't remember parts of my childhood, and I seldom asked because Mom wanted to forget her life with Dad, and I didn't want to hurt Andy's feelings by asking. Andy is my awesome stepdad.

Mom's marriage with Dad was difficult. He would drink and pin her arms behind her back and pull her hair, and when she couldn't take any more she would bounce back. She didn't dwell on sympathy. Instead, she shook off pain like it didn't hurt, but I knew it did.

It probably helped that Dad was sober enough to apologize the next day.

She thought her divorce would be the worst thing that ever happened to her, just like I thought it would be my only cross to bear. I was wrong. So was she.

9:30 p.m.
At the Dude Ranch

Brenda held her cards in her hand and stared across the table at Andy and two friends they'd met at the ranch. They were playing Hearts. Brenda had almost all spades—including the queen, the card nobody wanted to be stuck with unless they were going for all the tricks. Shania Twain played "That Don't Impress Me Much" on the radio. Brenda glanced at her watch. It was after 9:30 and the sun had finally set for the last day of their vacation. The room smelled of burned microwave popcorn.

"I still need to pack," Brenda said.

"Me too," her friend, Ginger, said.

Brenda hid her smile and strategized her hand. All she had to do was take the lead and watch her opponents follow suit. She'd take all the tricks and set everyone back twenty-six points.

The only problem was that the person with the two of clubs got to go first and she didn't have that card. *Darn.* She couldn't gain the lead. She had to throw off her spades. Andy took the first trick and played another club. But when Ginger threw a heart out onto Andy's lead, giving him a point, Brenda lost her opportunity to win.

Shoot.

Andy won that hand and gloated. "Do you want me to give you lessons?" he said to Brenda.

She smirked. "You rat." She hated to lose and he knew it. The music on the radio changed to George Strait's, "Write this Down."

While Ginger shuffled the cards for the next hand, Brenda asked Andy if the boys had packed yet.

"I doubt it," Andy said.

The cards were dealt. "Where are your older kids tonight?" Ginger asked. "I didn't see them around."

"A bunch of them went into town to a carnival." Brenda placed the cards in her hand in order by suit. She took a sip of her Coke and turned when the director of the ranch burst through the door. Everyone froze.

"What's wrong?" They all asked at the same time.

The director was frantic. "There's been an accident. A car was hit by a drunk driver, and your kids were involved."

Sirens shrilling in the distance drowned out the song on the radio. Brenda's heart flipped in her chest. She bolted out of her chair. "Are they okay?"

The director wrung her hands. "Someone who saw them said they looked okay, that they weren't bleeding, but I don't know."

"Where are they now?" Andy asked, jumping up to stand by Brenda.

"The accident was on the highway north, toward Durango."

Brenda was already rushing out the door, Andy holding her arm. "Where did they take them? He called over his shoulder.

"Most likely to Mercy Medical Center," the director said, "north on the highway about five miles."

Brenda fidgeted in their rented van as Andy turned onto the road out of the ranch. By the time they made it to the highway, the siren's blaring had stopped, but the traffic wasn't allowing them to move. They sat idle behind a long line of cars.

"How are we supposed to get through this?" Brenda said, biting her lip. Her head pounded. *How bad was the accident? Who was injured?* "Isn't there another way to the hospital?"

"This is the only road leading into town," Andy said. He reached over and patted Brenda's leg, flipped his emergency flashers on, and veered onto the shoulder of the road.

The night's darkness pressed into Brenda's fears.

Andy passed other vehicles.

People honked and flipped them the bird.

Andy rolled down his window and shouted to other drivers. "Our kids were in the accident! We have to get to the hospital."

A tow truck with flashing lights followed them along the shoulder.

Traffic parted and Andy continued on the shoulder until they came to the crash site in the middle of the road. Glass glittered and reflected off headlights from the oncoming cars. A purple truck sat at the curbside. A smashed truck faced the car.

Brenda gasped and clamped a hand over her mouth.

A police officer directed traffic.

Andy leaned out his window where the cop stood. "Our kids were in the accident. Is there a way to get to the hospital faster than this?"

The officer blew his whistle and waved another cop over. "Escort these people to the hospital." He stopped traffic until the young officer climbed into his car and led the way with his flashers blinking.

Andy followed.

"Did you see that car?" Brenda said. "There's nothing... left... of it. Certainly Kelly and Jason weren't in there." She trembled and her stomach churned acid.

Andy didn't answer.

Tears fell as Brenda cried. "Why did those kids have to go into town anyway?"

Brenda and Andy hurried into Mercy Medical Center's emergency entrance. The small ER waiting room smelled of stale coffee and sanitizer. Bloodied and bandaged teens cried and held each other. Some sat on the edge of their seats with tissues in their hands.

Brenda rushed up to the receptionist's desk. "My kids were brought in here from the accident—Kelly and Jason Craig. Can we see them?"

The receptionist, a middle-aged woman dressed in a wine-colored uniform, peered at them. "I'll let the doctor know you're here. Please have a seat."

Andy took Brenda's arm and led her to an open chair.

On her way, Brenda scanned the other people—mothers, fathers, and children. Some glanced at her. She approached two teens who had abrasions on their faces. "Were you in that accident?"

They nodded.

"What happened?"

They explained how the drunk driver in the truck had crossed the centerline and grazed the truck they were in.

"Were Kelly and Jason in the truck?" she asked them.

They frowned. "They were in the car, but they weren't bleeding," someone said.

Good, maybe they weren't hurt that badly.

Andy patted her arm.

The double ER doors opened and a dark-haired lady in flip-flops, shorts, and a bloodstained shirt stepped out and approached them.

"Are you Jason and Kelly's parents?" The lady's eyes brimmed with tears.

Brenda turned to her. "Yes."

"My name is Margo Philpott. I'm an OB nurse, but I happened to be at the crash site after it happened, so I'm volunteering right now." Her voice shook. "The ER is crazy because so many kids were injured, but the doctor asked me to give you an update." She paused. "Jason is unconscious and Kelly has a neck injury. The doctors are taking X-rays."

"They'll be okay though, right?" Brenda asked.

The nurse shrugged. "We don't know the extent of their injuries. The doctors have called in additional medical staff, and they're doing CT scans, blood tests, and evaluating each patient. We'll let you know when we know more."

"When can we see them?" Andy asked.

"Give the staff a few more minutes to finish the tests, and I'll bring you back." She patted Brenda's arm. "Hopefully it'll be soon."

Several minutes later, the nurse reappeared and waved for them to follow her.

Brenda trembled as Andy held her arm and they followed the nurse beyond the double doors. Someone moaned and shouted and a voice that sounded like Eric's cussed at someone. Machines beeped and swooshed. Hospital staff crossed in and out of curtained patient rooms, their brows furrowed, their postures harried. Someone rolled a gurney down the hallway with a sheet over a patient.

Brenda gasped. "Who's that?"

The nurse hesitated. "The driver of the car. He didn't make it." Tears filled her eyes. "Jason and Kelly are in the trauma rooms on this side." She pointed to the left.

Brenda burst into tears. Andy followed her into a room where Kelly lay on a gurney, wearing a neck brace, her eyes closed. They started toward her when a man in a white lab coat greeted them.

"Are you Kelly's parents?" the doctor asked.

"Yes, I'm her mother and this is her stepfather, Andy Krempp. What's wrong with her?"

"I'm Dr. Cartier. Unfortunately, Kelly has a spinal cord injury." He showed them the x-rays on the screen, pointing to the exact location. "She's sustained a C-4 fracture and this part of her spinal cord is bruised." He paused. "I'm sorry. It appears that she's paralyzed from her neck down."

Brenda's knees buckled and she fell into a heap on the floor. She envisioned Christopher Reeve, his motorized chair, and his labored breathing through a ventilator. Andy took her elbows and steadied her until she could stand again. Someone pulled up a chair for her to sit on.

"Can you fix it?" Brenda asked, her voice shaking.

Dr. Cartier shook his head. "We need to move her to a spine facility. The specialists there will be able to tell you more. We're not equipped to handle this type of injury here."

"Can another doctor fix it?" Brenda asked.

The doctor shrugged. "I don't know, but you can hope."

Brenda crossed to Kelly. Surely the doctor was wrong. He had to be. "Kelly, move your arm."

Kelly's eyes fluttered open, like they were trying to focus, but couldn't, like she couldn't comprehend Brenda's simple request.

"Why did you get in that car, Kelly?"

"What?" she asked, her voice barely above a whisper. "Everything tingles."

Brenda turned to the doctor. "What if you're wrong?"

The doctor shrugged. "I hope I am. Her cord doesn't appear to be severed, so she might regain some mobility."

"Kelly," Brenda moved to the end of the gurney. "Wiggle your toes."

Nothing.

"What about Jason?" Andy asked.

The doctor turned to him. "He suffered severe brain trauma and is critical right now. We've done an ECG and it shows that he has minimal brain activity. He needs to be transferred to a trauma center. The closest one is in Farmington, New Mexico. All we can do is keep him stable until we can airlift him to that facility."

"Is that where Kelly needs to go?"

"We could airlift her to a spine hospital in Colorado—the Craig Hospital—which is near Denver. Or we could airlift her to the same place Jason will go—the trauma center in New Mexico, which is about an hour away by car."

"What's the difference in hospitals?" Brenda asked, wiping her eyes with the back of her hand.

"Craig Hospital is one of the best hospitals for spine injuries, but not head trauma. But the hospital in New Mexico handles both head and neck injuries."

Brenda cried. "How can we be in two different places at one time?"

Andy took Brenda's hand. "Maybe we need to split up."

"How will that work? We still have Ryan, Ted, and Tyler to deal with." Brenda's voice climbed a notch.

"I could go to New Mexico with Jason and you could go to Colorado with Kelly," Andy said. "I'll call my parents to come out and help. They could take the other boys back home."

Brenda hiccupped a sob.

Andy turned to the doctor. "When do we need to let you know? I'd like to do a little research first."

"I understand," the doctor said, "but they need to go soon."

Brenda's stomach reeled. "Is Jason… going to…die?" Her words were barely audible.

The doctor shrugged. "He could go either way right now. I don't know."

"Can we see him?" Andy asked.

The doctor led Brenda and Andy to Jason's trauma room, which resembled Kelly's room. Hospital staff and emergency medical technicians raced in and out of patient rooms on their way.

Jason lay on a bed with a neck brace and tubes and wires projecting from his arms. A blood pressure monitor expanded and released around his arm.

Brenda approached him and placed her hand on his cheek. "Jay, it's Mom. Can you hear me?" She turned to Andy at her side. Tears spilled down her cheeks. "He looks like he's sleeping. He's not even banged up." She cried. "Why is this happening to us?"

Andy took a hold of her arm and tears filled his eyes too. "I don't know." He touched Jason's arm. "We're here for you, Jay. You're going to pull through, okay?"

Suddenly his whole body began to shake and convulse with spasms. Nurses rushed in. "He's having a seizure. You'll have to wait outside."

"Oh, my God," Brenda cried and dashed to the doorway, Andy beside her.

They watched an orderly hold Jason down while a nurse inserted meds into his IV bag.

Brenda buried her head in Andy's chest. "I can't believe this is happening."

Once Jason's body calmed, they went to his side and comforted him. Brenda took his hand. "We're here, Jason."

Eric shouted from another room.

"Eric. Can we see him?" Brenda said to a nearby nurse.

The nurse nodded. "He's in the room across the hall."

She and Andy went to his room. He was lying on a gurney. A doctor and an EMT were holding him down, trying to clamp his neck wound. Eric seemed disoriented, shouting obscenities at the drunk driver in the next room.

The drunk driver shouted back. A woman's voice from the drunken man's room told him to shut up or they would leave him there without care.

"We need to call Eric's mom," Brenda said to Andy. But she didn't know her phone number and Eric wasn't coherent enough to give it. She returned to Kelly's room. "What's Eric's mother's phone number?"

"Why?" Kelly asked, her voice barely audible.

"We need to let her know about the accident." Brenda's mind reeled. If Eric could never play basketball again, his family might blame them. The sooner she called the better.

Kelly recited the number and Andy jotted it down.

Brenda stepped into the hallway away from the kids and called Eric's mother.

Minutes later, Brenda consulted her brother, who was knowledgeable about orthopedic hospitals, and gained information about Craig Hospital versus San Juan Regional Medical Center in New Mexico. Craig was the better place for Kelly, but how could Brenda possibly manage being in two different places? How could she choose which child to stay with? Yes, she and Andy could split up, but she needed Andy with her. They needed to be together.

Either way, the decision intimidated her.

They finally decided to have both kids transferred to New Mexico. There was no feasible way to split up, especially being hundreds of miles from their home. It was bad enough that they were all the way out in Colorado. She couldn't imagine being separated too.

Chapter Five

Even when I walk through the darkest valley, I will not be afraid, for
you are close beside me.
Psalm 23:4 NLT

In the darkness, bits and pieces of my life appeared, random and disjointed.

First, I was a little girl, three years old, dressed in a swimsuit at my first pageant. I stood in a line with nineteen other three-, four-, and five-year-old girls at the Palos Heights poolside, the pool where Mom often showed off her perfect swan dive. The summer's sun had lightened my dark hair to a dirty blond and bronzed my skin.

Mom and Dad stood in the crowd, smiling and watching with the rest of the families, waiting for the winner to be announced. Mom held Jason at her hip, his fine hair the color of butter. Dad sported a Miller Lite in his palm.

"And the winner of the Miss Pink Tomato is," the announcer said,

"Kelly Craig."
The audience clapped. Cameras flashed.

Then the arguing started. Mom screamed at Dad. Dad's voice boomed after Mom. Harsh words spewed until Ryan was born, then Mom packed up me and my brothers and left Dad. We headed to Mom's hometown in Jasper, Indiana, a small German Catholic community.

Then I was eight, tumbling on the mats at gymnastics, working on my back handsprings, flipping my ponytail to the rhythm of the music.

Then I was thirteen, beaming because I'd performed my first back tuck.

In the next scene of my dark confusion, I skipped and bounced out to the center of the court with my squad, poms in hand, ready to cheer for the boys' basketball team. My heart raced and skipped at the excitement. Soon I'd be attending the National Cheerleading competition in Dallas. I spotted Mom, Andy, and my brothers applauding in the crowd.

Their cheers sent a chill along my arms. I tingled from my toes to the top of my head.

But wait. This was a different kind of tingling. My limbs felt as disjointed as the memories floating in my head. Voices loomed around me. They made no sense. The sound bounced and droned. I couldn't understand what anyone was saying.

Eric?

His strong, hard, and supportive arms embraced me. My fingers wandered up to his wavy hair and roamed down to the divot of his dimple on his check. My lips flickered over his parting ones, celebrating our two years together.

Suddenly, a loud noise thundered close to my ear, and a drill bored into the side of my head. I wanted to open my eyes, but they were too heavy. "Mom?"

Heels clicked on the floor. "I'm here, Kelly. Why did you get in that car?"

Car? What was she talking about? Something squeezed my arm. "What?"

"You were in an accident."

Accident? A dense fog floated in my mind. A vision of Eric, Jason, and me getting into the car and the headlight coming toward us rocketed into my memory. "What happened?"

"A drunk driver hit your car. Jason and Eric are in other trauma rooms."

"Trauma?"

"Eric will be fine. Thank God." She paused. "The last thing … we need … is being responsible for his …" She let her voice trail. "Jason … has a brain injury."

I didn't have to look at her to know she was crying. "Is he going to be okay?"

"We don't know." Her voice shook. "Can you move your toes?"

I wiggled my toes. Or thought I did.

"The doctor said … you're paral—." She sobbed too hard to speak.

I wanted to turn toward her, but my head was locked in a brace. "What?"

She sucked in a breath. "You are … you are paralyzed."

Paralyzed? That was beyond my comprehension. Surely not. But I was alive. Yes, I was alive. I pictured myself in a wheelchair struggling to roll up a hill. "I can't move my legs?"

Mom caressed my shoulder while choking out the words. "They say you'll be a quadriplegic. That means you won't be able to move your arms or legs."

I won't be able to move my arms? I tried to move them. They were moving, weren't they? No, they weren't. It was like someone had draped a heavy blanket over me. I saw Christopher Reeves sitting helpless in his chair. Would that be me?

The drugs fogged my mind and drooped my eyelids. Mom and the other voices faded into the distance.

"Kelly," a man said. "I'm the hospital chaplain. Can I pray with you?"

I slowly remembered where I was. Squinting my eyes open, I asked, "Am I going to die?"

He didn't answer. Did that mean I was dying? Everything was numb. Certainly I wasn't that bad. How could I be if I had no pain? Oh, yes. They were giving me pain medicine. That was the only explanation.

The chaplain recited the Lord's Prayer and waved the sign of the cross above my forehead.

After he left, I let myself fall asleep again hoping everything would be better when I woke.

"Kelly, I'm Dr. Cartier."

I raised my heavy lids. A man in a lab coat stood over me.

"We're transferring you to another hospital that is better equipped to handle your injury. You're breathing on your own. That's a good sign."

What? Breathing on my own was a good sign? Why wouldn't I be able to breathe on my own? I was beat-up, but not that bad. This would pass. I was young and in great shape. I'd heal quickly.

"Are you sure she's not okay?" Mom said. "She only looks bruised."

The doctor didn't answer.

"Kelly, try moving your arms," Mom said.

Didn't she ask me that a minute ago? I tried to move. I couldn't. "Mom?"

"I'm here," she said, lifting my arm, moving it up and down.

"How's Eric?"

"He's banged up, but he's going to be okay. I called his mom and told her what happened. His parents are coming out here."

Shutting my eyes, I prayed for the drugs to take me to that place where everything was safe and fun. I wanted to be enveloped in Eric's arms or sleep until it was time to wake up to the way everything was before.

Brenda and Andy stood side by side in Jason's trauma room. He was still fighting, but his life was on the edge. The machines swooshed and beeped, working to keep him alive.

The doctor entered the room. "Have you decided which child you want to transfer first?"

How could they possibly choose whom to send first? Brenda was supposed to be packing to go home now—not making life and death decisions for her children. "Does it matter?" she asked the doctor.

"Not really," he said. "There won't be a lot of time in between getting them there."

Brenda looked to Andy for a decision.

"Have them take Kelly first," Andy said. "You go with her. I'll wait with Jason until the chopper returns for him. Then I'll go back to Colorado Trails for the boys and drive to Farmington." He squeezed Brenda's shoulders. "Stay strong and keep Kelly and Jason upbeat. I'll get a hotel in Farmington and then meet you at the hospital."

Brenda nodded. "Okay." *Jason had to live. He just had to.* She turned to her son lying helpless before her and touched his cheek, noticing how his freckles seemed darker against his pale, pale skin. Would this be the last time she'd see him alive? Would this be the last time she'd touch his warm body and feel his breath against her palm? She bent and kissed him. "I don't want to leave, Jay, but I have to." She stopped to catch her breath and wiped her tears. "Andy will stay with you."

She sobbed again, her throat raw, leaning on Andy. "I wish he'd say something. Anything."

Andy put his arm around her.

She looked down and placed her finger in Jason's hand. "Squeeze my finger if you can hear me."

Nothing. He didn't budge.

She wiped her tears again. "Jay, give me a sign that you're going to be okay."

He didn't move.

She pressed her wet face into Andy's chest.

He held her tight, rubbed her back, and wiped his own tears. "Be strong. I'll be with you soon. San Juan Medical Center is only an hour away."

She nodded, forcing herself to stop crying. She had to fight to stay positive and strong for her kids.

Andy walked her back to Kelly's room and went to her bedside. Tears filled his eyes as he gently leaned over Kelly and kissed her forehead. "I'll see you in New Mexico."

"Okay," Kelly said, her voice small.

Brenda sucked in a breath and prayed, *God, please let my children live.* Her legs drooped like cooked noodles so she reached for the chair Andy scooted toward her. Two men arrived in blue uniforms, pulling a gurney alongside of them.

"Is this Kelly Craig?" one man asked.

"Yes, I'm her mother, Brenda." She stayed seated, clinging to the chair for composure. "This is Andy, Kelly's stepfather."

The man holding a clipboard and a pen nodded and introduced himself and his coworker. "We're the helicopter emergency technicians. I need you to sign the transfer papers." He handed Brenda the form. "We've made all the arrangements for a safe and smooth transition. Do you have any questions?"

Brenda shook her head. Andy stayed silent.

"Are you going with us?" one man asked.

"I am," Brenda said. She signed the form, her fingers trembling. "Andy is staying here."

Andy squeezed her shoulder.

"The ride is about fifteen minutes from the time we leave here until the moment we land," the tech said. "You're in good hands. We do this every day and have for years."

Even though he sounded reassuring, Brenda balled her hands into fists trying to stop them from shaking.

The tech moved to Kelly's bedside. "Kelly, we're going to transport you now. You'll feel the bed moving, but stay calm. This won't take long."

"Okay," Kelly said.

They placed the board beneath her, switched the IV tubes from the hospital bed to their gurney, and transferred her.

"Oh, gosh. Oh gosh," Kelly said. Every bump jolted her body. Even though she couldn't move, she still felt the pain that seared her neck.

After the tech locked Kelly in place, he wrapped her in blankets and turned to Brenda. "Here's a pair of ear plugs." He handed Brenda a little plastic package. "The chopper is loud."

Brenda took the plugs and opened the bag, while the tech placed plugs in Kelly's ears.

One of the Mercy Hospital nurses appeared with discharge papers. She promised Brenda she'd take good care of Jason until he was transferred. Brenda thanked her.

Andy waved one last time and turned to go.

Brenda sucked in another sob and followed the techs out of the room. She hated leaving her husband and son. This was it. She might never see Jason again.

The men escorted her and Kelly up the elevator that led to the roof, to the helipad where the chopper waited. As they exited the elevator, the noise of the engine roared from the exit door across the room.

They wheeled Kelly to the door. "The sound will make communicating almost impossible," the medic said to Brenda. "Are you ready?"

She nodded, but she wasn't ready for any of this. She loathed heights and shoved her hands deep into her jean's pockets to stop her nervousness, swallowed hard, and nodded for the man to proceed.

The medic opened the door that led to the chopper and out into the inky night. The whir and wind sucked Brenda's breath away. They motioned for her to climb into the back and fasten herself into a seat behind the pilot.

She'd never been this scared in her life—frightened for her children, her family, and her own life as the aircraft ascended into the skies. She squeezed her eyes tight and swallowed the bile rising in her throat. Adrenaline fisted inside her until she dared to open her eyes. The world twinkled below her.

The chopper glided across the cities, floating above the world's realities and problems. Oh, how she wished it could carry her back to their lives before the accident, back to their home, their healthy family, and safety.

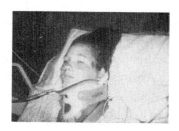

Chapter Six

Determine that the thing can and shall be done and then... find the way.
Abraham Lincoln

I was six years old, curled up in a ball on my bed, wearing my Barbie pajamas and giggling.

Dad bounded in the room to tuck me in, his heavy feet stomping. "Are you ready?" he asked in his deep, raspy, teasing voice.

I giggled and rolled into a tight ball. "Yes."

He lifted me into his arms high off the bed. "Here goes the cannonball."

I pinched my eyes shut in anticipation.

"Look out below," he said, and dropped me.

On the way down, my stomach dove like a roller coaster. I bounced and rolled on my bed and squealed. "Do it again."

He did it again and again, each time laughing and playing in his childish way.

My stomach kept flipping dizzily, but I couldn't see his face anymore.

I regained consciousness when the chopper landed and realized the stomach flutters were from the chopper pivoting, rotating, and swirling. The medics wheeled me into the San Juan Regional Medical Center in Farmington, New Mexico. After settling me into a room with Mom at my side, a doctor entered and explained the surgery to us.

"I'll insert screws and plates into your vertebrae so you can sit and keep your head up," he said.

I wanted to shout at him to hurry up and fix me so I could get on with my life and get to Arizona with Eric. This was really messing up my plans. I looked at Mom.

She swept a piece of hair off of my face and wiped my tears with her finger tips.

The doctor said they would perform surgery as soon as possible. All we could do was wait.

Brenda watched the nurses prep Kelly in a trauma room. They checked her vitals, urine bag, IV fluids, and neck brace, and jotted notes in her files. They talked to Kelly and seemed to see the person in the patient. For that, Brenda was grateful.

The surgeon introduced himself and asked Brenda if she had questions.

She didn't have experience with this sort of thing or time to research the procedure. The only question that came to mind was, "Will the surgery help her walk again?"

"We don't know. Her vertebra is fractured, but her spinal cord is only bruised, which is better than severed. This is called an incomplete injury, which means her recovery might be better than if it had been severed. It's still too early to know. Unfortunately, a neck fracture isn't like a broken leg that will heal in nine weeks in a cast and after the pins are inserted. This surgery is serious and necessary so she doesn't cause more damage to her neck. It'll give her the ability to hold her head up.

"What makes this surgery serious is that her spine is exposed. With any surgery, there is a risk of death, there's a risk that I could cause more damage, and she could end up with less mobility." He paused. "Or I could stabilize everything and she could regain mobility, but it can take up to a year for us to know what her final limitations are."

Brenda bit her lip and nodded, not trusting her voice. Tears streamed down her face, and she sucked in a sob.

"We can hope." He patted her arm. "I have to tell you everything that could go wrong before I perform the surgery. Before you sign the papers you need to know the risks."

She nodded. *I will pray.* "What exactly will you do?"

"I'll make a posterior cervical incision from here." He demonstrated and pointed to the back of his head. "It'll be about a six-inch incision. We'll have to shave the back of her head, but not all of it—only the area at the base of her hairline. We'll fuse the bones and take a graft from her hip. The surgery usually takes about four hours, but it'll be a few hours before we're ready to operate, so if you want to go have something to eat or a cup of coffee and return here, we'll let you know when we're ready to take her in."

"Is there a chapel here?"

The surgeon gave her directions.

Brenda turned to Kelly. "I'll be back in about fifteen minutes. I have to make a few phone calls and check to see where Jason will be."

After Brenda called family to beg for prayers, she followed the doctor's directions and took the elevator up to the chapel. The only thing she could do to help was pray. Miracles happened every day. Why not now? When the elevator door clanked open, she found the sign that indicated where the chapel was and followed the long corridor. Outside the dark double doors was a gold-plated sign, *Chapel.* She let herself in.

It was a quiet room, dimly lit, with rows of kneelers and a large wooden cross at the small altar. Several other people knelt with their heads bent in prayer. Brenda took a seat in a pew away from the others and knelt facing the crucifix.

At least Kelly was alive. Brenda couldn't give up hope that she'd make it through the surgery and hopefully be able to walk again. But what about Jason? Would he live? Certainly things would turn out okay. They had to. Yes, her children were injured, but they were strong. They'd always been strong. But were they strong enough?

Was she?

Her whole body trembled at what could happen next. She closed her eyes, but the room spun. She opened them again, focused on the crucifix, and prayed the Lord's Prayer.

Tragedy had never found its way into her life. She'd never lost a loved one. Pushing Kelly in a wheelchair or preparing Jason's funeral was unfathomable. Although she went to church every Sunday, Brenda had never prayed for something this close and personal, something so huge. Not only one life—but two. How was she supposed to pray? Should she bargain with God? Did that ever work? She prayed the prayers she knew well and wished she had a rosary, wished that she knew all the prayers to recite—not just the Lord's Prayer and the Hail Mary. She would learn the others soon, but for now she recited what she could.

Lord, we need two miracles. Please heal my children and let them live, God. They're both young and have their whole lives ahead of them. I promise that if You grant this request, I'll be at Your side for the rest of my life.

The thought of Kelly never walking down the aisle on her wedding day or Jason never throwing a football again jarred the knot in her throat. Tears spilled a slow stream down her face, but the sound of a chopper whirring overhead made her swallow hard and wipe her tears. It must be Jason. He needed her. She had to be strong.

(Me and my brothers before the accident)

Chapter Seven

Family means no one gets left behind or forgotten.
David Ogden Stiers

When the accident happened, twelve-year-old Ryan Craig was forced to stay at the ranch in the room to look after Ted and Tyler, his half-brothers. They stayed awake until almost one a.m. waiting for Mom and Andy, but fell asleep, not knowing what had happened to Kelly and Jason. Rumors whirled around the ranch that someone had died.

Ryan woke to a gentle nudge and opened his eyes. "Andy."

"We have to check out of our cabin. I'm taking you guys to the hospital."

Andy's cowlick spiked above his right ear, and his eyes were puffy and blood shot. Ryan doubted Andy had slept. "How are they?" Ryan lumbered out of bed.

Six-year-old Ted and eight-year-old Tyler woke and climbed out of their bunks to listen too.

"A chopper transferred Kelly and Jason to a different hospital located about an hour from here," Andy said. "Mom's there. We're going there now."

"What's wrong with them?" Ryan asked.

Andy cleared his throat and explained their injuries. "The doctors aren't sure Jason will make it."

Jason? Football player Jason? Not going to live? That seemed impossible.

Andy stooped over the suitcases opened on the floor. "You already packed. Thanks. Did you take everything out of the drawers? Even Jason's stuff?"

"Yep. Everything is there," Ryan said. *Everything except Jason's hidden stash of whiskey.*

The phone rang and Andy answered. He shared what had happened, his voice cracked, and he broke down, sobbing into the phone.

Ryan had never seen Andy cry. The air in the room turned hot and suffocated Ryan. His breath caught. Was Jason really going to die? Was Kelly?

Ryan sat in the back seat with Tyler and Ted while Andy drove to New Mexico. It seemed to take forever to get there. No one spoke for most of the way. Andy drove for miles across the sandy desert, crossing large rivers until they came upon a tall, massive L-shaped building. A large sign out front read, *San Juan Regional Medical Center.*

Inside, the receptionist told them that Kelly was in Room 200.

Andy sighed deeply, probably relieved she was still alive.

They took the elevator.

Kelly lay on a bed wearing a silver neck brace, staring up at the ceiling. Wires and IV tubes jetted from her still and body. Beeps echoed off the walls from a machine beside her bed. She didn't look hurt, except for the black and blue marks streaked across her arms. Ryan didn't get close enough for Kelly to see him. He stood toward the door, observing. He doubted Kelly even knew he was there. Mom sat in a chair at Kelly's side wearing the same clothes she'd worn the night before, her eyes swollen and bloodshot like Andy's. She glanced at Ryan and his brothers and then at Andy crossed the room and sat beside her.

"Jason is in room 240," she said.

"It feels like I'm moving, but I'm not." Kelly's voice sounded weak and small.

"Move your hand." Mom tapped Kelly's left hand.

Nothing.

"What about the other one?"

Nothing.

"Move your leg. Try," Mom insisted.

When Kelly didn't move, Ryan turned away, uncertain where to look. How could Kelly look uninjured yet be unable to move?

A man in a white lab coat entered the room and Mom and Andy eagerly looked up at him. He reached for Kelly's chart at the foot of her bed and skimmed its contents. He introduced himself as her surgeon. "Do you have any final questions before we take her into surgery?"

Mom and Andy stood, stepped toward him, and spoke to the doctor in hushed tones. After he left, they crossed the room and sat by Kelly again.

Minutes later, Andy's parents arrived—Grandma and Grandpa Krempp. They rushed past Ryan and his brothers at the door and headed toward Andy. Several nurses hurried into the room and squeezed Ryan farther away from Kelly.

Andy turned toward Ryan. "Why don't you boys go to the waiting room across the hall? We'll be there soon."

Tyler and Ted inched forward and huddled near Mom. Ryan slipped out and wandered down the corridor in search of room 240.

Light-footed and uncertain, Ryan glanced at each door number until he found Jason's room. He peeked inside, past the gray walls to where his brother lay. Taking a deep breath, he moved into the room. White surgical taped tubes protruded from Jason's nose and mouth. A metal brace encircled his neck too. Beeps echoed off the cold walls like in

Kelly's room. Ryan covered his nose with his hand and wished he could open a window. He would have preferred the smell of Jay's football jersey after a workout rather than the antiseptic odors that stuffed the room.

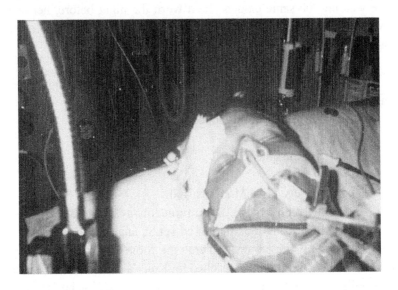

Jay lay flat on his back with his eyes closed. Ryan scooted a chair next to the bed. The boy in the bed didn't look like Jay. His face was puffy. Three wires trailed out the back of his head and hooked to a round gauge. Fluid drained from another tube out the back of his head into a bag. Ryan shuddered, fighting nausea. He choked back tears.

A lady in a white uniform entered. "Is he your brother?"

Ryan nodded.

"He looks different, doesn't he?" she said.

Ryan nodded again. "What are all those wires for?" He pointed to the back of Jay's head.

"They monitor the pressure in his brain." She pointed to the gauge at the front of his bed. "See this dial here?"

Ryan looked closer, watching the hand on the dial fluctuate by tiny increments.

"It tells us what his brain pressure is."

"Is it where it should be?" Ryan asked.

The nursed paused as if contemplating whether she should tell him or not. "We'd like for it to be between one and twenty millimeters." Ryan watched the dial fall a few notches than rise again, hovering around twenty-eight. "But it's higher than that now. What's going to happen?"

"We hope it doesn't stay there. We want the pressure to drop."

"Can he hear me if I talk to him?"

"Sure. I don't know what he'll understand, but it won't hurt." The nurse wrote something on a chart and left the room.

Ryan stared at the dial. Little by little, it escalated. After fifteen minutes, it climbed near the *thirty mm Hg* range again. He didn't know what the *mm* and the *Hg* meant, but it was way above the twenty mark.

"Come on, Bro, you can pull through. We know you can," Ryan cleared his throat. "If you wake up I promise not to breathe weird or flush the toilet at night and wake you up. I won't wear your boxers or steal your deodorant either."

Jason's body began to shake; first, his right arm quaked then his right leg. Then every body part hopped.

Ryan stood, trembling. "Nurse!" He was certain Jay's body would shake right off the bed. A loud, different, and continuous beep drowned out the other beeps. Ryan headed toward the door when the nurse rushed back into the room. More nurses followed. They held down Jay's body. It was like looking at a line of ants coming together on a tiny piece of sugar. Each one had a role, but everyone moved at once and their voices added to the beeps in the room.

A doctor arrived and gave orders for the nurse to put medicine into the bag hanging on the pole. Everything happened fast and was controlled quickly, but Ryan quivered. *What is happening to my family?*

The nurse stopped in the doorway where Ryan stood. "He had a seizure. This is common with head injuries. We have it under control now, but I'm sure that it was frightening to see. Are you okay?"

Ryan nodded. *No, I'm not.*

She squeezed his shoulder and left him standing stunned and afraid to reenter the room. He turned and dashed back to Kelly's room to be with the rest of his family.

Chapter Eight

It's gonna get harder before it gets easier.
But it will get better; you just gotta make it through the hard stuff
first.
Anonymous

Circular lights blared down on me. Hot searing pain stabbed my neck. I cried out, but my voice came out garbled and weak. My lips were parched.

"We're giving you something for pain right now, Kelly," the nurse said. She shot the fluid from a needle into my IV bag and the pain ebbed.

"It's all over, Kelly," the surgeon said, his blue mask resting on his forehead below his surgical cap. "You did well. I put five screws and two plates in at the back of your neck. I used bone from your hip and fused C-3 to C-4 and C-4 to C-5. Your hip and neck will be sore here." He pointed to his hip and the back of his neck. "It'll take a while to recover. The nurses will slowly elevate you to a more upright position, and eventually you'll start physical therapy, but for now, think baby steps."

Will I walk? I tried to remember if he'd told me. Maybe I missed that part of the conversation. The drugs were probably making me forget. Before I could ask him, the surgeon faded into darkness.

When I opened my eyes again, I was in a different location. They must have wheeled me somewhere else, but I didn't know where, and I didn't know how much time had passed. My head was locked in a brace, so I was unable to figure out my surroundings. Where was Mom? What day was it? Was it morning or night? Was it yesterday that Eric and I were riding horses together?

Then in a blink, everything rushed back—the accident, the surgery. Eric was still at the other hospital, recovering. Was he okay? *I need you, Eric. Dear God, please make this nightmare go away. Why me?* I closed my eyes, working to succumb to the drugs.

Suddenly, a glob of phlegm caught in the back of my throat. I had to cough, but I couldn't. My eyes flicked open. Fluorescent lights. Suspended ceiling. I couldn't turn my head. I was drowning! Who was there? Anyone? I needed to sit up. To cough. Choking. I can't. Breathe. Please. Someone help me. Where was the call button? There wasn't one. Even if there was, I couldn't press it. I was trapped inside my own body. No air. I couldn't even…cry… out.

I saw myself from above—outside of my body, my hair gnarled and splayed on the pillow. A silver brace encircled my neck, its appendages sitting on my shoulders, lifting my chin. Tubes sprouting like spider tentacles twisting around my body. Was this how I would die?

Two nurses rushed to my side. "We have to intubate you," one nurse said. "Stay calm."

Stay calm? I wanted to shout the worse swear word not in the dictionary. If only. I. Could. Breathe.

One nurse approached me with a long tube. "I'm going to insert this through your nose to clear your windpipe. Try to relax."

My eyes must have bulged, but after the tube was inserted, the mucous thinned, and I could finally breathe. The air filled my lungs and tears dripped down my face.

Never in my life had fear strangled and gripped my life so closely. The realization that I could no longer rely on myself for anything slammed into my chest. And even though I could finally breathe, the air in my lungs thinned. I was more alone than I'd ever been.

A Few Days Later

In my dream, I was at a basketball game waiting for Eric in the Assembly Hall outside the team locker room. His parents, sisters, the other team members' families, and I waited. IU had won. Bob Knight was giving his team a victory speech.

Finally, Eric bounded out of the locker room, smiling his heart-melting grin, carrying his gym bag. He headed straight for me—not his mother, not his sisters, or some other girl—but me. It was such a little thing, but one that made me a little more secure about his loyalty toward me. Rumors had spread that he'd been unfaithful, and he knew how much that bothered me, but for now, I was all his. He wrapped his arms around me and planted a kiss on my cheek.

"Congratulations," I said, smelling his spicy aftershave.

Someone took my hand. I could feel the pressure. It jarred me from my dream.

"Kelly?"

"Eric?" He was here? I opened my eyes to see him standing over me, his head and neck wrapped in thick white bandages.

"Hey," he said and squeezed my arm.

"You're here." Relief rushed over me. Emotions fisted my heart. Tears filled my eyes. "What happened to your head?"

"They put over two hundred sutures in my ear down to here." He pointed to his neck. "My ear almost tore off."

"What about your arm? What are the doctors saying?" How would he play ball?

"Yeah, my wrist is messed up, but it'll be okay. It's nothing compared to what you're going through." He took my hand. "I hate seeing you this way."

"Who are you here with?" It was easier to change the subject, to talk about him.

"Both of my parents brought me, but I didn't want to go back to Indiana before I saw you."

"Does your arm hurt?" It had to heal soon. Every day mattered if he was to make the NBA. It was his lifelong dream, and I was his biggest cheerleader.

"No," he said. "What about you? Are you in pain?"

"It's like I'm moving all the time, but I'm not. If you touch me I can feel your fingers but it's like someone or something is holding me down and I can't budge." I couldn't tell him that every tiny movement seared with hot pain. It was better not to think about it.

"You remember my speech, Kelly?" He paused, and it sounded like he had a bubble in his throat.

Yes, I knew his speech, the motivational one that he gave to students when he traveled to schools. The one he'd practiced on me for the last year. "Yes."

He recited it to me now, emphasizing the strength and reaching-for-goals parts. "You can do this. One day we'll look back on this and see how far we've come." He coached me, telling me what I needed to hear, being my cheerleader instead of the other way around.

Tears dripped down the sides of my face and his.

He squeezed my hand. "I can't stay long." He took a deep breath. "I have to see a surgeon about my hand. Your mom says they're transferring you to Chicago. I'll see you there. I promise."

I wanted him to lie beside me, to hold me, to tell me that everything would be better soon, but there were tubes and IV bags projecting from all around my body, reminding me that everything was far from okay.

"I don't want to leave you." He cried and shook with gasping sobs.

I cried with him. I didn't want him to leave, either. *I hate this, God. Why did this have to happen to us? Why did this have to ruin our plans?*

He reached for a tissue and blotted his eyes, then mine. "What a way to end the most wonderful vacation in my life."

Before he left, he kissed me and told me he loved me.

For the next few days, the drugs looped through my memory. Parts of my life floated in and out of my dreams. Random moments of my cheerleading life surfaced.

I was a sophomore in high school attending the national cheerleading championships. Our coach let a few of the underclassman, like me, go to watch and prepare us for when it would be our turn to go. We, and our competitors, stayed at the Hyatt where the event took place.

The night before the competition, we were told to go to our assigned rooms around 8:00 p.m. and stay there until morning. When I told my roommates my plans for the night, they giggled. I was the class clown, so they weren't surprised, but this was something I'd never done before.

We gathered around the phone in the room. "The team from Georgia is in room 320. I'm calling them first."

A friend gave me a high five.

I dialed 9-320. A girl answered.

"This is Judge Campbell." I disguised my voice. "I'm going over my notes for the competition tomorrow and need to know which stunts you'll perform in your routine." I held my finger over my mouth so the other girls would stay quiet and waited for the girl in room 320 to respond.

She paused briefly, but then told me everything.

"Thank you. Good luck tomorrow," I said.

After I hung up, my friends squealed and gathered around to read my notes.

I did this several more times before someone banged on our door. "Lights out."

The next day, our coach gathered me, and the team, behind the stage. "Last night someone made prank phone calls to the other teams.

This is wrong. It's poor sportsmanship."

Someone snickered. For years after, we laughed and laughed about this.

Coach never did.

The dream shifted to a gym full of cheerleaders training to teach for the National Cheerleader Association. I stood in the middle of the room with my hands tied behind my back. In training, I had to learn how to teach using only words. Without moving, I described our cheer routine in full detail and the other cheerleaders had to perform the exact movements. I needed to prove I could use words to teach instead of using my body.

When I woke in my hospital bed, I had the same sensation—that my hands were tied behind my back. But they weren't. They were at my side, free to move, but unable to move. My real life had become the imaginary training lesson.

In order to get what I wanted I had to use my voice to instruct others how to help me. I couldn't rely on my body.

I succumbed to the drugs again, to the glow of the medicine, feeling its warmth course through my veins.

Camp had been way more fun.

Chapter Nine

Siblings are the people who teach us about fairness and cooperation
and kindness and caring—quite often the hard way.
Pamela Dugdale

A Few Days Later

The phone rang. I imagined myself lifting it from the cradle and holding it to my ear. Was it Eric? Had I talked to him today? I craved his soothing voice, the one thing that brightened my day, the one I looked forward to the most.

When he called, Mom held the phone to my ear. He gave me pep talks and told me he loved me. Mom couldn't hold the phone all the time, so she propped it against a pillow and left the room to give me privacy. But the phone would go crooked.

"Kelly? Are you there?"

I'd have to wait until Mom came back to straighten it, but by that time all I could hear was the disappointing beep indicating that he'd hung up. I hated being separated from him.

Friends called every day too. They asked how I was.

"Good." I lied. There wasn't anything new to report. The doctors repeatedly told the newspapers I was in critical condition. My progress was almost nonexistent, but I couldn't admit it. It was easier to ask them questions about their lives. "How did cheerleading camp go? Who got best cheerleader? Who was the top team this year?" I wished I could be there with them.

"I'm not going to make it to teach at camp next week," I told my cheer friend when she called. "Will you let the NCA know?"

She laughed. "They already know, Kelly. You're all over the news."

Really? I had no idea. It was probably because of Eric. The media followed him relentlessly.

A nurse came in on her day off to check on me. She said she saw our story on TV.

Jason was still in a coma. He wasn't responding to anyone or anything. They put him in a room down the hall from mine to make it easier for Mom and Andy to go back and forth between us.

"Do you want to see him?" a nurse asked me one day. "I'll wheel you down to his room, but I need to warn you. He won't look like Jason. He has tubes going in and out of his nose and his mouth. His face is swollen. He looks…different."

"I want to see him." She didn't realize how strong I was, and I'd known Jason for seventeen years. I doubted his appearance would shock me.

She double-checked my IV bags, unlocked my bed, and rolled me down the hallway. Because my head was slightly elevated, I could watch where we were going, but going over the smallest bumps jolted me with burning pain. Sick of living in a fog, I'd tried to quit taking the pain pills, but I winced every time the bed shook.

When she wheeled me into the hallway, I welcomed the change of scenery. The air seemed healthier and the smells different. Was someone eating McDonald's french fries? How long had it been since I'd eaten fries?

"Going for a stroll, Kelly?" a nurse at her station asked.

"She's going to see Jason," my nurse responded.

The nurse at the desk furrowed her brow and rose from her paperwork. "Is… she uh, ready… for that?" She followed us down the hall and into Jason's room.

I wished they'd quit babying me.

Machines beeped and swished. Jay lay on his back, his eyes closed, and his face pasty white—almost the color of his sheets. He looked different.

Every nurse in the room had her eyes on me. Were they waiting for me to fall to pieces and break down sobbing? I kept my expression stoic, determined to show them how tough I was. I could handle this, but I wouldn't talk to him now, not with a room filled with ogling spectators.

I pictured him walking back to the cabin at the dude ranch and not getting into the car before the accident. Why had Eric coaxed him to come along? I should have insisted that he stay behind. Typically, we never hung out with him. If he hadn't come, would my injuries be different? Maybe I would've been behind John, maybe I would be lying in a coma.

But Jason loved Eric and hung on his every word. Nothing I could have said would have dissuaded him from joining us.

I secretly wished I could trade places with him and wake from my coma like the actors in *Days of our Lives*, back to the way life used to be, able to walk and slowly remember.

Everything was wrong.

The nurses let me stay with him for several minutes before they wheeled me to my stale room. On my way out, I wished all our woes could end as they do in soap operas.

Little by little, the nursing staff raised the level of my head in bed. The goal was to get me to a sitting position. Each time they made a trivial adjustment, the room spun. The last thing I wanted was to vomit. I'd choke to death. It took hours after each modification for the dizziness to subside. It took days before they inched my bed up to a full sitting position. After I finally acclimated to sitting upright, I was ready to leave the San Juan Regional Center.

The next transition was to transfer me to the Rehabilitation Institute of Chicago (RIC), but they didn't have a bed for me, so Christ Hospital in Chicago was the best option until a bed became available. Mom and I flew to Chicago by Learjet to Christ Hospital. Andy stayed in New Mexico with Jason because his brain pressure couldn't withstand the cabin pressure in a plane.

"You were born at this hospital," Mom said when we arrived.

Really? I didn't know much about my early childhood before I was seven, when Mom was still married to Dad. Would I see more of Dad's family since I'd be in Chicago? I still remembered the day we left.

It was the day after Christmas. Mom drove our van out of Chicago. Jason, Ryan, and I were in the backseat. It took six hours to get to rural Jasper, Indiana—a city only eleven square miles and surrounded by rows of corn, beans, and chicken farms. That's where Mom grew up, where her family lived, and where she said we'd be starting our new life. We'd gone to Jasper many times before to visit Mom's family, but never to live there.

Ryan was a toddler and Jason was five. I sat in the middle between them and entertained Ryan, but I picked on Jason—pulling his hair and pinching him when Mom wasn't looking.

I didn't realize how our lives would change and how important the Jasper community would become in my life.

As we got closer, the scenery became hillier and the grass greener, less snow-covered. Cows meandered in herds through fenced pastures along the roadside.

"What's that smell?" Jason asked. "You need to change Ryan's diaper."

Mom glanced in the rearview mirror. "That's cow manure. The farmers fertilize their fields with it."

"What's manure?" Jason asked.

"Do-do," she said.

Did I hear her wrong? "They put poo on their plants?"

"It makes them grow faster and bigger," Mom said.

"Yuck," Jason said. "No wonder why I don't like vegetables."

For most of the trip, we stayed more silent than usual because Mom wasn't in a singing mood. She often sang with the radio, inserting her own words for the lyrics, but not that day. She'd left Dad before, but usually it was for a day and we'd stay at a friend's house. This time she packed our van full of our summer and winter clothes, toys, dishes and towels, and anything else she could squeeze in.

Mom and Dad were both athletes and met in college. Dad was a lineman for Murray State's football team; Mom ran track and studied recreational fitness. She broke Indiana's high school long jump record her sophomore year. After they married, they lived in a suburb of Chicago so Dad could work for the family business, which was located there. A year later, I came along.

From the time I could walk, I exercised alongside Mom in front of the TV. We huffed through sit-ups, toe stretches, and the splits while we watched *My Little Pony* or *Strawberry Shortcake*. Mom enrolled me in everything girlie—baton lessons, jazz, tap, ballet, and gymnastics, but I liked gymnastics the most. I put on my little leotard and went to the gym with the other girls my age, and we'd line up single file in front of the mats. I watched every detail of their moves and aspired to be better than they were.

I practiced standing on my head or my hands and watched my brother upside down. If one of the girls in class could do a better cartwheel than I could, I worked harder and practiced extra at home. I flipped cartwheels in the living room and in the kitchen. Sometimes furniture was knocked over or vases flew off end tables. Then the next time I'd go to class, I'd watch that girl to see how I compared. Most of the time my efforts paid off.

I sat in the back seat of our van heading to Jasper with no idea how the city's gymnastics programs would improve my skills. When we turned off highway 56 into my grandparents' gravel driveway, Grandma's waist-high underwear waved in the wind on her clothesline. There, before the whole town, flapped Grandpa's underwear, Grandma's worn-out bras, towels, and sheets. Even though Grandma owned a dryer, she insisted on letting the sun and wind dry her laundry. Sometimes it made the towels so crisp that they chafed my skin after a shower.

We jumped out of the car and Grandma hugged me into her big bosom. Grandpa patted me hard on the back, unaware of his strength—practically knocking me to the floor. He fried his famous chicken in the warehouse—the large building at the back of the property—where he kept his deep fryer and walk-in cooler. We loved Grandma and Grandpa. They let us drink soda pop and run in the yard.

We only stayed with my grandparents a few days before we moved into an apartment. It was smaller and quieter than our big home in Chicago. Mom and Ryan stayed in one bedroom, and Jason and I had to share the other. It was the first time that we had to sleep in the same room, and we hated it. Our twin beds touched in one corner. We fought all the time. Most times it was over nothing, except we both liked to be right. Something small could end up escalating until we were wrestling on the ground. He liked to throw Hot Wheels cars at my head.

"Stop it." Mom said. "I don't know any brothers and sisters who fight like you do."

She probably wondered what kind of guy would marry a woman with three bratty kids.

When I started school, I was the only one in my classroom who had divorced parents, and I wanted to keep it a secret. I didn't want to be different from the other kids. But they found out because Dad was never was around.

Mom found a full-time job, and after school, we went to stay with a lady who babysat for ten kids. We hung out in her basement and did homework until Mom came to pick us up. She'd never worked full time, so when she arrived at the end of the day, I sprinted into her arms.

My wounds began to heal at Christ Hospital and the staff tended to my needs, but Mom rarely left the room during the day. She constantly moved my legs and arms, trying to keep them in motion. She said my muscles would atrophy if she didn't work them. It was probably her way to do something positive, but I didn't care. I didn't want her to leave me.

Slowly, visitors began to arrive. Dad and his wife, Dawne, came with their two daughters, my half sisters. Dawne seemed to really care about me and wanted to help. Dad cared, too, but it was awkward being with him. After the divorce, I resented him, and because of the distance, he became a stranger.

As I grew, Dawne bridged the gap between Dad and me. I didn't trust him after what he did to Mom, but I liked Dawne. I trusted her. When I visited them in the summers and on holidays, she treated me like family, included me in activities, and introduced me to other people as her daughter. She didn't ask personal questions about Mom or my family either. She taught me life lessons. One was to drive in the city with my car doors locked at all times.

Gramps, on Dad's side, was another visitor. He was a part of my early childhood that I did remember. Seeing him made the memories roll back to me—him babysitting me, slipping me twenty-dollar bills.

When he saw me lying in bed, his voice shook. "I hate seeing you in pain."

"I'm okay." I tried to reassure him. "What have you been doing?"

We chatted about many things, but one of his favorite quotes kept surfacing. "If you don't use it, you'll lose it."

He didn't mention the quote now, but seeing him made me remember his wise words. If I couldn't figure out a way to move soon I'd lose the ability forever. It had already started. Each day my muscles deteriorated. I hoped the doctors would give me the green light to work at walking again—soon.

One day the nurses dressed me, and leaned me forward in bed to put on a shirt. My head lay hunched over my legs and I saw my thighs, the ones I used to think were too big. Now they resembled sticks. Already. In a little over a week I'd lost all the muscle that I'd spent a lifetime building.

"Skinny legs and I can't even show them off." I said.

No one laughed.

In the mornings, the staff did my bathroom. They gave me enemas and wiped my bottom. Privacy was nonexistent.

The next night a tornado funneled down on the hospital. Sirens blared overhead. The loudspeaker announcer called a code and the staff ran around moving patients into the hallway. It reminded me of when Jason and I were little and there was a tornado warning. We put on our helmets, grabbed our piggy banks, and ran to the basement to take cover. But now, I wasn't afraid. Nothing could be as bad as what I'd gone through already.

Okay God, is this how my story ends? It probably wouldn't matter if I died now anyway.

But that didn't happen. The hospital only suffered minor external damages, and I was moved back to my room in the same bed, in the same damaged body.

Jason arrived a few days after me. Even though his brain pressure had decreased, he still wasn't responding. The newspapers updated his condition from critical to stable. I was finally listed as serious, but stable.

"He won't be the same Jason we knew," Mom said. "All that stuff you see about waking from a coma on TV is fiction, Kelly. The nurses said a coma is like swimming through peanut butter. He might not remember who you are or be able to talk. He might not be able to do anything for himself. The longer he's in the coma, the worse he'll be."

She said it matter-of-factly, but tears brimmed in her eyes. I could tell she was trying to accept it. Maybe saying it aloud helped it seem more real.

I didn't know what to expect. I couldn't picture him waking up a different person. Maybe he would lose his mean streak. Maybe switching places with him wasn't better either.

Dad's mom, Jayne, created a large journal that she kept near Jason's door. Visitors signed in, left messages, charting the dates and times they were there. People visited every day; most drove all the way from Jasper. Some visitors wrote a prayer in the journal or left cards. They described what Jason did that day or what he looked like at the time. Jayne thought it would be great for Jason to read when he woke up.

Would he wake up?

Mom read the notes in the journal to me. I should have been grateful, but I wasn't. I didn't want to be where I was.

(Andy with me, Jason, and Ryan)

Chapter Ten

Recovery is a process. It takes time. It takes patience. It takes
everything you've got.
More Than Skin Deep

July 20, 1999
Ten Days after the Accident

Even though my status was upgraded to stable, the constant part about me was that I couldn't move. I wanted to tell my friends that I experienced the most miniscule improvement. I wanted to hurry my therapy. Waiting at Christ Hospital was not only painful physically, but emotionally too. I needed to get back to Eric. Sitting around forced my mind to drift to unwelcome places—who was he with, was he cheating on me? I had to get back to Indiana. Soon.

Eleven days after the accident, I was transferred to the Rehab

Institute by ambulance. But President Clinton was in town and traffic slowed to a crawl for almost an hour. I pretended not to care, but I hated the tech's pity-filled stare and his probing questions about what had happened. Mom answered for a while, but then we both stayed silent. Staring at the ceiling of an ambulance for over an hour was worse than counting sheep.

Once I was assigned to a room at RIC, there was a constant influx of nurses taking my vitals, asking me questions, assessing my needs. A physical therapist read my chart and said, "Wow, with your injuries you're lucky you can breathe on your own."

I didn't feel lucky.

Nurses, therapists, and dietitians introduced themselves to us. The staff said I would have occupational, physical, and psychological therapy.

Bring it.

"Our job is to teach you how to cope with your disabilities," one therapist said.

If you say so. But they didn't know what I was capable of doing. They didn't know me. Once I got going, there was no stopping me. Last year I placed ninth in the national cheerleading competitions. I knew how to flip and tuck and maneuver stunts they'd never tried.

Besides, my injuries were different from the other spine patients. My spinal cord had only been *bruised* and my neck had been surgically pinned back together. There was a chance I'd walk again. They'd soon see my determination, and I'd be out of there.

Doctors and nurses asked me questions in past tense, "What *was* your major in college? Where *did* you attend?"

That part of my life was *not* over. I corrected them and said, "My major *is* elementary education."

The first morning, the trainer took me to the therapy room where other patients worked with weights and machines. Patients grunted as they lifted barbells. Metal clanked against metal. Eyes were pinched shut from exertion. Some tried to move their arms. Others tried to move legs. All were paralyzed in some way.

My first session was to hit a balloon back and forth with a partner while sitting up, but a tech had to hold me in an upright position because I couldn't do it on my own.

When they sat me up the room spun, my vision went black, and my head bobbed onto my chest. The next thing I remembered was lying down on the exam table, staring up at the ceiling. "What happened?"

"You fainted," the tech said. "It's called postural hypotension. Your blood pressure dropped because you've been lying in bed for a while. It's common after a spinal cord injury."

"How long will that be a problem?"

"It most likely won't happen often. The problem typically resolves itself." He reached for my shoulders. "Let's sit you up again, but we'll take it slower this time. Let us know if you start to feel dizzy again."

The next time, I managed not to faint. The tech held me while I tried to hit the balloon. On the outside, I stayed calm, but inside I died. This was more difficult than anything I had ever done. I couldn't hit the balloon. I couldn't move.

Slowly, at the end of the first week, my right bicep only flickered. I regained limited use of my left arm and hand, but could only wiggle my fingers. I couldn't grip anything. I couldn't push my call light or the elevator button. All I could do was lift my left arm and pretend to push my hair back with the edge of my palm.

"At least that's something," Mom said. "Maybe it's a sign that you will regain more mobility." She smiled wider than she had in days.

I smiled. Hope was my only friend.

My appetite returned, and I craved Gino's Pizza from Gino's East, two blocks from the hospital. They delivered, which made it easy for Mom and perfect for me because I craved it every day. It was the best way to get more spinach in my diet, too, since I was low on iron. Mom cut up the pieces, put it on a plate, and set it in my lap. Therapists showed her how to insert a fork between my wrist and hand guard so I could try to feed myself. But I was right-handed and the only mobility I had was with my left hand, and those fingers didn't move either, so stabbing my food and getting it in my mouth was a challenge.

One day when I was in the therapy room at RIC, a man entered looking for a woman. He called out her name.

"That's me," said a spinal patient who was working at a therapy table.

The man handed her an envelope.

"What's this?" she nodded toward the envelope.

"I'm sorry." The man said and turned to go.

The woman's eyes filled with tears. She turned to her tech. "Will you open the envelope for me?"

The tech nodded and slowly opened the envelope, then placed the papers in the patient's lap.

The woman glanced at the letter and tears streamed faster. "He wants a divorce. The jerk." She shouted after the deliveryman. "After all I've gone through with that bastard, he's dumping me because of the accident?" She swept her arm and flung the papers to the floor in one awkward motion. "He should rot in hell." The woman's face turned as red as the fire alarm knobs on the wall.

I wanted to cry for her. Even though I never knew her husband, I disliked him immensely. *What kind of person ditches his loved one when she needs him the most?*

The staff at RIC also provided sessions with speakers to help patients and families prepare for returning home.

"Are you going to the meeting today?" my nurse asked Mom.

"What's it about?" Mom asked.

"Making your home handicap accessible."

"Yes, we'll go," Mom said.

What?

Mom and Andy wheeled me into the room where the speaker talked about ramps, bathrooms large enough to accommodate a shower chair, automatic door entries, electric-powered wheelchairs, eating utensils, accessible beds, TVs, voice activated phones, and adaptive technology. Shortly after the meeting, my parents called a contractor back home and began making the changes that were needed to accommodate me.

Anger filled me. Why didn't they believe that I'd conquer this? Did they have such little faith in my ability, my determination? I couldn't believe they were contemplating making drastic changes to the house by turning the dining room into my bedroom.

The next day, therapists conducted sessions on sex for the disabled and therapy for quads who wanted to have an active sex life. Seriously? I wanted no part of that teaching session. I wasn't like the other patients. I could feel. Wasn't that half the battle? I simply needed my despondent muscles to correspond with my drive. I wasn't an *it,* and besides, I'd walk again. Soon.

The staff said what I was going through was normal. It was called denial, but I didn't care what they called it. I would prove them all wrong. I would work hard and improve until I could take care of myself again.

I couldn't look at Mom or talk to her when she began to make the changes to the house. I wanted to slam a door or walk away. If only I could. Her actions fueled my competitive edge. I was an athlete, darn it, and with that came an abundance of coordination, determination, and perseverance.

Mom and Andy were told that I would go home with a urine bag attached to my leg like the one I'd worn since the accident, the one with the thick tube that continually drained urine into the bag. If the nurses removed the bag, Mom would have to catheterize me every four hours. Tears stung my eyes.

Mom made me go with her to a class on how to catheterize me, but when Andy showed up, I didn't understand. "What are you doing here?"

"I need to learn too," he said. "What if Mom isn't home and it's time to empty your bladder?"

"Where's Mom going to go?" I asked him, but I knew what he meant. She had a job, responsibilities, and she couldn't be with me every waking moment. If she wasn't home, I needed to rely on Andy too. I prayed that never happened. Andy was an amazing stepdad, but I didn't want him to have to handle the intimate details of my life.

Andy and Mom were high school sweethearts. They dated a little in college, but once they'd gone to different colleges, each went their own way. After we moved back to Jasper, it didn't take long before the divorce was final and Andy and Mom started dating. Andy had never married. When people asked him why he hadn't married, he said he'd never met anyone that interested him the way Mom had. Some people in Jasper believed he was secretly waiting for her to return.

He'd heard Mom was having marital problems, but never interfered. He wanted things to work out for her, especially because of us kids.

It was weird watching Mom date. In the beginning, we objected. We were used to having all her attention because Dad was seldom around. Now Andy was taking a lot of her attention. To get noticed, I picked fights with Jason. We rolled on the ground, wrestled, boxed, and pulled hair more than we had before.

Once when Andy took us to a putt-putt miniature golf course, Jason kept counting my strokes, provoking me, so I chased him through the play area swinging my club at him.

It didn't take Andy long to catch on that our fighting was simply a tactic for more attention. To harness our energy he bought us a trampoline for Christmas. He also brought us treats—big bags of juicy Florida oranges, our favorite ice cream, or the latest movie.

He taught us how to perform card tricks and build card castles. One card trick I loved was when he stacked them on his wrist and magically slid them up to his elbow. In the summer, he pretended to eat bugs and we laughed. He asked questions to learn what we liked and that made us feel important. He understood and respected that Mom made us her first priority.

The more I saw Andy, the more I accepted him and liked him. The more often he came over the more he disciplined us. Time-outs became a dual parent activity.

When I was nine, Jason, Ryan, Mom, Andy, and I took a day trip to Angel Mounds in Evansville, an Indian burial site. After a day of sightseeing, we loaded into the car. Jason, Ryan, and I were playing in the back seat under an old sheet that we'd draped across the top of the seats, our makeshift fort.

Mom turned on the radio and heard Linda Ronstadt singing, "All My Life." She looked at Andy and said, "I want this song at our wedding."

Wedding?

Andy didn't drive away. Instead, he reached behind his seat and plucked a bag from the floorboard. Paper crinkled and he took out a little gray box.

"What's that?" Mom asked.

He opened the box to reveal a sparkling diamond ring.

I elbowed Jason who was oblivious to what was going on in the front seat.

"What?" he asked.

I nodded to Mom and Andy.

"Will you marry me?" Andy said to Mom.

"Say yes!" I shouted.

Jason chanted. "Mom and Andy sitting in the tree, K-I-S-S-I-N-G, first comes love, then comes marriage, then comes the baby in the baby carriage."

Mom laughed and took the ring box. She studied the ring with tears in her eyes and smiled. "It's beautiful, Andy."

"Say yes, Mom." I repeated.

Andy chuckled.

"Yes," Mom said and hugged him. "I'll marry you."

He slipped the ring on her finger and they kissed.

"Yuck." Jason said.

Andy knew that marrying Mom meant marrying us too. He couldn't escape us; he was outnumbered, but he didn't seem to care. He said he wanted the whole package.

But catheterizing me—that was going beyond fatherhood duties. I didn't want any part of it and hoped it never happened.

Steve Schanwald, the vice president of marketing for the Chicago Bulls, was Eric's friend. When he heard what had happened to Eric and realized I was in the hospital, he arranged for Steve Kerr to visit me the next time Eric came to see me. Steve Kerr was a star basketball player who'd dribbled beside Magic Johnson and Michael Jordan.

Word traveled all over the hospital that the basketball star was there to see me. Nurses, techs, and other hospital staff suddenly needed to check on my progress and stopped by to see me. Even after Steve's visit, the hospital staff treated me differently, like I was a star, someone who mattered.

Candy helped attract fans too. We figured out quickly that the staff visited my room more often when we kept candy to share with them. The nurses got to know my family and me really well, which helped in my care.

Jason and I received loads of mail, cards, gifts, and flowers. Someone brought me a book about a football player who became addicted to Vicodin after a neck injury.

Mom's voice chirped in my ear, "Don't stay on those pain meds."

When I was a child, she often scared Jason and me and said, "Drugs will make your brain bleed. One of you will have your father's addict gene. Who's it going to be? Will it be you, Kelly? Jason? It's up to you to fight it."

As a child, I was gullible enough to believe her threat, and now her warning boomed in my mind. I started skipping pain med doses, but the pain slowed my progress. The nurses wanted me to stay ahead of the pain, so one nurse suggested that I take Tylenol with codeine instead of the heavier stuff. I agreed and the transition helped keep the pain at bay, but calmed my fears of addiction, too.

Chapter Eleven

Nothing tends more to cement the hearts of Christians than praying together. Never do they love one another so well as when they witness the outpouring of each other's hearts in prayer.
Charles Finney

Brenda hated leaving her children at the hospital, but she needed clean, fresh clothing, and Andy convinced her that it would be healthy for them both to return to Jasper. Sister Betty and Father Kane from Precious Blood Church, a few blocks from their home, had organized a vigil for Jason and Kelly.

"The kids are in good hands here," Andy said. "We'll only be gone a few days."

When they arrived in Jasper it was evening, but the sun hadn't set yet. Most of the parking spots at Precious Blood were taken. People had parked on the grass and along the road. The church was so crowded that some people congregated outside the open church doors. The sound of the organ's dissonant chords drifted outside.

Brenda spotted Ryan waiting for them at the door. She hadn't seen him since the accident. They embraced, and when Ryan's shoulders shook with sobs, she wept with him.

Sister Betty whispered, "There's a seat in the front pew for you." She ushered them into the church.

When they entered, a hush fell. Emotions flickered on the faces of the congregation, their features distorted from the reflection of the candles they held. Not one person spoke. No one smiled. Never had Brenda seen a community so determined to make a difference, so solemn in prayer. She'd never known high school students to give up their personal time on a school night to pray, either.

She sighed deeply. She wasn't alone. While she and Andy had been coping with the complexities of the tragedy, these people—many of whom she didn't know—cared enough to pray for them, arrange novenas (prayers for nine successive days), and attend the vigil. She was lifted by their presence and was certain that God's light reflected in the candles they held.

Moved by her community and comforted by their support, tears rolled down her cheeks and dripped off her chin. Andy's eyes were filled with tears too.

From that moment on, she and Andy agreed to spend more time noticing the good things happening around them. It was too easy to become caught up in the negative parts of the tragedy. Instead, they found time to talk about something good that happened like when someone sent a card, made a meal, or helped with their other children.

When Mom and Andy traveled back to Indiana, Dad's wife, Dawne, left her daughters with a sitter and spent time with me in the hospital. Her companionship helped my depression.

"I want to write Eric a poem for our three-year anniversary," I said. "If I do, will you get it in print for me?"

"I know of a place that will print it in calligraphy. Would that work?"

"Perfect. Could you put it in a frame, too?"

Dawne agreed and wrote down the words that I dictated. A few days later, she had the gift matted and framed, hours before Eric arrived.

July 27, 1999
Seventeen Days after the Accident

I couldn't wait to give Eric the poem, but first he had something for me. We were alone in my hospital room, not the most romantic setting, but Lake Michigan's waves lapped against the shore outside my window, and the door was shut. That was the best we could do.

He no longer had bandages on his head, but the evidence of the accident was present in the long red-glaring scar along his neck and his wrist splint.

He reached into his pocket, pulled out a little ring, and held it up for me to see. It had two hearts and a little baby diamond in the middle of it. He slipped it on my finger and stared at me with such smoldering intensity that tears burned my eyes. I ached to wrap my arms around him. This gift wasn't just a ring. It was a symbol of his love, of his commitment to me. He believed in me. He knew that I would heal. He wasn't giving up on me.

"Look in that bag over there," I said, moving my arm toward the bag that leaned against the wall.

He opened the bag and took out the framed poem. As he read the words, his eyes turned red and welled with tears. "This is the best gift anyone has ever given me."

I believed him, but a few days later when Mom read a newspaper article about the poem, I beamed at how much it had meant to him.

"Listen to what *The Journal Gazette* wrote about Eric." Mom read aloud to me, "This is the best gift he's ever gotten. Not basketball. Not a scholarship. Not even the good fortune to escape the fatal three-car accident that injured him, his girlfriend, his girlfriend's brother, and killed the driver of their car. No, what Eric reveres most these days is the framed poem Kelly Craig gave him earlier this week."

The paper showed a picture of Eric smiling, sitting in a chair without me by his side.

I mourned for him. My arms ached to be around him.

The worst parts of his visits were the goodbyes. When it was time for him to go that day, I said, "Wait. There's a song I want you to listen to. It reminds me of you."

"Who sings it?"

"Garth Brooks. It's called, 'It's Your Song.' "

He placed the headphones over his ears and hit play. His eyes held mine, and his tears flowed, turning his face a deep shade of red.

The power of the lyrics fit our lives. The lyrics spoke of how Eric's voice gave me wings, when I was afraid he gave me courage, he was my *somebody* who believed in me. I wouldn't let him down, and anytime I doubted myself I'd think of him—the light that shined, the song guiding my heart, that my dreams would come true with God's angel—him.

Each level at the rehab center had different types of patients, but all were learning how to live with their new disabilities. Jason finally arrived at RIC and since he was only seventeen years old, he had to stay on a different floor, the pediatric one. Mom and Andy took turns visiting our rooms, but each evening they left for a hotel.

The darkness of night often found me the most vulnerable. During the day, when a weak moment bombarded me, I smiled through the pain, promising myself I could give in to the sadness later when no one was around. I loathed drama and refused to show one weak moment.

Visitors commented on how strong I was, and when one of my fingers twitched or a limb trembled, they cheered and said it was a sign that finally the neurons were kicking in, that the charged electrodes were finding the paths of mobility.

But when evening came and the buzz of shift changes and visitors ceased, and I still couldn't move, I swallowed the lump of night meds and gave in to the sadness of my life. I cried. I cursed God and secretly envied my friends' lives—the ease at which their bodies worked.

Jerry Springer hosted abusers, drama queens, and criminals on his show. Why did bad things happen to people like me and not to idiots like them?

Jay Leno was the one who kept me laughing. I watched his show when I wanted to cry and laughed instead. The next morning I woke realizing that I'd gotten through the night without tears.

The Brady Bunch and *Gilligan's Island* reruns kept me sane during the quiet time in the day. They brought a sense of familiarity to a strange place. I looked forward to *Who Wants to Be a Millionaire?* too, and found myself watching the clock so I wouldn't miss it.

It didn't take the therapists long to assess my abilities and realize that no matter what they did, I wasn't progressing.

Hope faded.

The techs concentrated on teaching me techniques to cope with my limitations at home. They took me and a group of disabled patients on day trips to the Navy Pier and into the heart of Chicago, where the wind blew Lake Michigan's water, shoppers rushed, horns honked, and taxies screeched as they blurred in and out of traffic. The smell of car exhaust wafted from the streets like a poisoned cloud. Some patients oohed and aahed about never seeing Chicago before.

In late September, on Indian summer days, Mom shuttled me outside on little jaunts around Chicago to perk my spirits and warm my chronically-chilled body. She wrapped a blanket around my legs and pushed me along the pitted sidewalks, the cracks jarring me sideways. Oftentimes, we had to stop at a curb because there was no way to get me down. Mom got creative, turned the chair around, and asked able-bodied people to help lift me off the curb. But there were many times when no one was around to help, and Mom had to take me back to the hospital. The slightest curb limited my ability and impacted my mood and experiences.

I pushed and worked on improving my abilities, but to no avail.

Chapter Twelve

No test or temptation that comes your way is beyond the course of what others have had to face. All you need to remember is that God will never let you down; He'll never let you be pushed past your limit; He'll always be there to help you come through it.
1 Corinthians 10:13 MSG

Three Months after the Accident

Someone sent the above Bible verse to me in a card. How was I supposed to believe the message? No one I knew had ever gone through what I was going through. They had the use of their extremities, they didn't have to face what I was facing, and I was past my limit.

Practically my whole life I tumbled, cartwheeled, and flipped into back tucks and front walkovers. I could bounce into the air and land on my feet, but now I couldn't put one foot in front of the other.

Maybe if I believed in God more deeply He would grant me the ability to walk again. *Hurry up, God. You can send a miracle my way anytime now.*

When early October arrived, the leaves turned to copper and wine, and for the first time I noticed how deep their colors were, and how the chill of winter loomed nearby and settled in my bones. Maybe I paid more attention to the changes because everything swirled in slow motion, pausing my life, and freezing my progress.

With fall's breeze, the reality of my new life blew in, and after ten weeks at RIC, it was time to go home. I had to leave my new friends, the support system of abundant helpers—all who had become my confidence—and face the friends back home who'd prayed for me, who'd cheered for me to make progress.

How would I face them without feeling like a failure?

Mom brushed my hair and applied my make-up while Andy collected the cards and gifts scattered in the room.

Mom flashed the mirror in front of me.

"Could you soften the blush on this side?" I asked, moving my braced arm to indicate which side.

She blotted my cheek with a tissue, tucked my makeup away, and gathered the rest of the clutter.

I gave my room one last glance. Stark walls, clanking metal beds and trays, a parking lot window view on one side, and Lake Michigan's whitecaps on the other—a safe but chilly haven.

The floor nurses gathered around and voiced their well wishes. "You know where to reach us if you have any questions. You'll do fine. We'll keep you in our prayers." They turned to Mom and asked her to sign another paper.

Andy loaded the car while Mom wheeled me to say goodbye to Jason. "There isn't much more they can do for him," Mom said. "He'll come back to Jasper soon." She pressed her fingers into her temples. He was still nonresponsive, but every now and then, he squeezed Mom's finger—once for yes and twice for no, but it was difficult to determine if his responses were random or if he really understood.

Mom pushed me closer to him, tears trailing down her cheeks.

"I'll see you at home, Jay. Wake up soon." I refused to cry.

The familiar sounds of the rehab wing faded as reality rustled along the walls of the hospital, followed me down the whirring elevator shaft and out the front door where Andy waited in the open air, the large sky looming above me, poised to swallow me whole. Not only were my limbs paralyzed, but my tears also lay dormant, frozen behind a smile, suspended in fear. If I let them flow, I'd never stop.

Andy lifted me into the back seat of the car and strapped me in, grunting as he exhaled.

I had to face everyone in three hours. Eric and the rest of my family and friends waited for me in Indianapolis at the Plum Creek Golf Course, at Finish Line Celebrity Golf Outing, a sponsored benefit for Jason and me.

Medical bills were pouring in. Jason and I would have lifetime expenses for our injuries. We'd have to pay caretakers, doctors, hospitals, and building contractors to remodel our home.

Eric's friend Mike, a marketing guy for NIKE, had worked mega hours to coordinate the fundraising event. One of Eric's friends, who worked for Finish Line, helped get them to sponsor the event too. Mom said many people spent hours putting it together.

The event was everyone's way of saying *we care*.

Pro basketball players, a few Colts and Pacer players, Gene Keady, John Calipari, Slick Leonard, Reggie Miller, Tom Izzo, and Payton Manning were a few of the big names invited and supposedly attending. My brothers and friends were excited to meet the stars.

I was thankful for all the work that went into the event, but people were raising money for a life I didn't want.

While Andy drove to Indianapolis, I watched the yellow line in the road, paranoid that someone would cross it and hit us, squeezing my eyes shut every time a car came close to the line. I couldn't keep myself straight. Every bump jarred me enough to knock me lopsided until my head bobbed to the side.

Mom turned to say panicked. "Kelly! Andy, pull over. She's falling down."

Andy stopped the car. Mom propped pillows and suitcases around me to keep me from drooping and Andy drove on.

When we arrived at the golf course, the sun was warm and the temperature better than most Indiana October days, but the trees were bare and my heart spun like the leaves chasing each other in circles on the pavement. I couldn't wait to see Eric.

Family and friends greeted me like I was some kind of rock star. But I could tell I disappointed them. They'd counted on me to improve, and I had nothing to show for it. Over and over again people said, "We're sorry, Kelly. How are you doing?"

I wanted them to say, "You're doing great, Kelly. Look how far you've come. We can tell how hard you've worked."

Their sympathy suffocated me. I smiled to keep from crying.

The view from my chair distorted the faces of friends I'd known for years. No one looked the same. Nostrils flared from a different perspective. Hugs were awkward and nonexistent, as if people were afraid to touch me. And everyone looked down at me.

The focus shifted when the celebs arrived—on them, instead of me. My sorority sisters pitched in and helped serve food and beverages, each bringing a piece of my past with them, reminding me that they cared, and how important I was to them. I pressed them with questions about their lives, vicariously living in their excitement, pressing the gloom of my frustration and inadequacy deep.

Relatives asked about the pros and if they could take pictures with them.

People wore shirts that said, "We love Kelly and Jason."

Someone lifted me onto a golf cart next to Eric, but there was no brace or support to keep me from falling over. Every bump jostled my position, knocking me crooked. The urine bag strapped to my thigh yanked on the tender skin between my legs, reminding me of my status, of my vulnerability. Eric kept a stiff arm around me.

The day wore on. Clouds dotted the sky. Tree limbs fluttered in the breeze. Bees buzzed around open pop cans. The crowd grew. Cameras flashed. Golfers swung and swore as they tore divots in the grass. Some laughed. And inside, my heart ached for Eric to smile at me the way he used to, to hold me with longing, and to gaze into my eyes until my breath caught. But he didn't. His eyes remained dim and his touch cool. He stayed by my side, but the energy between us had thinned.

He drove around the course, greeting the coaches and players he knew, showing them the personality that I loved. This was his circle of friends. This was where he wanted to be—among the greatest athletes and coaches in the Midwest.

An Indianapolis TV crew perched their broadcasting equipment on the covered porch of the country club's dining area ready to broadcast live from the event. The sports announcers interviewed coaches and Eric and me. One reporter asked Eric if I was going to go to Arizona, which Eric and I hadn't discussed.

He held my hand, massaging my fingers affectionately, and shifted his gaze to me.

I waited, holding my breath.

"Kelly has to continue with her therapy," Eric said. "She's really not in a position to travel. Her focus has to be on herself, on walking again. My focus has to be on playing, but it's hard. It's the hardest thing I've had to do." He paused to inhale. "They say there is a reason for everything, but I don't understand how anything good could come out of this."

The interview continued, but my head ached. I wanted to go to Arizona. I didn't want him to leave me behind. I remained poised in my chair, smiling for the camera, convincing others that my injuries were only temporary, that the doctors weren't sure how much more mobility I'd regain. "Eric's right. For now, I have work to do to get back to walking again."

I wanted to scream at Eric. *Don't leave me. Please, don't go. I need you.* But I needed to let him go.

When the event was over, Eric went to the hotel with my family and me and stayed in my room. We nestled side by side in bed with our clothes on.

"Kiss me," I said.

He pressed his lips to mine, but the passion was gone, only a stiff cardboard sensation without a hint of spark remained. He was only going through the motions to please me. I was losing him.

I couldn't breathe. What should I do? The room spun. Hurry. Think of something. How do I convince him that I'm the same person—that I would walk again? I couldn't reach over and run my fingers through his hair or hold him close to make him believe me. I couldn't move. I wanted to bargain with him—if I prove I will walk again, will you stay with me?

Reality seared its dark eyes into my soul. All I could do was suck in a wretched sob.

He drew me closer in his arms.

I didn't want his pity.

What had I expected? I was sporting a diaper and a leg bag, and I couldn't walk.

The air in my chest tightened. Determination reared its head. I couldn't give up. I bit my lip and swallowed my tears. He was in love with me once. I hadn't changed. And what about his marriage proposal? The funny one, the one with the twisty tie and his baby diamond earring he'd taken off and given to me when he asked me to go to Arizona with him? Certainly he remembered. I was the same person, so why wouldn't he still love me?

"I love you," he said, as if reading my mind. But his words were empty vapors evaporating in the air. What did they really mean?

There was nothing I could do but pray for a miracle.

Chapter Thirteen

Out of suffering have emerged the strongest souls; the most massive
characters are seared with scars.
Kahlil Gibran

When we finally returned to our home in Jasper, nothing was the same.

Posters and banners were draped across walls and doors welcoming me, but I didn't want them. I wanted to crawl up the stairs, take a hot shower, slink into my bed, and burrow under the covers. But that wasn't within my ability. I had to sit where I was parked until someone moved me.

But first I had to ask.

RIC had given us a packet on how to order a motorized wheelchair, but before we could order the chair, someone had to measure me. And before that could happen, Mom had to call the rehab facility in Evansville to make an appointment.

Meanwhile, I sat in my manual chair watching the construction workers tear up the dining room for my new living quarters. They pounded nails, drilled screws into drywall and added doors, walls, and a bathroom. With each bang and crunch, my head throbbed, and my hope splintered.

One construction worker told Andy he was donating a large wheelchair access door to the garage. Typically, they were three thousand dollars.

"Thanks," Andy and Mom said.

The man looked to me, maybe hoping for a thank you or a smile—something to acknowledge my appreciation, but no way. I didn't want the damn door. I didn't want any part of a wheelchair life. If I could have, I would have turned my back to him.

Since my room wasn't ready yet, I slept on the sofa in the family room. After the lights were out and the house was still, tears rolled out of the corner of my eyes, down the sides of my face, trickling into my ears. Eventually I fell asleep, but I woke trapped under the sheets with short bursts of leg spasms. I was smothering hot.

"Mom!" I shouted, breathlessly.

Andy snored from down the hallway.

"Mom." I called again, trying to thrust the thick air out of my lungs to gain volume, to push through the heat under the covers. No one heard. There were no nurses to help. I hollered one more time.

Finally, Andy came. He entered the family room half awake. "What's wrong?"

"I…need…to roll to my other side."

He smoothed back the covers from my face and I gulped in the fresh air. Then he carefully lifted me, turned my body in the other direction, and placed the pillows between my knees and thighs.

How would I get help every…single…night? How would I breathe through the panic attacks?

I used to wake early and bounce out of bed, but now I waited on the couch and stared at a speck of sunshine that peeked through the slatted window blinds. The world woke. Birds chattered. Dogs barked. Coffee brewed in the kitchen, dripping and hissing. My brothers' feet pattered above me in their rooms and then down the stairs, getting ready for school.

But I couldn't move. It wasn't up to me to decide when I could rise. It was up to whoever helped me.

When Mom was ready, she took my arms and flung me into a sitting position, but the motion was so quick my head bobbed and everything went black.

"Kelly!" Mom shouted. "Andy, come quick. There's something wrong with Kelly."

Andy ran into the room.

"Her eyes went up in her head," Mom said, her voice quivering. "What did I do?"

Andy propped a pillow behind me and leaned me back. "You didn't do anything, Brenda. This is all new to us."

I opened my eyes. "I'm okay. I fainted."

"She probably got up too quickly," Andy said. "That's all."

He was right.

Mom cried. "I don't know what I'm doing. How am I supposed to know how to do this?"

None of us did. Not me. Not Mom. Not Andy. Or my brothers. There was no manual that showed us how to switch to this new life. We were all blind.

"We'll get help soon." Andy rubbed Mom's shoulder.

The RIC staff had recommended we find a nurse to get me up in the morning, give me a shower, and do my bathroom. Otherwise, Mom and Andy would burn out. But with all the activity going on, we hadn't started the interviews yet. They slowly lifted me to a sitting position again and Mom emptied my leg bag.

Once I was dressed, Mom pivoted me into my chair, brought me food, and placed me in front of the TV so I could pretend my life was as normal as the actors in their shows.

Taking my clothes off and dressing me in the morning was like dressing a life-sized Barbie doll. I had to give instructions to whoever was taking care of me on the best way to manage the task. RIC trained us that it was easy to break an arm, a finger, or a wrist if I twisted the wrong way.

Days ran together. People came and went. Aunt Missy and Aunt Shari pitched in to care for me. Neighbors brought dinners. Life for others continued as if nothing had happened. Airplanes flew over the house. Cars zoomed by. People went to work. Friends went to school.

Nothing paused but me. Day after day, I sat in front of the TV near the warmth of the fireplace.

One day, my brothers went to school and Mom left for the grocery store. Before Andy went to take a shower he asked, "Will you be okay?"

I nodded. *As okay as I'll ever be.*

Two minutes after he left, my legs started to spasm. It had happened before, but not often, and I never knew when it would start or how long it would last. The only way to stop them from trembling was to apply pressure, something I couldn't do.

The tremors started in my lower legs and moved up to my thighs, slowly shaking my entire body. I slipped further and further forward, unable to stop the momentum, falling out of my chair onto the tile in front of the fireplace. My head thumped like a bowling ball.

With my cheek against the floor, tears fell, and in that moment, I wanted to die. What kind of life was this? What good was a life that needed constant care from others?

Five minutes later, Andy's footsteps sounded across the kitchen floor and paused as if wondering where I was. He could probably see the empty chair, but not me because the sofa blocked his view. "Kelly?"

"Down here." My words muffled against the floor.

"Kelly!" He hurried around the sofa to my side and lifted me back into my chair. "Are you hurt?"

"No." I couldn't look at him.

He brushed the hair out of my eyes. "What happened?"

I told him about the tremors.

He held me and patted my head. "I shouldn't have left you alone."

"You can't stay at my side all the time. I'm okay now."

He whooshed a heavy sigh. "Thank God. Who knows how long you would have been on the floor if I hadn't been home. You need to wear the safety seat belt."

I hated the unsightly lap belt with the bright red center buckle. The belt wrinkled my shirt. But maybe he was right. Some things were more important than fashion. "Okay. Strap me in."

After that incident, the safety restraint became a part of my wardrobe—red buckle and all.

Eventually my room was complete with bed, desk, and a hanging TV. The view smacked me with the truth: my condition was permanent.

Photo frames of my younger self hung on the walls—taunting me about a life I'd never know again. Me in a cheerleading uniform. My senior high school photo. I wanted to smash the frames on the floor.

If only I could.

The bed was a hospital bed from Great-Grandma's house. She'd used it during a period of illness, but for now, it was mine. It came complete with a crank to lift my head and another crank to raise my feet. *Oh, goody.*

The out-of body sensation returned. I was suspended from the ceiling looking down from above, like the motions of my life were a dream. That feeling became survival—especially the day I needed a bath.

My shower chair hadn't arrived yet and there was no easy way to bathe me. From my bed, Mom unbuttoned my shirt and slipped my arms out, one at a time, then removed the rest of my clothes. She draped a sheet over me and hollered for Andy.

What was she doing? He was going to help? I squeezed my eyes shut.

He didn't say anything as he hoisted my near-naked body out of my bed and carried my 115 pounds of dead weight into their bathroom, huffing. He bent to place me in the warm water and knelt on the floor holding my naked body up. Mom bathed me, swishing the cloth in the water in a hurried fashion.

I stared at a speck above the tub wall, a tiny crack in the grout, pretending they weren't hunched over my naked body, and that this was happening to someone else.

It was the longest bath of my life.

Afterward, Andy lifted me out and together he and Mom dried me off, wiping my hair and blotting my tears.

Andy hoisted me into bed and turned the TV to ESPN.

No one said a word.

No one ever talked about those moments, the private and ordinary moments every able-bodied person took for granted.

In cheerleading, a tumbling pass included a round-off, back-handspring, and a full twist. It took me ten years of training to learn that maneuver, but what I had to do now was a hundred times more difficult, and it would take me a lot longer to get good at it, if I did at all.

The first Sunday I was home, Mom insisted I go to church with them, but I didn't want to go.

Growing up, our family went to church together every week. During Mass, my brothers and I stayed solemn, prayerful, and respectful—or else Mom would shoot us the "look." At communion, when the parishioners walked up to get the host, Jason and I knelt at our place and *people watched*. During many services, the people from a nearby home for the mentally challenged attended. They came to church in a van as a group and walked down the aisle for communion in single file. Most of them had some type of visible deformity—enlarged heads, limps and dragging feet, loud voices, drawn-in arms, or crossed eyes. Jason and I snickered as they walked by. Our bodies trembled from suppressed laughter until Mom would shoot us the look again.

When we returned home, we mocked those people and walked around the kitchen dragging our feet. We limped and beat our arms into our chests, distorted our voices, and grunted obnoxious sounds until we laughed, until we cried.

So when Mom said I had to go to church with them, I feared that people would make fun of me, too. *That's what I get.*

Andy pulled up to the circle drive at Precious Blood Church, put the car in Park, and unloaded my wheelchair from the trunk. He lifted me out of the car and onto the chair. People stopped. Stared. I was the freak at a show. People asked how I was doing, pity reflecting in their wrinkled brows.

I smiled.

When Ryan pushed me to our seats, every eye was on me. When it was time to shake hands to offer a sign of peace, people turned away from me like I was invisible.

Okay, God. Is this your way of getting back at me for making fun of the disabled people?

Even though I knew God didn't work that way, I couldn't stop the guilt from gnawing at me. How ignorant I'd been.

The mentally challenged and disabled people were the real heroes!

When we got home, Ryan took the video recorder out of its case and Ted, Tyler, and I staged mini plays about a day in the life of a quad, making fun of how I couldn't move, of me lying in my bed trying to sit up, of all the things I couldn't do. We called it, "Counter Attack."

In one scene, Tyler pushed me through the double doors of my bedroom as if I was exiting a western saloon. In another, Ryan covered me with a white blanket and rolled me into things. Tyler called me a Rolling Ghost. In another scene, Ryan lodged a tennis racquet under my chin and threw balls at the center of the racquet, just missing my face. It was stupid fun, but a way I could laugh at myself and try to forgive myself for the way I'd acted toward the disabled in our church.

Ryan used his sense of humor to make me smile. He did his best to make jokes and entertain me, which he was usually good at, but it was tough to laugh about anything. One night shortly after I came home, he lifted me out of my wheelchair to put me into bed. In his fun-loving way, he twirled me around trying to get me to laugh, but it only made me dizzy.

Mom came into the room. "How did you get in bed?"

"Ryan put me in."

She turned to Ryan. "Wasn't she too heavy?"

He shrugged.

"That was probably really stupid," Ryan said. "Now that she knows I can do it, I'll probably have to keep doing it."

Everyone took turns helping, but Ryan took extra turns. He brought me food and brushed my hair. He applied my lipstick and sponged my foundation. I taught him everything he didn't want to know about mascara and eyeliner. He held up the mirror and sighed impatiently while I inspected my face.

"Will you blot this spot right here?" I asked. "It's too thick."

He sighed louder.

I paid my brothers to bring me food, to fill my water bottle, or move me to another place in the house. They didn't see me any differently than their annoying sister who was constantly asking them to do things. They ignored me.

I called to them when they were in the lower level of our home, the room where they played pool, ping-pong, and video games. "It must be nice to be able to walk and play games!" I shouted down to them. *My blatant ploy to make them feel guilty.* I counted the seconds before one responded. It typically took less than five.

"I'll help you as soon as my lives are over," Tyler said. "I only have two more to go."

If only I had two lives.

Eric called often. My heart fluttered each time the phone rang, anticipating our conversation, wanting to be there for him. But I had to wait for others to answer the phone.

I shouted to my brothers. "Answer the phone!"

They were in the basement with their friends and didn't want to walk up to give me the phone and adjust it so I could talk. They often let it ring.

Didn't they realize that Eric's voice was the only thing I looked forward to?

When Eric and I finally talked, I rarely complained. I pasted on my upbeat voice and drummed up positive things to say about sports or national news. He no longer asked about my progress. He probably figured that if I didn't bring it up there was nothing new to report. I wanted to say, "I walked today," to give him hope, to give him a reason to stay true to me.

He talked about Arizona and his new team and how he didn't feel like he belonged there without me. He told me he missed me and we cried, and his words made me believe he still loved me.

But some days he didn't call, and I made excuses for him.

Mom asked, "Did Eric call today?"

"He's busy. He'll call when he can." I defended him, rationalizing why he hadn't called, but fear invaded my confidence. Had he met someone to replace me?

There was no way to know.

We hired a nurse and an aide from Jasper Memorial Hospital's

Home Care to take care of me Monday, Wednesday, and Friday mornings. Those were my *shower* days, the days I looked forward to because I loved a hot shower, but they were also my most *dreaded* days because the aide did my bowel program. It took them two hours to get me ready for the day. First, the nurse emptied and irrigated my bladder, then inserted an enema into my rectum. Once she was done, she left and the aide took over. The aide transferred me from the bed to the shower chair, and for the next ten minutes, she washed me in the shower from head to toe. After drying me off, she blow-dried my hair and styled it. Then she transferred me back to the bed to dress and stretch me.

Having help gave my parents and my aunts a break. They all needed to get back to their own lives. Tuesdays, Thursdays, Saturdays, and Sundays were my sleep-in days when Mom got me up later, when it was convenient for her.

I needed new clothes. Pants crept up my legs showing off my skinny ankles. Bras with a clasp in the back created sores. Shorts were out of the question because my legs were thin and atrophied. Shoes with heels elevated my bony knees and they had to be a half size bigger because my feet swelled. Belts were no longer needed because nothing was tucked in.

Before the accident, I carried my makeup kit in my purse. Now my purse consisted of Tylenol, my hand gear/wrist guard, and urine bags.

One night when Mom and Andy were gone, Ryan was home with his buddies hanging out in the lower level, watching sports and playing video games. I called down to him because it was late and I needed to get in bed. RIC had warned us about bedsores and the dangers of staying in one position too long.

He ignored my pleas.

"I'll pay you ten dollars if you come up here."

Nothing.

When Mom and Andy returned and realized Ryan hadn't transferred me to bed, they were incensed.

"Ryan. Get up here," Andy said.

The noise in the basement hushed at Andy's tone.

Ryan climbed the stairs to where Andy stood. "What?"

"You were supposed to transfer Kelly to her bed."

"I'm sick of taking care of her, putting on her makeup, doing her hair. Why is it always me? None of my friends have to do this crap."

"You're a part of this family," Mom said as she wheeled me into my room. "Everyone pitches in. That's what's expected."

"She needs to learn how to do her own makeup," Ryan complained, his face red.

Andy wanted to ground him, but I asked him not to. I didn't want Ryan to resent me.

Ryan wouldn't be the last person to get frustrated with my never-ending requests, but at least he spoke his mind, and I knew where he stood. I respected him for that. He was the only one brave enough to say it like it was.

Maybe he was right. Maybe I needed to learn how to do my own makeup. I hated needing his help, or anyone else's. I wished I could survive without anyone, but maybe it was time for me to try to do some things for myself.

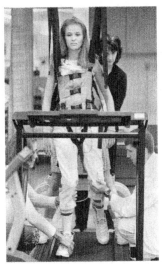

(David Pierini/*The Herald*)

Chapter Fourteen

Some see a hopeless end while others see an endless hope.
Unknown

My therapy continued on an outpatient basis at Memorial Hospital's rehab center in Jasper. I couldn't give up. Any day I hoped a neuron would find a path from my spine to my brain and instantly connect. Some days Mom drove me, and other days my aunts did.

One day a rehab tech said, "We're going to strap you in this machine over here." The tech pointed to a harness above a treadmill. "It simulates walking. It might feel strange to stand again, but let's see what you can do."

I couldn't wait to stand.

Two techs strapped me in the harness and clipped the supports around me. Two other techs planted my feet beside each other on a treadmill. Slowly, they rigged me up to a standing position. I could finally see at eye level again. It was such a rush of sensory stimulation—seeing and hearing from a different level, feeling my body erect and taking the pressure off my tailbone. Oh, how I wished I could stand forever.

The techs groaned in their efforts to help stimulate a walking motion. Maybe now that my body was aligned something would happen. Excited, I willed my muscles to work and concentrated on putting one foot in front of the other. Hope propelled me to grunt and surge forward.

But the only thing that moved was my blood pressure from the failed effort.

I didn't show the techs my disappointment or my frustration, and I didn't complain, but inside I wept.

The occupational therapist worked to help me build muscle and mobility in my left hand. She set an easel with paper in front of me, and a palette of paint beside me. Pineapples had been my favorite object to draw in high school. I drew them during class when I should have been paying attention.

After the tech placed a brush in my wrist guard, and nodded for me to begin, I worked at painting a pineapple. The first few drawings didn't resemble the fruit—they were simply a blend of yellow and green brush strokes. But the more I painted, the better I got.

One day, when Aunt Missy came to pick me up, she saw my drawing. "You painted that?"

I nodded.

"That's really good, Kelly."

I chuckled. "You can have it."

"Really?"

I nodded again.

"Thanks."

"Did you know that the pineapple is a welcoming sign?" A tech asked. "It means, welcome to my home."

"I never knew that," I said.

Months later, I was in Aunt Missy's home and saw my pineapple painting matted and framed in her hallway. I hadn't realized the drawing meant so much to her. After that day, I painted pineapples often and gave them away as gifts to my friends and family. The pineapple became my signature artwork. It was the only visible metric of my improved mobility.

The insurance company decided that Jason no longer qualified for benefits at a specialized facility. Since he hadn't shown improvement, they wouldn't invest more dollars into his therapy.

"What are we supposed to do?" Mom asked.

"You'll have to bring him home," the doctor at RIC said.

Mom cried. "How are we supposed to manage him, Kelly, and our three other children?"

Jason had feeding tubes, aspirators, and the threat of bedsores and was a solid six feet tall. He needed skilled care, but where would Mom find it?

Dr. Campbell, a physician who practiced medicine at Jasper Memorial Hospital, took a personal interest in Jason's case and found a way to bring him to the hospital for more inpatient rehab. "Specialists claim that brain-trauma patients typically respond better if they're surrounded by people." He coordinated the efforts to bring Jason out of his coma by finding volunteers to help.

Bev Luegers, a friend of our family, organized a program where a volunteer was at Jason's bedside around the clock. Volunteers read to Jason, prayed, sang to him, and talked to him about current events. He was rarely alone.

Some of the volunteers who came and read to him didn't know our family, but they knew Jason could hear voices and they were told that the interaction of people in his room might help bring him out of his coma, and they wanted to help. People wanted to be a part of his healing.

Mom occasionally left me alone to watch Ted and Tyler, so she could visit Jason and work with him. "I'll be back in an hour," she said to me one day.

When she left, I said to Ted, "Do you want to bake brownies?" His eyes lit up. "Yeah."

Since I couldn't see on top of the counter and he wasn't tall enough to load the ingredients there, I told him to set everything on the floor. "Take the brownie box out of the corner cupboard and place it in my lap."

Step by step, he listened to my instructions and set the ingredients on the floor: the brownie mix, an egg, oil, and a cup of water. He carried a mixing bowl, spatula, and mixer to the floor too. I taught him how to set the timer and turn the oven to 350 degrees. He folded the ingredients together and used the hand mixer to blend them, then scooped the batter into a pan and stood on his tiptoes to place it in the oven.

Afterward, he handed me a beater and kept one for himself and together we licked the dough and laughed while the house filled with the sweet aroma of chocolate. My mouth watered.

Mom came home in time to help cut the brownies. "Ted, I can't believe you made these."

"Kelly told me what to do."

Mom turned to me. "Nice work." But when she saw the mess on the floor, she cringed. "Who's going to clean this up?"

Ted shrugged and looked at me.

"I'll have to sit this one out," I said, laughing.

Ted helped Mom clean up the mess, but the next time we baked together (and we did many more times), Ted placed a vinyl tablecloth on the floor first. That way all he had to do was take it outside and shake it.

Baking with Ted was the first time in a long time I'd done something positive. The experience made Ted and me closer, but it also helped me to see that I could still teach, that I didn't need to physically move to create something, that my voice had power.

I spent a lot of time in the kitchen near the candy drawer too, sitting around while Mom cooked or cleaned. After meals, I loved to have something sweet and Mom knew it. One day after lunch, she slipped me a Lemon Head before she ran the sweeper. (Lemon Heads are little lemon-tasting candies shaped like a ball.)

As I sucked on the candy, I remembered Mom's visits to my elementary school when she'd sneak a piece of candy into my desk. She was the coolest mom. It made all the other kids jealous.

But today, the candy lodged in my windpipe. I gasped. I couldn't…breathe. I flailed my arm in jerky motions. *Mom!*

"Kelly?" She shut off the vacuum cleaner.

A friend of the family who was visiting at the time stepped behind me, wrapped her arms below my rib cage, and jerked me toward her, administering the Heimlich maneuver.

The lemon ball shot out of my mouth and clattered on the wood floor. I sucked in a ragged breath. Tears streamed down my cheeks. Quadriplegics don't have the lung force to cough or sneeze the way able-bodied people do. My cough sounded like a bird chirp—quick, soft, and a little melodic.

"Oh, my gosh, Kelly. You could have choked to death."

Wouldn't the headlines have been ironic?

Girl sustains blunt force trauma from drunk driver and survives, but dies from a Lemon Head.

I never ate another Lemon Head. (But I still eat Skittles—the wild berry flavor in the purple bag—never alone though, just in case.)

My new life continued. Nights were the worst, and darkness my enemy, dragging on forever, especially when my cries went unanswered and I didn't get turned. I coped by praying. "Oh God, steer my thoughts in another direction so I won't focus on my discomfort."

Soon, I fell back to sleep—unless there was a fly in my room. Then it was torture because it pestered me all night.

(David Pierini/*The Herald*)

Chapter Fifteen

Our prayers may be awkward. Our attempts may be feeble. But since the power of prayer is in the One who hears it and not in the one who says it, our prayers do make a difference.
Max Lucado

I wasn't the only one who had to adjust to my new life.

Mom struggled, but her battle was different than mine and her path for recovery was different, too. She not only had to deal with the day-to-day difficulties of seeing to my needs, but her hopes and dreams for my future shattered. She wanted to see me happy and independent. She wanted me to fall in love, have a family, and eventually give her grandchildren. She thought she'd have an active lifetime with me—taking spinning classes together, hiking along the Patoka River, and going on family vacations.

She believed in miracles and searched for a way to make my life an active one. She wanted to help me beat all the odds and walk again.

Her faith gave me strength.

People from all over the US wrote to her sending prayers and hope. They told her about the miracles that happened to their sisters, brothers, and daughters. Daily, my mother read letters and cards a stranger had sent about someone they knew and how a miracle had healed them.

Mom and my aunts—Missy and Shari—took me to rehab, exercise reflexologists, chiropractors, and spiritual healers. Mom's faith grew stronger and louder. It was like she'd made a deal with God—if He let Jason and me live, she'd devote her life to Him. She believed that if she prayed for a miracle then God would oblige. She attended Mass multiple times a week. She went to church some mornings to sit and pray the rosary. She attended novenas. She conversed with other spiritual followers who encouraged her to attend well-known conferences where a specific leader conducted miracles.

She said, "Kelly, so and so is in Evansville. Let's go. He's a proven healer."

She drove me an hour from our home to attend one conference. We wore heavy coats, hats, and mittens because the weather had turned cold. After we found a parking spot, Mom transferred me from the car to my chair and strapped me in.

"We have to hurry. We're late." She took hold of my wheelchair and steered it down a sidewalk path to the conference center. When we started to cross the street, the right wheels of my chair wedged in a rut on the edge of the curb.

"Slow down." I said, as my chair teetered.

"Oh, no!" Mom tried to navigate me back onto the concrete, but lost control.

It happened fast, but I saw it coming in slow motion. The chair went down on its side with me still strapped in. My shoulder hit the dirt first. My head followed. Dirt embedded in my cheek and a bruise swelled, but more than anything my anger seethed. How could she do this?

Standing at the edge of the street, she attempted to right the wheelchair but didn't have the strength. "I need help!" She shouted into the wind. No one was around except for passing cars.

One car slowed.

"Maybe these people will help," she said.

The man in the car pulled up to the street light and pulled over to the curb. Instead of helping, he shook his head like he was annoyed that Mom was in his way. He peeled out and sped off.

What a jerk," Mom said. "Maybe I should call 9-1-1."

"Get me up," I said, my face still planted in the dirt.

"I can't, Kelly. The chair is too heavy." She tried again without success.

Humiliated, I closed my eyes.

Another man pulled his car up to the curb, put his flashers on, and jumped out. "Can I help you?"

"Yes, please. I can't get her chair up by myself," Mom said. She laughed nervously.

Together Mom and the stranger righted my chair.

Mom thanked him.

"Are you okay?" he asked me.

"Yes, I'm fine." My voice shook. "Thank you."

After the man drove off, I said, "Take me home. You're crazy. It's too cold to be here, and now my head hurts."

"We didn't come all this way to turn around. We're going. You're okay." She brushed the dirt off my face and shook my hair loose where dirt particles lay imbedded.

I tasted dirt and spit it out, but I told myself it would be worth it, that after I met the healer none of this would matter. Mom was right. We needed to get there.

She raced into the pavilion area and into the warm building to the sign with an arrow pointing to the auditorium. Mom followed the sign and we went in. Hundreds of people sat listening to the speaker.

After the man gave a speech about faith and healing, he invited sick and disabled people to come to the stage to be healed. Mom pushed me into the line and gradually we made our way to the front.

The man prayed over me. "Stand, my child. You are healed. You can walk now."

That was it? Just like that? I didn't feel any different. Was he crazy?

He tried to lift me, but the restraint kept me in place. I wasn't going anywhere. Even if the restraint wasn't on, I still couldn't move.

In the car on the way home, my hope faded. Mom stayed silent.

This should have worked. I should be walking. I tried not to cry.

"Stay positive, Kelly. Keep praying," Mom said. "In God's time you will heal."

But when would that be? What was taking Him so long?

"Let's go to Holy Love," Mom announced another day. "On a pilgrimage."

"What's that?"

"It's a sacred place where you can go and ask Blessed Mary to heal you. It's in Cleveland, Ohio, and it's supposed to be a holy land."

It sounded perfect. Maybe this was where I'd heal.

"People go there from all around the world. Some see visions. Some are healed from arthritis, heart problems, and other ailments. We have to go," Mom said.

"Okay."

A lady from Mom's Bible study had brought a pamphlet about the place to Mom's group. She read parts of it to me. "There's the Lake of Tears and the Sorrowful Mother Shrine there. It's Mary's favorite place on earth, designed by heaven. They claim that the water has healing abilities."

"You don't have to plunge me in it, do you?"

She laughed. "No, we'll sprinkle it on your head." She continued to read. "Each person who visits the spring and shrine will be affected. Heaven knows and will give each person what she needs."

I couldn't wait to go. Mom's faith was contagious, and her enthusiasm sold me.

She took me there.

The rosary was at midnight, which was the time when the healing and the visions supposedly took place. Winter shared a glimpse of her icy breath even though it was only November, and my teeth chattered. I prayed fervently. Others around me prayed the Our Father and Hail Mary. The intensity of the faith-filled people lifted my spirits and spiked my hope.

"Did you see that?" Mom asked after the last prayer.

"What?"

"A million twinkling lights. You didn't see them?" Her words raced excitedly.

I shook my head.

"I can't believe you didn't see anything." Her enthusiasm caused others around us to chatter.

The lady next to us smiled. "I saw them too." Tears filled her eyes.

"Maybe I blinked," I said. Why hadn't I seen what Mom had? The brochure said no person left without being affected in some way. I tried to move my toes, my legs, but I couldn't. Why hadn't something happened to me? If God knew what I needed, why couldn't I walk now? Didn't He think I needed to walk?

"Kelly," Mom said, "You have to believe or none of this will help."

"I thought I did." But maybe I needed to pray more.

Disappointment covered me like a heavy coat, weighing down on my faith, choking my belief that God was with me and would give me what I needed. Where was He?

Christopher Reeves sent me his picture and a letter, encouraging me to attend a conference he was hosting in New York to learn more about the studies they were doing for people with spinal cord injuries.

"We need to go," Mom said.

Who was I to argue?

We went.

Traveling by plane as a quadriplegic was a new experience. The whole pat-me-down thing at security was a bigger deal. People stared at me while I waited in line. Their eyes roamed over my body and my chair like I was a piece of unfamiliar luggage. Did I have something on my face? Was my hair standing up? Did I do something wrong? No, they were gawking at me because I was paralyzed. The terminal police took forever to check me, too, so the ogles seemed to go on forever. In addition to checking for explosives, security had to inspect my chair too.

Before we boarded, I had to give up my chair so they could store it in the belly of the plane. They replaced it for a narrow one that could squeeze down the center aisle. Rules were that the flight staff had to transfer me to the skinny chair.

Trusting a stranger to move my body meant I had to allow their hands to touch me. I doubted many able-bodied people would be up for that experience, especially if they valued their private space. If the person transferring me didn't bend the proper way, I could miss the chair, fall to the floor, or scrape my bottom on something. And if that staff person had body odor or wore strong perfume, I wore their stench all day or until I took a shower—which never happened on vacation because I couldn't travel with my shower chair.

Mom and I had to sit in different parts of the plane. I sat in the back in an aisle seat next to a middle-aged man. When the plane landed, the force jarred me forward until my head was almost touching my knees. The lap belt kept me in the seat, but there wasn't a shoulder harness to keep my upper body from lurching forward.

With my body hunched over, I said to the man next to me, "Excuse me, sir." My words came out muffled in my lap. "Would it be too much trouble for you to push me back up?"

Nothing. He must not have heard me. I tried again. "Can you help me?"

Still nothing.

I inhaled deeply and forced my words to sound louder. "Sir, could you help me?"

"Me?" he asked.

Whom else would I be talking to? "Yes, please. Could you push my shoulders back into the seat? I'm a quadriplegic."

He hesitated, then turned in his chair and lifted my shoulders to a sitting position.

"Ah," I said. "Now I can see the world again. Thank you." I laughed.

He didn't. His brow creased as if horrified. "Does that happen often?"

"Nope. That was the first time."

The people sitting across the aisle stared, their mouths agape.

"I became a quad a few months ago. I'm still learning what my limitations are."

He nodded. "Were you hit by a drunk driver?"

"Yes."

"I heard something on the news about you. I'm sorry," he said, and asked me questions about the accident, the driver, and the other kids in the car.

Mom and I laughed later about the man's expression and me bent over in my lap. If I didn't keep humor in my pocket I'd be sucked into the pity—and that wasn't an option.

At the conference, we met people who were injured in accidents—surfing, motorcycle, and construction work—some had sat in their chairs for decades, waiting and hoping for research to find ways to heal them. There were fewer females than males at the conference—and even fewer people my age.

Christopher's mother spoke. Her message was articulate, her presence poised, her delivery organized. She spoke about implanting chips, radical surgeries, and raising funds for research dollars. She shared what they were doing to find a cure. The foundation needed volunteers. Guinea pigs. Would I consider helping?

No, I wasn't up for a radical surgery in China, or anything else they mentioned, but the conference opened my eyes to a problem in the world that I'd never paid attention to before. I wasn't alone. There were many people like me sitting in chairs waiting for a miracle.

Did they have faith? Were they praying?

We met many other handicapped people while we were there, too, but one man stood out. He was an outgoing sort of guy. He wrecked his motorcycle going 100 mph. He said, "After my accident, I decided to do something with my life and studied to be an attorney to help disabled people. I snow ski too."

That didn't surprise me. He was more adventuresome than me.

"There's a lot more that you could do too, Kelly."

"Thanks, but I'm going to walk again."

He frowned. "You should stop hoping for something that might not happen. Try to focus on what you have right now because you're missing out on some pretty amazing things."

It was like he'd slapped me. *How dare he shoot down my dreams of walking again?* I wanted him to turn away, to move away from me, but he didn't. He stared at me like he was waiting for me to say something. His words were the kind that only bold and unfiltered people said, the insensitive ones.

After he left, his words clung to me, the sting of his slap burning my cheeks for days. I seethed inside at the man's attitude, at how brazen he was for saying what he'd said, for thinking I was wallowing, for hinting that I wasn't accepting my limitations. Who was he to tell me what I should and shouldn't focus on? He didn't know me.

Then it hit me. He was a quad, just like me, different than any able-bodied person giving advice. His limitations weren't a whole lot different than mine, yet he hadn't waited to walk again.

The more I thought about what he'd said, the more sense it made. I didn't want to get to the end of my one and only life and feel that I wasted it because I was bitter about my circumstances. I saw a quote, "Stop waiting for Friday, for summer, for someone to find love with you, for life. Happiness is achieved when you stop waiting for it and make the most of the moment you are in now," and decided I didn't want to wait. I needed to find something positive to do while I worked on my mobility.

But what?

Mom's growing faith rubbed off on my brothers and me in different ways. We prayed more often as a family, but there were still times my brothers and I made fun of Mom's over-the-top faith healing antics, too—not in front of her, but on our own.

Late one night, everyone had gone to bed, and I was too hot to sleep. There was nothing I could do but pray. *God, please send someone to check on me. Please God.*

Two minutes later, the stairs creaked. "Who's there?" I said.

"Me."

"Tyler?"

"Yes."

"Come here, please." I made sure my voice sounded desperate.

Tyler entered my room. "What?"

"The Holy Spirit is in you. I prayed for God to send someone to help me right now and here you are." I used my most dramatic voice.

"Yeah, yeah. What do you need?" he asked, sighing.

"Seriously, Ty, God sent you to me on purpose."

He paused for a brief moment as if weighing my sincerity.

"You've been chosen. Maybe God has made you a healer."

"Stop it, Kelly, you're scaring me."

"Think about it. Why did you come downstairs?"

He shrugged. "I'm not sure."

"See. It's because God called you to heal me."

"Okay, then," he said, sighed loudly, and placed his hands on my legs. "Rise!"

I laughed and did my best to pretend to be dramatically lifted.

He laughed too. "What do you really want?"

"Can you take my top cover off?"

He adjusted my blankets and pillow and went back to bed.

Deep down I knew Mom was right. God had a plan and I needed to find it. I needed to feel it, breathe it, and become a part of His plan, but I didn't know how. I sighed. If only healing was as simple as Tyler planting his hands on my legs.

It took Mom several more healing trips before she realized that I wouldn't heal until I was ready and she was the only person benefiting from all the traveling. She believed in miracles and so did I, but the healers weren't working. I had to find a different way.

"You have to forgive and let go, Kelly," she said.

I thought I had, but if that meant accepting my limitations, I couldn't. I wasn't ready to give up the Kelly Craig I had been before the accident.

I wanted her back!

(David Pierini/*The Herald)*

Chapter Sixteen

Each one should use whatever gift he has received to serve others,
faithfully administering God's grace in its various forms.
1 Peter 4:10 NIV

Mom and my aunts told me, "Use your voice, Kelly. You could travel to schools and talk about the consequences of drinking and driving."

I wanted no part of that freak show. Everyone would gawk at me with pity in their eyes, just like they had at church and the airport. It made me sick to my stomach. Mom and my aunts wanted to give me purpose—something to focus on, which I understood, but I stood firm. I was not going anywhere.

They didn't give up. They wrote the speech for me and set the date. My first presentation would be at Jasper Middle School. I finally agreed to speak because I didn't want to let them down. They were doing so much for me—taking me to therapy, doing my bathroom, getting me dressed, feeding me. I could do this one small thing for them.

When Mom pulled up in front of the school, I smiled through my anxiety, wishing I could stay in the car and hide. Life was different in the chair, and I wasn't sure how to be me.

I went through the motions while they helped me out of the car, positioned my chair, and pushed me through the double doors.

Students gathered in the gymnasium—the same place I'd cheered and hung out for years. They hushed when I entered. I swallowed the lump in my throat. Every eye was on me—every...pitiful...stare.

Missy adjusted the mic and the principal introduced me.

I wanted the students to stare at me with their mouths agape, in awe over my athletic ability—the way others had before. But they stared at my chair and me with frowns and empty pride.

Don't dwell on it.

I began speaking. At first, my voice came out small, but by the third sentence my voice amplified and the words came out more forceful. I told the students about our vacation, how I used to cheer, and how Jason played football.

"Look at me now," I said. "I can't brush my own teeth or comb my hair. One person did this. One person who chose to drink and drive." I paused for effect. "Did you know that every two minutes a person dies because of a drunk driver?"

As the story flowed, passion fueled my energy and my adrenaline soared. I'd forgotten how I loved the speech class I took at IU and the powerful feeling it gave me to have an audience's attention.

Maybe Mom and my aunts were right. Maybe this was something I could do with my life, something that would give me a reason to go on. Maybe God needed more people to share the message about drinking and driving, and it was my responsibility to contribute.

After the speech, students rushed to me with probing questions. They asked silly questions like, "How do you go to the bathroom?" and "How do you take a shower?" but also serious questions, "Can you have children?" and "Have you talked to the drunk driver?"

One girl asked, "Are you in pain?"

Thankfully I wasn't in physical pain, but emotional pain was a different story, but it was safer not to talk about that.

Adults probably had the same questions the student had, but were afraid to ask. I realized how little some people knew about the life of a quadriplegic, and I didn't mind sharing. More people needed to understand. Maybe I'd seek more speaking engagements. If I honored God by speaking on the consequences of drunk driving, would I heal faster? Would he grant me a miracle?

I didn't know the answers, but praying about them would help.

Eric called and asked questions: "What did you do in therapy today?"

"I wiggled my left toes yesterday. The doctor says it is a good sign to have movement below my injury. He said I have more movement than most C-4 fractures. I have the mobility of a C-7 injury."

"That's great," he said, sounding as hopeful as I felt that progress might continue.

"How's your hand?" I asked. "What do the doctors say about you playing ball?"

"I should have a full recovery, but it'll take time. I feel bad that I'm okay and you aren't."

"That's silly," I said.

"I'm thinking about transferring to Iowa. If I'm in Iowa I'll be closer to you and my dad, plus Steve Alford's offered me a spot on the team. What do you think?"

"I think you have to do what's right for you." But it didn't matter where he was. He wasn't with me. His life was going on and mine wasn't.

My parents decided to fly him out to see me for Thanksgiving, probably hoping to cheer me up. It had been four months since the accident. He agreed to come. Seeing him in my home sent my heart soaring—his dimpled smile, his wavy hair, the way he dominated the room—it brought back all the reasons I loved him. My goal was to act as able-bodied as possible so he could see that my personality was the same, that I was the same girl he fell in love with.

Before dinner, we hung out with my family and talked about basketball and his career, and how he decided to transfer to Iowa. After we ate the usual turkey and stuffing dinner, we hung out in my room. He talked about people I didn't know, mentioning the names of strangers, reminding me of how his life had taken a different path, one without me.

Before Mom went to bed, she transferred me to my bed and left Eric and me alone.

He sat on the edge holding my hand.

"Are you seeing other girls?" There, I asked the one question that sat on my chest.

He hesitated and turned my hand over. "I'd be lying if I said no. I'm sorry. I love you, Kelly, and I always will, but I can't handle the responsibilities of being with someone who needs…" His voice trailed. "I'm too young. I want to be that man everyone wants me to be, but I can't."

It was like he'd sucker punched me. What an idiot I'd been to think he would stay with me.

"It's like you died," he said, tears filling his eyes.

I wanted to beat my fists into his chest. I hadn't died. I was alive and in love with him. I refused to cry. How could he love me unconditionally and then leave me?

I knew then that we were over. God was making it clear that I needed to cut him out of my life. No more phone calls. No more contact. Could I do that?

Letting go meant letting go of a huge chunk of the old Kelly. I'd held on to her for too long, and I wasn't sure I was ready to let her go. If I let her go, I'd have to let go of my hope, and I wasn't ready to do that.

Later that night, after he'd gone upstairs to sleep in my old room, I let go. I succumbed to the tears and the hope. I cried until my chin trembled, my eyes swelled and my nose dripped onto the pillow. I pitied myself and my inability to wipe my face with a tissue. My chest ached with a sharp cramp, and I wondered if my heart was dying from the pain. Could that happen?

If Eric wouldn't love me, who would? Would anyone accept me for me, see the *me* behind the chair?

And I didn't mean only guys. What about an employer, a friend, a brother? Was everyone I knew on the verge of letting me go because of my disability?

Was I too much work?

The walls in my room closed in around me like the stone wall around my heart.

The next morning, I said goodbye to Eric, never discussing the night before, pretending indifference. Hopelessness wore a mask. Depression gave me a stoic exterior.

But he continued to call. Some days I wondered if he was reconsidering our relationship, but then I saw something in the news about him. The media made him sound like an insensitive jerk for not standing by my side. He had survivor's guilt because he could do all the things I couldn't.

At the same time, I noticed that one of my cheer friends had disappeared from my life, and I grew suspicious. "Have you heard from her?" I asked him.

He sighed heavily. "I saw her at a party and we cried about you and your situation. One thing led to another." He let his voice trail.

"You slept with her?"

His silence was the answer.

I loathed my friend for what she did. I wanted to call her up and scream at her, slap my hand across her face. I should have hated Eric, too, but I couldn't. I wanted him so desperately I would have forgiven him.

What an idiot. Where was my dignity? If I wanted to move on, I had to be strong. Heat coursed through my body and propelled my words.

"Quit calling me," I said. "You're staying in touch because you feel guilty, but that's not helping me. It gives me false hope. I can't live this way." I took a deep breath. "For my sake, please quit calling." I wanted to shout, L*ove me like you said you did. Don't leave me. I need you.* He cried, but I kept my composure and hung up.

When Mom put me to bed that night, the loss covered me, but left me as hollow as my spinal injury. Maybe it was better to not feel at all.

The lyrics to the Garth Brooks song slammed into my mind, the song I'd shared with Eric months before. When I was afraid he gave me courage, he was my *somebody* who believed in me. I wouldn't let him down. Anytime I doubted myself, I'd think of him. What a joke. I was wrong. The song that was guiding my heart was not about Eric; the song was about God!

God was the only person I could rely on, the only person who would never leave me.

But where was He? Did he know my heart? Did he hear my prayers?

Just like my hope for a relationship with Eric, my rehab dwindled. When I returned to Jasper I had it every day, then I went three times a week, twice a week, and eventually I didn't go at all.

I immersed myself in perfecting my speeches by studying motivational speakers. One speaker I studied was John Wooden. One of his tools was the *Pyramid of Success*, a triangle spreadsheet that included fifteen blocks of favorable traits. On the bottom were the following words with their definitions: industriousness, friendship, loyalty, cooperation, and enthusiasm. The pyramid included all the necessary personality traits a person had to attain in order to be successful—at the top was one block titled "*competitive greatness.*" By following this pyramid, John Wooden believed the person would reach success.

This quote was at the top, "Success is peace of mind which is a direct result of self-satisfaction in knowing you did your best to become the best that you are capable of becoming."

At one speaking event, someone took my photo with Mr. Wooden's pyramid draped in my lap. Several weeks later, I received this letter from Mr. Wooden:

Dear Kelly,

Our mutual friends, the Easts, were by yesterday and brought some photos of you with my pyramid in your lap. It pleases me that you have enjoyed my idea of what success should be and what I consider the necessary steps to reach that plateau.

We are all equal as far as having the opportunity of making the most of what we have under the conditions that exist for us, rather than complaining about what we don't have.

My father gave me and my brothers two sets of threes:
1. Don't whine, don't complain, and don't make excuses. Make the effort to do the best of which we are capable under the conditions that exist at the time.
2. Don't lie, don't cheat, and don't steal and you will always have a clear conscience.
3. I also remember a verse he quoted —
"When I look back, it seems to me
all the grief that had to be—
made me, when the pain was over
I was stronger than I was before."

The Easts spoke highly of your courage.
If we have faith, family, and friends, our needs are filled.
In His name with best wishes and love,

John Wooden

He included the pyramid in his note and wrote these words on it:

> For Kelly—with congratulations on your positive outlook. Why—we can't understand, but we must believe in who directs our path.
>
> Best wishes, John Wooden

When Andy saw the letter, his eyes grew as big as golf balls.
"Do you know who this guy is?" he asked.
"The head basketball coach for UCLA?"
"Yes, but more. He's a legend, the greatest coach of all time." Andy cited Wooden's accomplishments. "He's in the basketball Hall of Fame, Kelly. Can I take this letter to work with me?"
I laughed. "Sure." For the next half hour, I researched Coach Wooden in detail. His winning basketball statistics and positive messages were unmatched. Although I'd never met him, his words inspired me and the fact that he took time to send me, a nobody, a personal message made me sit a little taller and hum a tune.
He'd influenced many people in his career. Could I do the same? Could I be a person with all the attributes on Mr. Wooden's pyramid?
I wasn't sure, but I wanted to try.

Chapter Seventeen

Coincidence is God's way of being anonymous.
Laura Pederson, *Best Bet*

January 2000
University of Illinois, Champaign

Most weekdays started the same way for Shawn Schaefer his senior year at the University of Illinois at Champaign—with a bowl of sweetened cereal and ESPN news. But after being gone for Christmas vacation—late nights, glazed ham, pecan pies, chocolate cakes, family, and gifts—he dawdled at the kitchen table, not thrilled to get back to the principles of taxation and public policy, exams, and vending machine food.

A segment on ESPN caught his attention. An attractive dark-haired girl with a soft voice said, "We were at a dude ranch…best vacation…a drunk driver crossed the center line."

The reporter began. "Today we're interviewing Eric Miller, Mr. Basketball from Indiana, after his near-death experience in a car accident where his girlfriend, Kelly Craig, became paralyzed."

The reporter asked Eric questions about his injuries, his career, and when he met his girlfriend.

"Kelly saw me on TV at a dunking contest." He smiled. "She told her Mom she wanted to date me some day." He chuckled. "All I can think about now is Kelly and her brother. It's tough for me to even go to the grocery store because people recognize me and want to talk about everything. I can never get my mind off of Kelly." He paused.

"Somebody could give me five or ten million dollars, and I'd give it all back and more just for things to be the way they used to be."

The camera switched to the girl in her home. They asked her another question. "Did Bob Knight call you after the accident?"

"His secretary called and left a message that he was trying to get a hold of me, and said he would call back, but he never did," Kelly said. She remained poised and fluid in her answers, showing no emotion.

The news reporter continued. "Miller has made three trips to Chicago to visit Kelly."

The camera switched to Eric again. "She's an athletic girl. She could do anything you asked, run, flips, anything. It's heartbreaking to see her in bed, not able to do any of that stuff. I pray every night that she'll be able to walk again. It makes me wonder, why am I able to do all these things? Why am I so lucky?" He stared into the camera. "Please keep Kelly and Jason in your prayers."

Shawn wondered too. Why did bad things happen to good people?

Kelly said, "Eric and I can't have a normal boyfriend and girlfriend relationship. He's in Arizona and I'm in Indiana. But we remain good friends."

Shawn suspected that there was more to the story. It was what she didn't say that had more meaning. He admired how she was able to tell only a part of the story, professional enough to blur the lines, and not to slam Bob Knight either.

The camera shifted to reveal the scar along Eric's ear and neck. "If it hadn't been for the nurse," Miller said, "I would have bled to death."

Kelly spoke about her injuries. "It will be a long hard road, and I don't know where or when, but I'll walk again."

Shawn watched Kelly's responses. "Wow," he said to his roommate who was walking through the room. "Look how composed she is even though...how is she staying positive?"

"Yeah, hey, I better go," his roommate said. "I gotta get to class. I'll catch you later." He picked up his books and left Shawn alone in the apartment.

Shawn took his cereal bowl to the sink, rinsed it out, then grabbed the TV guide on the dented console. He flipped to the page about the ESPN special. *Great, it'll be on tonight too. I can tape it then.*

As he gathered his books for class, he thought about an automobile accident he'd been in coming home from his high school Christmas dance. He'd fallen asleep at the wheel in his 1992 Chevy Cavalier and crashed into an oncoming minivan going fifty-five miles per hour. He didn't remember the scene, only the blood. No matter how hard he tried, he couldn't remember anything that happened that day or weeks after.

The accident had changed him.

He spent days in the hospital recovering from facial surgery to repair broken bones. Metal plates were implanted under his right eye. The right side of his nose had to be realigned, too. Finally the doctors told his parents that he could go home.

"We won't know the extent of his injuries for some time," the doctor said. "We'll have to wait and see if he fully recovers."

For four weeks, Shawn walked, talked, ate, and slept, yet he didn't remember the accident. Shortly thereafter, he became the old Shawn on the outside, but deep inside he'd grown a more compassionate heart. He felt for the girl on TV, he understood her underlying fears and respected her courage.

He could have ended up the same way.

Glancing at the TV one last time, he programmed the video recorder timer for 7:00 p.m.—when the ESPN piece would air again. He'd watch it and jot down the town she lived in so he could send her a card.

Later that evening, Shawn returned to his apartment and played the ESPN segment again, ready to write down the city where Kelly lived. Watching the piece for the second time made the story feel even more real. Yes, people on TV often put on a facade, but this girl seemed real.

Jasper, Indiana. That was the town she lived in. He jotted it down.

It was normal for him to send cards to friends and family, but this was the first time he wanted to send a card to a complete stranger, especially someone he saw on TV. He chuckled to himself, but logged on to his computer anyway.

First, he typed her name and city in the search bar at Google, but couldn't find a "Craig" with the first name Kelly. He wrote down all the Craig's he could find in Jasper with their phone numbers. He called each one and asked if they knew Kelly. Some were kind and said no, but others simply hung up.

He dialed 411 to search further, but the operator told him there was no listing for Kelly Craig in Jasper. Puzzled and disappointed, he told himself he'd try again another time. For now, he had accounting homework, and if he wanted to graduate in May, he'd better get back to work.

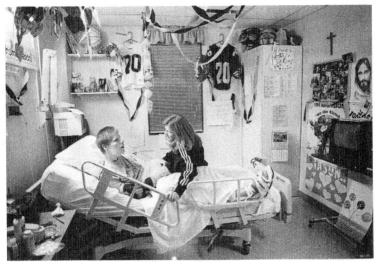

(David Pierini/*The Herald*)

Chapter Eighteen

*Sometimes courage doesn't always roar. Sometimes courage is the
little voice at the end of the day that says I'll try again tomorrow.*
Mary Anne Radmacher

If a paralyzed person didn't have to worry about going to the
bathroom, life would be easier. Most people think that people in
wheelchairs can be transferred to a toilet when they have to go, but that
doesn't happen. Toileting takes muscles, and people in wheelchairs
don't have working muscles, so other methods have to be used.

When I left RIC, I had a catheter. My bladder was never full, but
that meant the bag always had urine in it. Even though the bag was
tucked under my pant leg and nobody saw it, I knew it was there.

That might sound like an easy way to control the problem, but it
wasn't for many reasons. First, the tube made a terrible fashion
statement, and I couldn't wear underwear. Besides the cosmetic
reasons, the tube yanked at the tender skin between my legs and

burned. It didn't feel natural. I often called the nurses at the hospital to check the tubing, certain there was a problem.

"Unfortunately," a nurse said while making a home visit, "that's the nature of the device. We could remove it, but then someone would have to catheterize you every four hours."

I looked at Mom standing next to the nurse. "What do you think?"

"They showed us how to do that at RIC," Mom said, standing in my bedroom, "but I need someone to show me again. I forgot how."

"You'd do that?" I asked, hating for her to have to commit to one more thing.

"It'll be less of a hassle for you, Kelly. It'll be worth it."

I couldn't wait to have it removed. As soon as it was gone, the burning pain stopped and freedom returned.

Mom and Andy watched another video demonstration on how to catheterize me to refresh their memories, and the nurses helped when they had questions.

In the beginning, Mom couldn't find the urethral meatus to insert the tube, but eventually she got better. But at each potty break, she had to lift me onto the bed, pull down my slacks, sterilize the tubing, and deposit the urine in the toilet.

One day, when Andy was the only one home with me, and Mom wouldn't be home soon, I had to urinate. The nightmare came true. Andy had to perform the task.

As he placed me on the bed and pulled down my slacks, I tried not to think about what he was doing. I stared at a shelf in my room pretending I was far away, and that Andy was a stranger, not my stepfather, and this was happening to someone besides me.

Carefully, he tried to insert the tube.

"You're not there," I said.

"Sorry." He tried again.

"You're still in the wrong…"

"Damn!"

Five more times he tried. Five more times he failed, each time losing more patience. I stayed calm, hoping it would help him, but he sighed and mumbled under his breath until finally he was successful. I hated knowing that I'd caused his frustration.

Once he directed the tube properly, the energy in the room relaxed, and the next time he had to help it got easier for both of us. So easy, in fact, that I chose him to go with me to the Final Four basketball tournament.

After the ESPN interview, they sent me two tickets to the Final Four tournament in Indy at the RCA Dome. I asked Andy to go because he was the only one who could transfer me in and out of the van and my chair, and onto the ground if I needed to be catheterized.

Dawne's brother starred in a CBS show titled, *Windfall,* and let us visit their suite at the games. An actor from *Happy Gilmore*, the one who played Shooter and a girl who starred in *Dumb and Dumber* were there too.

Luckily for me, the suites were on the same level as the handicap floor, which made it easy for us to go back and forth and mingle with the stars.

Eric was at the tournament, too. We'd arranged to see each other, but during the game, he hung out with his friends in the seats below us. I watched him instead of the players, observing the quirks of his personality, aware of my fragile feelings, still hurt and disappointed that I mattered so little to him.

He stopped by the suite at halftime, eager to meet the stars, but not to spend time with me. "This is cool, Kelly. Usually I'm the one with the connections. But this was all you."

"Whatever." I didn't know how to act around him, how to be casual about someone I'd wanted to spend my life with. How was I supposed to pretend to be someone different? In order to keep my distance and guard my heart I pretended he didn't matter. If changing my personality would have brought him back I might have tried, but I didn't know how, and I didn't want to. He wasn't the guy I thought he was, but I'd been too close to see his flaws. Now, in watching him from a distance, I was able to see his real character.

At halftime, Andy took me to the unisex handicapped bathroom, lifted me to the floor, and catheterized me. It was strange lying on a public bathroom floor, but I didn't have any other options. I'd gotten used to awkward places and situations, and Andy had improved at performing the never-ending procedure. The only awkward part of my life I couldn't get used to was not having Eric in it. Even though I saw who he really was, how our interests weren't the same, and how I was better off without him, the sting of his breakup continued to burn my cheeks as if it happened yesterday. Would I ever be able to move on and forget him?

The community continued to visit Jason at Jasper Memorial and slowly he showed signs of improvement. Most comas don't last more than two to four weeks, but Jason had been almost unresponsive for seven months. The doctors told us that the majority of people who score a three or four (like Jason) on the Glasgow Coma Scale (a scale used to determine the severity of comas) within the first twenty-four hours of going into a coma are likely to die or remain in a vegetative state.

However, ever since Jason moved to Jasper and was surrounded by people in our town, he showed gradual signs of awareness. At first, he smiled like he recognized voices. He moved his body when people asked, he squeezed Mom's hand once for yes and twice for no, and he followed simple commands and nodded.

Mom asked him questions. "Give me a thumbs-up if you can hear me."

It took him a long time to react, but he gave her the signal.

His high school friends visited and asked him questions, and he smiled, especially at the girls.

Therapists and family encouraged and cheered for each milestone. Eventually, his eyes opened and although his reactions were slow, he seemed to know what was going on around him, but he couldn't speak. Hospital staff taught him sign language. He spelled words when he wanted something.

Tubes were removed and therapists exercised him. One day when Mom and I were in rehab, Jason was there too. Two techs held his arms while he stumbled on the treadmill. He grimaced through each miniscule movement. With his legs turned in and his bent body, he took slow, jerky steps and moaned.

"Put your lips together," Mom said. "Make an mmm sound."

He clamped his mouth shut. "Mmmmmooooooommmmmmm," he blurted. His vocalization was drawn out and distorted, but it was the first word he'd spoken in nine months.

Mom cried. "You did it, Jason! You did it!"

The therapists in the room cheered. Some cried. Tears filled my eyes, too. The word was small but brought immense hope.

He spoke more after that, but his words were often unrecognizable. People asked him to spell the word he was trying to say. One word took minutes to speak and longer for us to understand. He traced letters in the air and contorted his body into letter shapes to help us comprehend him.

When family visited, he knew who they were, nodded, and spoke their names in drawn-out grunts. People quizzed him about events in his life, and he nodded because he remembered.

He drooled, had trouble swallowing, and choked often, which made eating a challenge.

Walking was difficult because his muscles spontaneously contracted causing his legs and hands to turn in. An orthopedic doctor built dynamic casts for his arms and legs to work as braces to help straighten his limbs. The doctor changed the casts regularly to increase Jason's range of motion.

His recovery was gradual and it was difficult to notice each microscopic achievement.

Not too long after he began talking, he said to Mom, "I saw Him."

"Who?" Mom asked.

"God."

"What did He look like?" Mom prodded.

"Bright lights… and I saw His face. He told me…"—Jason's words were slow and choppy—"I… wasn't ready to go there yet… I had to go back."

Mom sat stunned and wondered what it was that God wanted Jason to do with his life. She cried and secretly wondered if she'd prayed for the wrong miracle right after the accident. Should she have prayed for

God's will instead of praying for God to keep Jason alive? If she had prayed for God's will, would Jason be in heaven now?

The Jason I once knew no longer existed. This one looked like Jason, but acted far different from the one who left us the day of the accident.

(Photo from *The Durango Herald*, April 8, 2000)

Chapter Nineteen

When you don't have a vision or a plan for the future, your mind has no choice but to dwell in the past.
Steve Maraboli

April 2000
Durango, Colorado
The Trial

Many people called to see how Jason and I were doing, many of whom I'd never met. One man, Bill Brown, called on behalf of the Advocacy for Victims in Colorado. He was a patrol officer who knew about the accident. He informed us that there was support for victims of drinking and driving accidents—financial support to travel to the trial. They paid for Mom, Andy, and me to fly to Colorado and stay at a hotel. They paid for Eric to fly there too.

The night before the trial, Eric took me to the movies. I prayed he would reach for my hand, but when he didn't I was angry that I'd wanted him to. Where was my dignity? He didn't want any part of me. When would I accept that? Our conversations were strained. He talked about his new friends, strangers, about his transfer from Arizona to his new school in Iowa, his new basketball coach.

When the movie ended, he brought me back to my room without a kiss. The magic between us was gone forever.

The next day, I heard he'd gone out with the other people who were there for the trial after he brought me back. They'd all left me behind. I smiled when they talked about where they'd gone and what they'd done. Pretending I didn't care was getting easier every day.

In the courtroom, before the judge entered, the victims sat on one side, the driver and his family on the other. Each side had about five rows all facing where the judge would sit. It was the ugliest reunion because we were all there to relive the nightmare of our lives. I shuddered.

The driver, dressed in an orange prison uniform, sat next to his attorney, his head bent. News articles said he hadn't graduated from high school and was only twenty-two. Several of the kids in the accident whispered about the defendant's family. Rumor was that he had a daughter. They speculated on whether she was in the courtroom.

Most people who knew me didn't see the dark poison of depression seeping into my pores. Some days my attitude flipped-flopped in mere seconds. In each of those weak moments, all my problems led back to one person's carelessness. I knew I was supposed to stay positive and only dwell on those things I could do, but that wasn't reality. In my real world, I traveled down the *negative* hall more than I wanted to.

I hoped attending the trial would help me vent my frustrations and help me accept my disability. Mom said I needed to forgive him, but I wasn't sure that would help. Forgiveness couldn't bring back my legs, and I wanted to show the driver what he'd done to my life, to say my peace, to make sure that justice was served. I wanted to support John's family too. If they wanted vindication for their son's death, I would be there for them.

If you aren't ready for the worst consequence then don't do the crime. Every action has a reaction. I made a mental note of these sentences to put in my speech. The drunk driver was simply a drunk driver, not a person. We all make choices.

Today would be his worst hangover.

At 2:30, court was in session. Our attorney, Ms. Law, began. The judge asked her what he should expect that afternoon. She explained that John's family, the doctor, and many of the victims wanted to address the court. The court agreed to let her proceed.

John's father spoke first about his son's life, John's childhood treehouses, how he'd climbed Mount LeConte, scuba dived, and snow skied.

John's mother showed us photos of John at Christmas and at the lake the year before the accident. When she showed us the last photo of John that was taken at the dude ranch with JoAnne, the ranch hand in the front seat with John, Mrs. Hollberg's eyes filled with tears. "That's the last picture we have of him alive. It makes it more personal to see him."

Many of us nodded in agreement.

"I don't hate Mr. Ridgewall," she said. "He did a stupid thing and should serve time for what he did while he's here on earth, even though he may be punished somewhere else later on. But that's not up to me."

The judge thanked her and invited John's sister to speak. She shared what she missed about her brother—photos, e-mails, and told us how his guitar sits by the front door because no one wants to move it. His sister had a baby girl four months after John's death. The baby has John's long fingers and toes, which is a constant reminder that a part of John still lives.

John's other sister spoke too. "His death was senseless and unnecessary. Everyone has the right to make his or her own choice. The Durango court should set an example that it's not okay to drink and drive and that people who kill and maim others should get punished for those offenses."

Another man who'd worked at the ranch, who'd also been at the accident scene and at the hospital, spoke. He described the scene and how he helped the officer before following them to Mercy Medical Center. "The hospital staff had to cut JoAnne's clothes to determine the severity of her injuries and she was screaming at Mr. Ridgewall who was swearing at her. When I heard Ridgewall say, 'Excuse me," to the police, "these people won't quit f—ing with me,' I had to leave the room. I wanted to jump on the bed and pound him. I never felt that kind of anger toward anyone in my life, and I don't hate him now, but he killed someone and drastically changed the lives of everybody in this courtroom, and he needs to be punished." He lowered his voice. "The defendant should receive the maximum sentence for his crime. It's something that everybody else has to live with for the rest of their lives, and he should have to too."

Stephanie, the driver of the purple truck—the truck I should have gone in—spoke next. "I relive the crash in my sleep. I wake in the middle of the night, frantic with fear. It's difficult for me to feel safe; I don't want to drive in the dark; I imagine headlights coming head-on into my lane."

I knew what she meant. I had the same fears. Some people with my injuries choose to drive, but I doubted I would ever be brave enough for that experience.

Then it was Eric's turn to speak. He moved to the front, his six-foot, seven-inch frame towering over everyone. "We're not dealing with an ideal citizen here. He's allegedly been in trouble before for kicking someone in the ribs."

We'd heard this rumor.

Eric glared at Mr. Ridgewall. "If I had been responsible for an accident like this, I'd want my life taken instead of taking someone else's life. It would be a personal hell to live every day knowing that I took someone's life and hurt all these people. Even if you get the maximum amount of jail—which is thirty-six years—you wouldn't be able to experience what you've dished out.

"I hope you receive the maximum sentence. You're sitting there looking down right now, but if you look me in my eyes you'd see the pain..." Eric shook his head. "—I can't describe how you changed everybody's lives."

Eric's face turned red and tears spilled down his cheeks. "I know I'm lucky to be standing here today. Not a day goes by that I don't feel guilty that I'm okay when I know what Kelly has to go through every day, or when I think of the Hollberg family. I have four beautiful sisters, and I can't imagine any one of them being taken away from me. I sit alone at night crying because of what's happened.

"I've never had to experience jail time, and I don't know what you do in jail, but I'm sure you'll have time to write a letter to the victims." He paused. "That's what irks me the most—that you never apologized. I hope the Durango court gives you the maximum sentence."

The judge thanked him and Eric returned to his seat.

"Your honor?" A man said and stood.

"You want to make a statement?" the judge asked.

"My name is Tim Williams. He moved to the front of the room. "I'm grateful you're letting me speak. In terms of suffering, I don't deserve the amount of time that these good people do," he waved at me and the other victims. "But I hope what I have to say is of value to them.

"I'm here as a victim's advocate for our local chapter of Mothers Against Drunk Driving. I'm also here as a firefighter and EMT with Animas Fire here in Durango, and I'm here because I care about justice and mercy."

"I don't know where Zach Ridgewall will eat his next meal, but I do know he will be able to feed himself, he won't have to be fed through a stomach tube the way that Jason was being fed. Both Jason, Kelly, and the driver deserve justice, but who deserves your mercy?"

The judge thanked Mr. Williams and he returned to his seat.

The ER doctor wanted to speak about Ridgewall's head injury, his level of intoxication, and his behavior in the emergency room, but the defendant's attorney objected. "Whatever the doctor knows about Mr. Ridgewall is privileged, and Mr. Ridgewall hasn't waived any privileges. The doctor is inappropriate and unprofessional to give statements about a patient who hasn't given him the right. It's in clear violation of the statute."

Ridgewall's attorney and the doctor argued, but in the end, the court allowed the doctor to say this, "I spent two hours with Mr. Ridgewall in the ER and he had no remorse. The only concern he expressed was his fear of jail. I've been working in the ER for twenty-two years, and I can't recall ever seeing the level of insensitivity that I experienced from

Mr. Ridgewall that night."

It was my turn to speak next. Mom pushed me up to the podium and stood behind me. We faced Mr. Ridgewall. Mom had said she didn't want to say anything, but once we got in front of everyone, she spoke, the whole time playing with my ponytail. She rehashed the events of the night of the accident and how apprehensive she was to go back to Durango for the trial. She ended with, "We're praying for you, Mr. Ridgewall." She squeezed my shoulder, indicating it was my turn.

A lump knotted in my throat. I swallowed it down, but my voice came out soft. "I don't have anything prepared to say to you," I glowered at Mr. Ridgewall, my voice shaking. "I'll speak from my heart and you can roll a day in my life."

For the next few minutes, I told him what Jason and I had gone through immediately after the accident up until the present. "This is how you changed my perfect life into hell."

Mr. Ridgewall's head dropped and his shoulders shook like he was crying, but I didn't care. What about my tears?

"My brother is still in the hospital. My mom can't handle both of us at one time. I'm totally dependent on my family. I can't eat when I want to eat; I can't have a drink of water or sit and have hot chocolate unless someone brings it to me. I'm confined to this wheelchair, and there's nothing I do I can do for myself. I have to have adaptive equipment, help to go to the bathroom— stuff you take for granted. Even though you're going to jail, you'll get out one day and you'll be fine. But I'll still be in my wheelchair and Jason will never be the same.

"For *nine* months I've had to endure life in this chair, and I'm sick of it." I paused to catch my breath. My voice trembled and tears fell. "We will pray that when you go to bed at night, you think about what you did."

The judge nodded. "Thank you, Kelly."

Mom wheeled me back to the seating area and blotted my face with a tissue.

Andy stood next and asked to speak. "I want to tell you a little about Jason." He told the court what kind of athlete Jason had been and how he was progressing with his injuries. "He's still fighting. He's still hospitalized. When will he get out? I don't know. He has a long way to go. The doctor told us that his symptoms are similar to Parkinson's disease, which affects his speech. He can't walk. He's trying, but he's rigid, his ankles are turned in. He has limited movement with his arms too. They're turned in. He works every day to try to get better.

"His therapy changed at the new hospital, and he's responding a little more. He suffered damage to the part of his brain that controls speech. How will that affect the rest of his life? I don't know. The doctor said he won't talk like he used to. There's a good chance that he'll be with us for the rest of his life. He won't have the opportunity to go to college, he probably won't have the opportunity to live on his own, and he may not work either. He tells us he wants to go home, but he has to improve a lot before that can happen. It takes a tremendous amount of time to take care of him. He can't do anything. We're hoping that he will improve.

"Kelly won't have the college life she had, but she's a remarkable girl. I know she'll get through this and continue on. We have hope that she'll get better and that there will be some miracle that will help her walk someday and use her right arm.

"I know you have a tough decision," he said to the judge, "one that will affect Zach Ridgewall's life. But his decision really affected our lives forever.

"What's a good sentence? I don't know, but I asked Jason what he thought. He said Mr. Ridgewall should die. I said, 'Are you sure that's what you said?' because he's difficult to understand, but Jason nodded. I asked him to spell it to me, just to be sure I understood him correctly. Using sign language, he spelled D-I-E, and then he said, 'Go to hell.'

"We're asking the state of Colorado to make a decision that Mr. Ridgewall not be released until the state is one hundred percent positive he won't be a threat to society, because right now we think he is."

Andy returned to his seat.

"Thank you, Mr. Krempp," the judge said.

Our attorney handed the court photos of the accident vehicles and victims. "In the state of Colorado, vehicular homicide is considered a reckless crime. It involves causing the death of a person, but we treat it as a lesser offense, and we don't even treat it as a knowing offense, we treat it as reckless. In this case, the voluntary consumption of alcohol by Mr. Ridgewall is the reckless act—or one of the reckless acts that he's accused of.

"There is a large range of sentences that are available to you today, and in this jurisdiction there has been everything from probation to prison time to community corrections. As a judge, you have sentenced four people involved in a vehicular homicide. You probably remember them, and I think you could probably distinguish those cases from this case.

"You take each case separately, look at it, examine it, and decide what you believe is appropriate. So far, you haven't had a case that you believed a substantial and lengthy prison sentence was appropriate.

"For that reason, I want to tell you about all of the opportunities the driver had that day to avoid the death of John Hollberg and the serious injury of all the people who have talked to you today and the people who can't be here to talk to you."

The attorney recapped Mr. Ridgewall's events the night of the accident—how much he drank, and the opportunities he'd had to relinquish his keys. "That is all I have to say, your Honor."

Zach Ridgewall's attorney stood. "Your Honor, I have a few comments, then Mr. Ridgewall would like to address the court."

"I wish it had been explained that the first time Mr. Ridgewall came to court, the judge told him—in county court—not to contact any of these people. It was an order of this Court that he was restrained from contacting any of you, any of the victims in this case." He turned and nodded toward me, then faced the judge again. "Your Honor, Mr. Ridgewall has no significant criminal history. He is a young man, twenty-two years old. Has no felony convictions, has no history of drinking and driving convictions. In fact, Judge," he turned to me and my family again, "I appreciate the comments of the people who have been up here," he turned back to the judge, "but Mr. Ridgewall is a very nice young man. He's a very respectful young man. He's been employed.

"It might be easy and understandable to demonize Mr. Ridgewall, but he's not a demon. He's a young man who was working at the time of this incident and drank too much.

"We don't discount any of the things that the people have said with regard to what has happened to them. But he—Your Honor, while he's been in jail, he's done what he could. He has been attending AA meetings; he's worked toward his GED.

"And Your Honor, as he indicated in the statements to the Court, he's mortified about what happened and ashamed of his behavior, not that he remembers it well.

"And Judge, from our perspective, we would ask the Court to discount some of the statements or descriptions of his behavior that evening, not because he was intoxicated, but that the things that he may have said and the attitudes that he may have had are not reflective of him, since he had a significant head injury that evening.

"Mr. Ridgewall had to be cut out of the car, and he doesn't remember going to court three days later. Things have cleared up for him and he has good clarity now, but he was injured in that accident. And from everything I know—my experience with him and everything that people have told me, he is not at all the kind of person who would be making the kind of statements that have been ascribed to him.

"Your Honor, twenty years in prison is not going to heal anybody. We gave the court a brief summary of other similar cases. There are ten in this decade, in which the sentences range from five to seven years, and often community corrections are imposed. Mr. Ridgewall didn't intentionally injure others. This was a reckless act—to get drunk and get behind the wheel.

"In terms of justice, it would be unjust to Mr. Ridgewall to sentence him more simply because of the social status of the victims or the publicity that might have been engendered. That would be unjust to consider those things in sentencing Mr. Ridgewall. We ask the Court to sentence him consistent with the sentences that others similarly situated have received."

He paused. "Mr. Ridgewall would like to address the Court."

The drunk driver stood beside his attorney, facing the judge. "I would like to tell the family members and the people who were in the wreck that I'm very sorry for what I did. If I could change anything that night, I would. I wish it was me rather than any of you." He turned to face me, and the others. "I wish I could go back and change that day. I will never drink again.

"With the medical staff that night, I'm very sorry for my actions. I feel terrible about it, and I don't know how to repay anybody about that. I'm sorry." His voice broke into a sob. "Very sorry." Slowly, he sank into his chair next to his attorney.

Had his attorneys prepped him to sound that way, to look shameful? Or was he really sincere?

The judge said, "Mr. Ridgewall, I don't have words to try and describe or summarize the pain that you've caused. The folks that have spoken today have done that far better than I ever could. And I don't have the authority under the law to sentence you long enough to satisfy their very understandable and just cries for retribution.

"But it is also true that if sentencing were left to our emotions and to our feelings, and the understandable feeling of all involved, that there would be no undue punishment. But that is not the law, and the law requires me to consider other things today as well, and I will consider those in making my decision as to what to do.

"The law differentiates between deliberate action and reckless action. Your actions were reckless. The law distinguishes between a person who sets out to kill and a person who kills through their own recklessness. The law distinguishes between a person who sets out to harm somebody and a person who harms someone through their own recklessness.

"I accept that you didn't set out to hurt anybody on July tenth, but on July tenth you did drink yourself into a state of intoxication, you drank until you were belligerent, and you were aggressive and in defiance of good judgment. On several occasions that day, you decided to drive your car and you drove it recklessly and you caused the injuries as described today.

"It's a miracle that there aren't more people out here as your victims. I've heard you today, and I've read the things you've written in the court papers leading up to this sentencing. You don't have a serious criminal history, and as far as I can tell in the reports that have been provided to me, you've never gotten a traffic ticket in the state of Colorado. I can tell you very clearly that if you had been—if you had been accused or charged or convicted of drunk driving in the past, that this would be a very different day, that your sentence would be longer.

"I'm going to sentence you to prison today. You will be released from prison at a time when most of your life is still ahead of you. You'll have your health, you'll have a chance to do something with your life, raise your daughter.

"I'm going to sentence you to prison because you deserve it, because you've hurt these people, to punish you, and for the purpose of deterring others so that people will know in our community that drunk driving, vehicular homicide, and vehicular assault are serious crimes. You do those things; you're going to get punished.

"I'm going to enter judgment of conviction against you pursuant to your guilty pleas to vehicular homicide and vehicular assault. Those convictions will be on your permanent criminal record.

"As far as restitution goes, I don't know that restitution can ever be made, but I will permit the district attorney to submit figures to me and request restitution. I'll consider those as they come.

"For the offense of vehicular homicide for killing John Hollberg, I sentence you to the Department of Corrections for a period of nine years.

"For the offense of vehicular assault for the terrible injuries you've caused Jason Craig, Kelly Craig, JoAnne McGuirk, Brian O'Hara, and Eric Miller, I sentence you to nine years in the Colorado Department of Corrections, to be served concurrently.

"That's the sentence of the Court. Court's in recess." He lifted the gavel and brought his hand down with a slam.

I sat stunned. Nine years plus nine years? Was it a total of eighteen?

A uniformed man led Mr. Ridgewall out of the courtroom. Our attorney turned to face those she represented. Someone asked her what nine years concurrently meant.

"It means he got a total of nine years." The attorney explained that concurrently meant he would serve them all at the same time. No more.

Nine years? That was all? In nine years he'd be able to walk right out of prison, brush his teeth, and do all the physical things I couldn't do. Was that supposed to be fair? After nine years I'd still be paralyzed, Jason would still have a brain injury, and John would still be dead. We looked at each other with our mouths open and our brows creased, puzzled.

I thought he'd get more. It wasn't that I wanted an eye for an eye, but a sincere apology would have helped. Was he remorseful—even though he said he was?

About three years after the trial, I received this letter from Mr. Ridgewall.

Dear Kelly,

I understand if you never wanted to hear from me again. I don't know if you have any hate towards me, but if you do, I understand. I wanted to write this letter to tell you how sorry I am for the pain I've caused to you from the car accident that happened July 10, 1999.

I've been wanting to write all of you who were involved in the car accident for a very long time. I was unable to due to a restraining order that is being held against me. The restraining order is still in effect. I just recently wrote the judge who sentenced me to prison a letter asking him if I could write each of you an apology letter. He said that would be a good idea so he contacted a lady to help me write these letters.

Kelly, I am so sorry for the pain I've caused to you, your brother, Jason, and all of your friends. I never wanted to hurt any of you. I still can't believe this happened. I am still trying to wake up from this bad dream.

I remember seeing you in the court during my sentencing and I remember seeing your brother on the videotape. Those pictures will stick with me for the rest of my life.

There is not a day that goes by that I don't think about all of you. I just want you to know that I will never forget what I have done or the pain I have caused to all of you.

I am truly sorry for what I have done and I know this prison sentence will never even come close to paying for what I've done.

I've been very concerned about your recovery. I hope you are doing well. I do care about how you are recovering from what I've caused.

I will never drink and drive again.

I am truly sorry for what I've done. I do care about your recovery.

Sincerely,

Zach Ridgewall

Was his letter the result of a judge-ordered or lawyer-ordered request to get him in good graces with the court? Were the courts considering a parole? I didn't know, but I found out months later that everyone in the accident received the same letter. There was no way to know what prompted him to write the letters, but it didn't matter. It wouldn't change anything.

Should I write him back? It wasn't up to me to forgive him. It wasn't my job to judge him either. He would have to deal with that in his own way. I opted not to send him a letter.

Jason, on the other hand, insisted on writing to the judge to plead that Mr. Ridgewall not be let out of jail early. Jason dictated a letter to Andy and Andy sent it. We don't know if the letter had an impact on Ridgewall's jail time.

It helped that we lived in a different state than Ridgewall and didn't hear news about him. I wanted to know that he hadn't done the same thing again, but if he had, there was nothing I could do about it anyway.

In my own way, I forgave him. He hadn't known me and deliberately tried to ruin my life. He'd made a stupid mistake, and I happened to be in his way.

Chapter Twenty

The darkest nights produce the brightest stars.
John Green, *The Fault in Our Stars*

For weeks after the trial, I stayed home feeling bitter and lonely, self-conscious, drifting in life as a spectator. It was easier to stay home because I could hide, and my life hurt less there. Days passed. I was a stranger in my own body, not knowing who I was or how I was supposed to act. I no longer felt freer than a kite in the wind, ready to take on the world. I was lost on a foreign island, alone, in a place I'd never been, wandering on a rocky terrain I didn't understand, searching for the basic survival skills.

A man from the rehab store in Evansville delivered my new wheelchair, the motorized one that was sized especially for me. As he wheeled it into the house, I cringed. It was a huge contraption with wide armrests and knobby controls. Thick large tires adorned the back and small ones on the front. It screamed, *Look at me, I'm disabled.* It smelled like a new doll on Christmas morning—plastic, rubber and vinyl—but this was not on my Santa list.

The man demonstrated the chair's features, explaining how to go forward, how to tilt backward, and how to move it sideways. He showed Mom how to adjust the footplates, the headrest, and how to point the joystick in the direction I wanted to travel. He showed us how to maneuver over different surfaces and curbs, how to move up and down slopes, and how to charge it. "When you're in a new location it's important to plan your route before you begin, so you know how to maneuver. Want to take it for a spin?"

"No, thank you." Having the ability to control my own position should have excited me, but the chair was a reminder that my condition was permanent. Giving in to this chair meant I was accepting my disability, and I couldn't.

He turned to Mom who sat beside me.

"Why not try?" she said to me. "It will give you more freedom."

"I'm fine right where I am."

The man shrugged and handed Mom his business card. "I understand. It's a big change. Here's my phone number if you have any questions."

"Kelly," Mom said. "Get in it now so you can get the feel for it, learn how to control it."

I didn't say anything.

The man hesitated. "Would you like me to transfer her?"

"I'll do it," Mom said, turning to me.

I couldn't fight her.

She transferred me.

The chair hugged me closer in the hips than the manual chair. I sat taller too.

The man showed Mom how to lock the brakes and pointed to the seat belt. Mom adjusted it to fit me.

I moved the control and jerked forward.

"It'll take a while to get used to," the man said. "It's like a new pair of shoes that fit differently at first, but eventually you'll wonder how you got along without it."

No, I didn't want to get used to it. What was I going to do with my life? Nothing was right. But anger wasn't the solution. The negative emotion drained me. I needed to move on and accept my new life, but how? What did I have left to focus on?

My family encouraged me to find positive events to look forward to every day. "Why don't you compete for Miss Strassenfest?" Mom suggested.

Should I?

For four days every hot August, the city of Jasper, known for its German heritage, filled with thousands of visitors who attended Strassenfest, German for *festival*. Even though Jasper was a small community, Strassenfest was one of the largest festivals in the state of Indiana. More than twenty-five thousand people packed the city's streets during this fun time. All the money it generated went back into the community—vintage baseball games, live music performances, food, and each year one girl was crowned Miss Strassenfest.

Since pageants had often been a part of my life and I wanted to pursue a speaking platform, I decided to compete for the title, but not without reservation. How would people view me as a wheelchair contestant? It shouldn't matter, but what if it did? I didn't want to win because the judges felt sorry for me.

As I prepared for the competition, memories of past festivals I shared with Eric hinged in the corners of my mind. To stay focused, friends drilled me with questions the judges might ask. They asked me about the classes I took in high school, the accident experience, and hurtled one question after another so I could prepare.

For the formal part of the competition, Mom found the perfect two-piece pale yellow dress in a magazine. Two pieces made it easier for her to do my bathroom. My friend, Annamarie, did my hair. Aunt Missy helped dress me and accessorize my outfits. Everything came together, and the competing became the perfect diversion.

Part of the competition was meeting with the judges separately for an interview. During that time, they asked each contestant questions pertaining to her interests and the courses she took in high school or college based on the resume she'd submitted to them.

Before that part of the competition, I approached the judging coordinator with a request. "Would it be okay if I went last?"

"Why's that?"

"I don't want the judges to give me high scores because I'm in a wheelchair. If I go last then they'll be able to hear all the other contestants first and compare me with them. Hopefully they won't be tempted to give me high marks because they feel sorry for me."

She nodded as if she understood. "We can honor that."

After everyone else participated in the private interviews, it was my turn. I sat in front of all ten judges.

They said hello and made small talk and then one judge said, "A few of us are IU fans. Could you sing their fight song for us?"

I never dreamt they'd ask me to do that. But it was an easy request. I began, "Indiana, our Indiana..." I sang the entire song.

They cheered and we laughed.

Another judge asked, "You were in the Girl Scouts for eleven years. That's a long time. What made you stay with them for that long, and what were the benefits?"

"The scouts taught me life skills—how to pitch a tent, how to work and get along with others and simple things like how to tie a knot. The badge incentive taught me how to work toward reaching a goal. I stayed in Scouts for a long time because Mom made me," I paused to smile, "but also because it would improve my leadership skills. There's value in being a part of a team."

I left the interview feeling positive, composed, and articulate—like I'd nailed the answers. It was a great feeling. Speaking to schools had done that for me—kept me calm when put on the spot, but I still had to get through the rest of the pageant.

The stage competition began.

Gene Koontz, the Strassenfest emcee of the pageant, welcomed the crowd. I positioned myself backstage with the other contestants, many of whom had become friends.

"Kelly Craig is our first contestant," Mr. Koontz said.

With his signal, I wheeled onto the stage and prayed my legs wouldn't spasm. I gazed out into the crowd, wearing the smile I'd practiced, handling the controls of my chair with the same finesse. The pianist played a song. I moved to the corner of the stage and paused for three seconds. The audience cheered and clapped. When I proceeded back to the center stage to the microphone, the pianist ceased playing. I positioned my mouth in front of the mic. "Welcome to the twenty-second Annual 2000 Strassenfest. I hope you have a safe and enjoyable time at the festival as you help celebrate Jasper's German heritage."

After I introduced myself, the nine other contestants walked on stage one at a time and introduced themselves. We all wore business attire. When everyone had spoken, we exited the stage and the emcee welcomed the Little Miss and Mister contestants for their competition.

The group of queen contestants gathered in the dressing room to change into sportswear apparel, our next event. When it was our turn again, I wheeled out first.

Mr. Koontz described what I was wearing—a coral short sleeve sweater by Ralph Lauren from Siebert's in Jasper, orange capris, sun glasses by Out of the Blue, and silver bracelets by Catherine Kay. Mom had crossed my pedicured, sandaled feet, finishing off my sporty look.

After this part of the pageant, the contestants returned to the dressing room for the final part of the competition—the evening gown, when I'd be asked an impromptu question in front of the live audience. When the Little Miss and Misters walked off stage, we returned to the stage.

"Contestant number one is Kelly Craig. She's twenty years old and the daughter of Brenda and Andy Krempp. She's using her cheerleading experience to teach cheerleaders. She's also a professional speaker on the dangers of drinking and driving. Her favorite parts of Strassenfest are the community involvement and the Optimist Club's giant cookies. "

The audience clapped and cheered again. I smiled wide.

Mr. Koontz held a small basket. "I will select a question out of here for everybody this time." He plucked a piece of paper from the basket.

I sat waiting, poised in front of the microphone, nervous but composed.

"Kelly, your question is, 'What would you like to have accomplished by your ten-year class reunion?' "

"First and foremost, I would love to walk into my ten-year class reunion, but beyond that, I would like to have accomplished and have my classmates see that I'm a successful teacher who loves her job and has a great family life, a family who supports me in all I do. Thank you."

I had to keep my answer to one minute, but was it too short? Had I said um, or uh? Had I said enough? I smiled and waited for the others to answer their questions.

After each girl answered her question, the judges brought out the Little Miss and Mister children and lined them up in front of us. The girls wore red dresses with white pinafores and each boy wore suspenders, shorts, knee-high socks, and a feathered, green hat, replicating the costume of the old German days. After the winners were announced, last year's Little Miss distributed the trophies and set the tiara on the new Little Miss who beamed.

Once the children were ushered off stage, Mr. Koontz introduced the queen judges. Many worked in Evansville, none were from Jasper, and all were involved in pageants; some were directors and pageant coaches, and others worked for talent agencies. Their pageant backgrounds were impressive. Certainly, they would be fair.

Kelly Flannigan, the 1999 Strassenfest queen, gave a short speech and thanked the community for the year. I prayed my bladder wouldn't leak while I waited for the final verdict.

"Miss Photogenic is Audra…Miss Congeniality is Natalie…Our second runner up is Amanda…The first runner up is Abby."

Maybe I was wrong. Maybe I hadn't nailed the interview. Maybe the judges had decided that it wouldn't be right to choose a wheelchair contestant as a winner. Doubts buzzed in my head. The other girls sparkled and twirled in their high-heeled shoes. Their dresses swayed and flowed, while mine wrinkled in my cumbersome chair.

"And the 2000 Ms. Strassenfest queen is Miss Kelly Craig."

The audience roared and whistled. I wheeled to the center stage blinking back tears; my heart soared. Last year's winner set the crown on my head and draped the banner around my shoulder. She placed a dozen roses in the crook of my arm. Pride fisted in my heart, and I raised my chin higher.

The Master of Ceremonies closed with, "On behalf of everyone here on the committee— thank you for being a part of the 2000 Strassenfest Pageant."

The crowd rushed the stage. Cameras flashed. Family and contestants congratulated me. My self-worth ascended.

Not soon after, there were rumors that I won the pageant because people felt sorry for me. I didn't want to believe it because I handled the interview well, but it hurt to hear what people were saying—until I received a card from a judge.

She congratulated me and wrote, "My wish for you is that your year as Queen be filled with the pride in knowing that this title was not given to you—you earned it."

I let her letter steer my emotions from doubt to self-confidence, knowing how hard I'd worked. I wanted to be recognized for an accomplishment and she understood.

During the days following the pageant, I participated in other festival events. I rode in an old model car during the parade, wore my crown, and waved until the sun blazed its hot rays on me and I wobbled with dizziness. Quadriplegics don't sweat below their level of injury. My body had no way to cool itself. I needed help.

My friends confiscated freeze pops, the colorful ones in the long plastic tubes, from the float ahead of us, and took turns sticking them down my back and laying them on my neck. It was exactly what I needed. My vertigo finally subsided.

For the remainder of the festival, I wore the crown and smiled because for the first time people didn't notice my chair. They weren't staring at me with pity. They were congratulating me on something I did. Maybe from then on I'd be the Kelly Craig who won the Strassenfest pageant and not the Kelly Craig who was in the accident.

The festival's theme was "Blending the Past with the Future," but it was my theme too. Finally, my past was blurring into a more vibrant future. People were beginning to see me, the person in the chair and not the chair. The chair was slowly becoming invisible. This was my future, the beginning of a Kelly Craig who would reach her goals, not a girl to feel sorry for.

After the pageant, I received many congratulatory cards and letters, but the words in this Hallmark card from a friend, stood out:

"Just as an experiment, stop for a minute and see yourself as I do. Step away from all that self-doubt, all the noise in your head, and notice how brave you are, how good, and how strong.
Can you see it?
Now look deeper. There's more. A light about you, almost. Something that separates you from the others. Your spirit shines.
Stop for a minute to believe.
There is magic inside you."

I wasn't sure about the magic part, but I believed God was directing my path and was happy with the trail I was wheeling down. He was shining the light on me so my message could be heard. I needed to make Him proud.

My voice led the way. It was the only bud that could flower into purpose. Could it give me a piece of my life back? I wasn't sure, but maybe if I focused on a speaking career to share my message with kids, I'd find out. If I could be a queen in a chair maybe I could be a teacher in a chair.

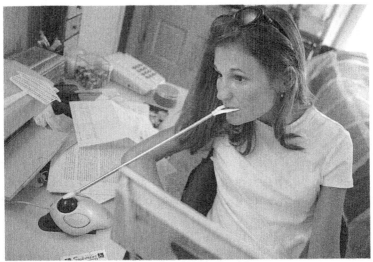

(David Pierini/*The Herald*)

Chapter Twenty-One

What lies behind us and what lies before us are small matters
compared to what lies within us.
Ralph Waldo Emerson

One late afternoon that summer, a friend talked me into walking to
another friend's house—about four blocks from mine where a group of
girls were gathered. I'd never rolled down a street before, but I was
getting used to the ease of the electric chair and the freedom it gave me.
When we left my house, it was early evening, the sun still shining, the
weather warm, but after we hung out for a while, night set in. It was
midnight when we started back to my house.

Crickets chirped, fireflies speckled the air with light, and summer
smells wafted along our way—newly cut grass, pool chlorine, and
roses. It was invigorating to be free enough to walk home. One friend
walked beside me as I rolled and the others followed in a car with the
flashers blinking.

Halfway home, a police officer spotted us crossing the road, turned on his flashers and pulled in front of us, forcing me to pull over to the side of the road. He got out of his car and approached us.

"Where are you going?"

"Home," I said.

"Where's that?" he asked.

I pointed in the direction of my house and gave him the address. Since when was it a crime to walk home? "Could you turn off your lights?" He would wake the neighbors, and I didn't want to be the talk of the town by morning. My cheeks heated, and I hadn't done anything wrong.

"No, Ma'am, I can't. You're blocking traffic and causing a hazard." He pointed to my friend's car behind us.

"Those are my friends," I said. "They're following me to make sure I get home safely. I'm not blocking traffic, and how am I any different than a cyclist?"

"You can't be doing it this way."

This was the way I moved. Was he going to give me a ticket? I bit my tongue, but wanted to ask him if my rights were different because I was in a chair. He was discriminating against me. I doubted he would have stopped a pedestrian walking home.

He didn't give me a ticket, but he followed us until we pulled into Mom's driveway and then he turned to go.

My friends were miffed, so they drove to the police station to report the officer. One friend said, "Kelly finally got the courage to leave her house and venture out in her chair and your officer hassles her for rolling home."

I didn't want them to make a big deal about it, but I liked that they were rooting for me. They returned to my house afterward and we hung out in the driveway. By this time, it was almost one a.m.

Fifteen minutes later, Mom hurried out of the house in her robe, her brows wrinkled. "Kelly, a policeman called and woke me up. What's going on?"

I told her what had happened. "Why did he call?" I asked.

"To say he was sorry."

"Good," someone said.

The incident made me realize how often disabled people were treated differently. It inspired me to use the incident in my speeches to bring awareness to people with disabilities.

Mom believed when children fell and skinned their knees, a wise parent kept a neutral expression. If the parent reacted with hysteria or jumped to aid the child, the child would assume his parents' opinion— that he'd suffered an awful experience. The child would most likely scream louder because of his parent's reaction.

However, if the parent knew the child was okay, the right thing was to smile, react calmly, and redirect the child. This inadvertently taught the child to pick himself up and brush off his scrapes when he fell. It taught him how to cope without screaming and crying.

I was raised in a home where Mom rarely focused on sympathy. Her thing was to keep moving and not dwell on the past, brush yourself off, and get up again.

There were moments soon after my injury when Mom's lack of attention irked me because I craved sympathy. I wanted her to understand what I had to go through every day.

Eventually I realized that if Mom had waited on me and pitied me I never would have rolled the way I did into my new life, so I wasn't terribly surprised when Mom said one day, "You should go back to school."

"Yeah, right. How?"

"If it's something you want, we'll figure it out, Kelly."

All my life I'd wanted to teach. She knew that. My friends were all away at college, but moving and living on a campus overwhelmed me. I was motivated to go, but I didn't know how to work out the logistics.

"It'll give you something to focus on."

There was that word again, *focus*. Having something to look forward to helped. Maybe I could commute and take a few classes. IU wasn't an option because it was two hours away, but what about the

University of Southern Indiana? It was a seventy-five minute commute. Mom scheduled an appointment with a counselor and took me for a tour.

The summer sun followed us, shining through my window along the highway. Touring the campus brought back memories of IU. Even though it had only been a little more than a year, it seemed a lifetime ago.

This campus was foreign and empty even though students and faculty walked by. At IU when I walked from class to class, there were over forty thousand students so I blended in. Here, I stood out. When I caught someone looking at me I smiled, but they looked away, as if embarrassed I'd caught them staring.

I wanted to shout, "I'm no different than you. I sit and you stand."

How many times had I walked past a disabled person without any regard for them as a person? Too many to count.

We went to the counseling office and met with an advisor who handled the paperwork transfer and arranged my schedule. The counselor told me which classes would transfer and which classes were required to graduate with an elementary education degree, but I wasn't sure I wanted to pursue that degree. Instead, I scheduled a radio broadcasting class in addition to a humanities class for elementary education. I wasn't ready to switch majors yet, but I wanted to keep an open mind to another degree that might help my professional speaking platform. Wasn't that the direction God wanted me to take?

Afterward, I rolled the path of where my classes were and learned the way. Next, we went to the nurse's office and explained my needs and that she would have to catheterize me every four hours. She showed us her office and assured us that she could assist me with my bladder.

At the end of our visit, my adrenaline spiked, which surprised me. I was more excited than I thought I'd be.

Mom shared the news with everyone.

But anxiety crept in. Who would take me? Mom had enough to do without following me to school for the next three years. She had a job and I couldn't drive.

"Hire someone to take you," Mom suggested.

Of course. But who?

Mom's aunt Martha Jane volunteered to drive me, bring me home, accompany me to classes, and take notes if she had to. She arranged her schedule so she was free the days and times of classes, and my plans fell into place.

My motorized chair became like a piece of clothing, a part of me, and my freedom. I didn't want to go anywhere without it. If I wanted to sit in the sun, I pressed a lever and rolled forward to the window or out the door. If my butt burned from sitting in the same spot, I tilted myself back. If I was ticked at Mom, I could wheel away and drive myself into the bathroom to stew.

Andy bought a water bottle with a long straw, filled it, and tucked it in the corner of my chair. I no longer had to ask someone for a drink. Every morning my nurse rinsed it and refilled it.

I couldn't wait to get my van, too. It would make me even more independent. Not that I was going to drive it, but because no one would have to lift me in and out of the car every time I went somewhere. And I wouldn't be pulled over by the cops for wheeling home.

Saying goodbye to my cute little Camry stung. It was only a car, but it had been a part of my teen and college life. It had carried books, cheer uniforms, friends, Eric—and all the memories of the words spoken there, the songs sung—memories of the life I still wanted.

It would be funny to be twenty years old and riding in a van. My friends and I used to make fun of people who drove vans. They were for moms with children, definitely not twenty-something adults.

Mom, Andy, and I went to Louisville, Kentucky to pick it up. The sales manager was also in a wheelchair. He showed us how to work the controls and lock me into the passenger seat.

All Mom had to do was press a button to disengage the side ramp and I could wheel myself in. The chair automatically locked in place. Simple.

"This will be great, Kelly." Mom told the manager how I was starting school in a few weeks and how difficult it had been getting me in and out of the car.

"We can modify a vehicle for you to drive," the man said.

I couldn't fathom the idea. I had limited wrist movement and no right triceps, but Joni Erickson Tada, who was also a quad, drove. I'd read about her and marveled at her courage. I wasn't so brave. I could hardly sit in a car without flinching at the oncoming traffic, let alone drive one. I couldn't do it. "Thanks. I've heard that, but I'm not ready."

"I understand," he said. "Have you heard of the Ms. Wheelchair pageant?"

I laughed. Was he serious?

"It's a real thing. You should compete. You're a beautiful girl."

"Thanks," I said.

"I noticed you're wearing a wedding ring," Mom said to him. "Are you married?"

"Sure am," he said.

"Wow, I bet your wife is awesome," Mom said.

He smiled. "She is, but so am I." Turning to me, he winked.

I wondered if he'd met his wife before or after his accident. Statistics showed that couples who met after they became disabled stayed together compared to those who married before the accident.

"You need all the techie tools to achieve optimum independence," the girl from the Vocational Rehabilitation Center said one day. "I can recommend a great IT guy who can get you set up for school with the latest and greatest gadgets."

Mom took his number and called him.

He came to the house, assessed my living arrangements, and took inventory of what I needed.

When he returned a week later, he brought a special phone with huge buttons. The downside was that the phone was placed in my room, the central part of the house, and since I used speakerphone, everyone heard my conversations. But still, it was an improvement. I no longer had to wait for someone to answer the phone for me.

Instead of lifting the receiver to answer the phone, all I had to do was get close to the receiver and say hello and it connected me to the caller. It was like magic.

When it worked.

The phone's software identified my voice, but it was fickle. I said hello, but had to wait two seconds and say hello again before it recognized me.

The tech also showed me a voice activated computer typing system, but it wasn't efficient, so I resorted to typing with a six-inch plastic stick that fit in my mouth and pecked one letter at a time. The tech brought a raised keyboard that sat about twelve inches off the desk, which made pecking easier.

He demonstrated the gadgets until he was confident I understood how to use them.

Slowly, I gained independence.

Before school began, I'd grown fond of one of the part-time aides, Karla Barnett, and I asked her to work as my full-time caregiver. She agreed and I paid her privately. She was able to keep her job at the hospital too, since she worked part time for them.

Every morning, six days a week, she showed up at my door, sometimes at 5:30 a.m. On Mondays, Wednesdays, and Fridays it took her two hours to get me ready because she did my bowel routine, but on the other days it took an hour. On Saturdays, a caretaker from Jasper Memorial came to help.

Martha Jane arrived at my house two days a week, drove me to school, and before classes she made sure I had a lap desk and a notebook. During lectures, to take notes, I asked someone from class to place a pen in the skinny part of my wrist guard between my pointer finger and thumb. I'd find the nicest girl, sit next to her, and ask her to help. "Excuse me; can you help me put this gear on my hand?"

"Sure. How?"

"It's easy. I'll show you. Take the strap and attach it…" The trick was to keep my voice calm and use my words effectively. Generally, people liked to help. And once I had my go-to person in each class, it was more enjoyable.

Using the wrist guard was the only way I could write since my fingers had no mobility.

I didn't talk to my professors about my disability. I wanted to be treated like everyone else and do the work on my own. I took my own notes, quizzes, and tests. Even though I used to be right-handed, I became good at being left-handed.

There were times when I had to wait near an elevator until another student came by to push the button for me. It was a simple task, but I didn't have the mobility to push most buttons. The last thing I wanted was to get in the elevator and have the doors close me in without a way to go anywhere, but it happened. All I could do was sit there and wait for the door to open.

When students stared at me, I asked, "Do you want to know what happened?" I was open about it because it was important for me to educate others about persons with disabilities.

One day while I was waiting in an elevator with my notebook open, a girl commented at my cursive.

"Do you take an art font class?"

"No. Why?" I asked.

"Your handwriting is cool."

"Thanks," I said.

"How do you write that way?"

I wanted to say, "*First you become a quad and lose all your right-handed ability, then you focus on perfecting the only side you have left. But I wouldn't recommend it.*" Instead, I smiled and said. "I guess it comes easy to me."

Some weekends I typed ten-page papers with my mouth stick—one key at a time.

The only time I needed help for a course was when I had to cut, staple, and glue projects together, but the final product was always my creation. I had the vision, bought the supplies, and found someone to be my hands, directing them with my voice as to how I wanted the final project to look. Mom helped the most.

The beginning of every semester was overwhelming when I'd get the syllabus for all my classes and go over the course requirements. I'd wonder how I was going to do all that.

But every semester I did. It helped not having a life outside of school. One semester I earned straight As, which was nothing like the old Kelly.

The first semester of taking elementary education classes left me with doubt. When I told people I wanted to teach elementary kids, they said, "Are you sure you don't want to be a reading specialist instead of a teacher?" One of my friends said, "Maybe you should change your major. How will you write on the board?"

I didn't want to let the accident define me, but how could I not? The disability permeated into every crack of my life. Maybe I should listen to the people who recommended I change my major. Maybe I should switch.

I sought the advice of a school counselor who also doubted my choice, so I changed my major to communications. Perhaps speaking about the consequences of driving drunk was what God wanted me to do.

A few days after I started the eight-week class at a radio station, I knew I'd made a mistake changing my major. I didn't like working with adults. I wanted to work with children. I'd changed my major because I was in a wheelchair, instead of doing what I really wanted. I allowed the wheelchair to define who I was. I transferred back to elementary ed. I would prove everyone wrong and become a teacher.

I would become an awesome teacher.

(Jenna and Me)

Chapter Twenty-Two

It is good to have an end to journey toward; but it is the journey that matters, in the end.
Ursula Le Guin

Jenna, a friend I met through Mom, decided to join me at USI the second year I attended. She drove my van, and we went together for the last few years. Jenna's mom and mine were good friends, but Jenna and I hadn't been friends in high school. She was two years younger, ran with a different crowd, and got pregnant in high school. We were very different, but came together because of unusual circumstances. She needed me and I needed her. Jenna and I had one huge thing in common—neither one of us envisioned that our lives would turn out the way they had. We became best friends fast.

Our trip to USI took seventy-five long minutes. For half of the way she cranked up her hippie music and we sang like rock stars. For the other half of the way she compromised and switched to my pop music and we sang like pop stars. "Nothing is Gonna Stop Us," by Starship became one of our favorites. Sometimes I asked her to skip to another song after thirty seconds, which drove her crazy, but variety helped make the best of the long haul.

Jenna was also an elementary ed major, but we only had a few classes together since I was a year ahead of her. We ate lunch together and shopped at the mall during our long breaks. We visited the mall so often that storeowners knew us by name.

Many mornings Jenna asked, "Did you study?"

"For three hours. What about you?"

"Nope. I'm screwed," she said. "If it wasn't for you I'd never be able to do this. I'd just stay home."

We helped each other get through it. She made it easy for me to go back to college and together we made it fun.

There were perks for people with disabilities in college. I was able to schedule my classes early, before the other students, and Jenna was paid to take me to school. Since Jenna drove me, she was allowed to schedule her classes first too.

My physical fitness class was held in the campus gym, but when I wheeled to the side doors, I couldn't open them. I waited for a student to walk by. Finally, one did. "Would you open the door for me, please?"

The girl held the door and I wheeled onto the gym floor where other students gathered. They turned and stared.

"Is this elementary phys ed?"

They nodded.

The teacher walked in and said hello, then turned to me. "Are you in this class?"

"Yes."

"They let you register for this class?"

I nodded.

"How am I supposed to teach you? We'll be doing physical activities. I don't mean any disrespect, but there's been a mistake. How can I teach you if you can't participate?"

My face heated, but I was so stunned and embarrassed by her attitude that my tongue stuck to the roof of my mouth. It was probably better not to say anything because I feared that I'd regret my words.

"You need to go back to scheduling and see if you can take another class in place of this one." She ushered me to the doors, opened them, and waved for me to leave.

I wheeled away seething at her lack of tack. She'd made up her mind that I was unteachable without giving me a chance. It made me more determined. I went directly to the Dean of Students. "I need to talk to him. Is he available?" I said to the secretary.

"You're in luck. He just returned from lunch and has a few minutes." She escorted me into his office.

I didn't waste time and wheeled up to his desk. "I've been told that I need to take something different besides my physical education class. However, it's a requirement for my degree."

"Who told you that you couldn't take the class?" He set his pen down.

I explained what the teacher had said. "I know I can teach gym. I've coached girls' cheerleading and gymnastics for years. Since my accident, I've coached girls who have won competitions. I know I can teach." Each word came out more forcefully. I inhaled sharply.

"I don't doubt that you can," he said.

"I don't need to jump and do flips to teach what to do. I have my voice, photos, movies of stunts, and my own personal experience. I'm totally capable." I couldn't stop my rant now that I had someone listening.

"I'll talk to the instructor," he said. "She'll have to revamp her class to accommodate you. I apologize. You have every right to take this course, and we'll make sure that we get it right. Give me today to talk to her, but plan on attending class tomorrow at the same time, and we'll get this straightened out."

I left his office exhausted and unnerved from the conflict, but relieved that I'd accomplished my goal.

The next day I returned to class and students stared, but I ignored them. The teacher didn't acknowledge me, but she saw me. She was probably upset that she had to revamp her lesson plan to accommodate me, but I didn't care. For the rest of that semester she only talked to me when she had to. I vowed to never treat my students the way she'd treated me.

I ended up with an A in her class. Years later, I heard she told her students, "If a girl in a wheelchair can pass this class, so can you."

Even though I'd acted confident about the gym class, doubts continued to sail like ping-pong balls across a table. One minute I was confident and the next I wasn't. How would I convince a principal to hire me? Would parents trust me to teach their children? If I could convince the dean, could I convince an employer?

I went through the motions of getting my teaching degree because it had always been my goal, and I needed to focus on something positive to keep me going, but there were days when I wondered if my teaching dream would come true.

For a while, I wouldn't face my fears. I went to class and buried my concerns, never expressing my deepest doubts.

But one day, when talking to my school advisor, he asked, "How are things going for you, Kelly?"

"Good."

"Are you ready for student teaching next year?"

"I'm nervous about the logistics of how it'll all work out."

"What do you mean?"

My advisor knew me well. He'd been with me for three years guiding me through my ups and downs. He never heard me voice a concern about my teaching ability. "What if I'm not a good teacher?"

"It's normal for you to have doubts. Everyone does. You'll make a great teacher. You already are. Think of how many students you've already mentored. You may not have your hands to do the work for you, but you have a teaching mind and voice. Nothing can stop that—it's who you are. Don't forget that."

He renewed my confidence, but the true test would come when I had to teach. I hoped that parents and teachers would be more open-minded than my PE teacher.

Chapter Twenty-Three

Decisions are made from either our mind or our heart. It would be nice if those two were always aligned, but that doesn't usually happen. When the two are at odds, I follow my heart. With Christ in your heart, you'll be at peace with where you end up.
Shawn Schaefer

Christmas 2000
Belleville, Illinois

Shawn was home from college on Christmas break and eager to see his family, eat home-cooked meals, and spend time with his sister, Shannon, and her fiancé, Tim. Tim had been diagnosed with non-Hodgkin's lymphoma five months earlier and was struggling with the diagnosis, the treatment, and was growing weary of all his appointments. His treatments left him nauseous and fatigued.

Tim's fight resembled a boxing match. After being knocked down numerous times, he got up and learned that the cancer was gone, but a few months later, the doctors told him the cancer was back and worse than before. Shannon was by his side through it all and at times took on the fight when Tim needed to rest.

Shawn took him to dinner, to an occasional appointment, and looked for any opportunity to drop off his favorite treat.

But Shawn's girlfriend, Haley, was having difficulty understanding how she fit into Shawn's life. She phoned him. "I realize that you have other places you want to be right now," she said, "but I can't handle being shut out."

"I need to be available for my sister and Tim," Shawn said. "Right now that seems more important. I know I'm not letting you in right now, and I'm sorry for that."

"I don't need to be your first priority, but I need to be one of them."

Shawn understood her feelings, but he also knew his heart. Spending time with Haley seemed wasteful and self-serving. Shannon and Tim needed him more. If he went out with Haley, he'd be thinking about Tim the whole time anyway.

"After three years together and overcoming long distances this past year we should be growing closer, but we're growing apart," she said, her voice cracking.

"I don't disagree. I love you, and don't want to cause you pain. I can't explain why I'm pushing you away. I might be making the biggest mistake of my life, but we need to go our separate ways. If we're meant to be together, then we'll find our way back to each other."

As Shawn hung up the phone, tears stung his eyes. Although he understood Haley's frustration, he couldn't change the way he felt, or where God was leading him.

He thought of Kelly, the girl he saw on ESPN earlier that year, and wondered how she was doing. How did she maintain such a positive attitude in the midst of her personal tragedy?

He paused and went to his computer, typed Kelly Craig in the space bar at Google and clicked through the old articles about her, marveling again at her strength. He browsed for an address, but came up empty again.

He took the letter he'd written to her months ago, the one he kept in his desk drawer, and reread it, wondering if he'd ever get the chance to send it to her.

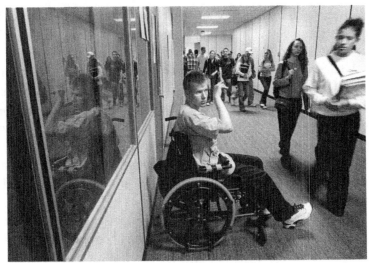

(David Pierini/*The Herald*)

Chapter Twenty-Four

I hate the words "handicapped" and "disabled." They imply that
you are less than whole.
I don't see myself that way at all.
Aimee Mullins

January-May 2001
Jason

Once Jason came home and was able to move more and communicate, he wanted to finish his senior year of high school, so Mom discussed the options with school administrators. It was decided that he'd take the required four classes necessary for a certificate of completion. He wasn't capable of obtaining an actual diploma and wouldn't know the difference, but it would give him purpose.

Mom and Andy had five children at home and two were disabled, plus Jason needed twenty-four-hour care. He couldn't be left alone. His short-term memory lagged. He couldn't remember what he had for breakfast, but he knew all his math facts.

His speech was severely impaired. Saying one word took a long time to pronounce and resembled the low groan of a whale. Most people couldn't understand what he was trying to say even though he understood everything they said to him. At school, he worked with a speech therapist who determined he couldn't enunciate the sounds /s/, /t/, /f/, and /k/, or /sh/ and /ch/ blends. He also had difficulty pronouncing sounds at the end of a word and other consonant blends.

To communicate, he used gestures or a communication board—a laminated board with the letters of the alphabet printed in large type. He pointed to the letters to create words. Oftentimes, it became a word-search game to understand him. He formed a word and we'd guess what he was trying to convey.

"Are you spelling one word or two?" his therapist asked.

Some days he didn't want to work on his speech and became belligerent with the therapist, but she asserted herself. "Take him to the principal," she said to Jason's assistant, Matt.

Matt was Jason's friend before the accident and now his personal assistant. He helped Jason with his homework and assisted him in classes. "Jason, cut the crap," Matt said. "You said you were ready to settle down and learn."

Jason nodded and listened to Matt, but still balled his hands into fists and glared. He didn't want to need help. He didn't want people to stare at him. "I'm not special; I'm normal." But his classes were with learning-disabled students, and the special needs bus he used to call the *short* bus picked him up every day and brought him home.

At first, he refused to take the bus because he used to make fun of the kids who rode on it. "I'm not retarded," he said to Mom.

"If you want to go to school you have to take the bus," Mom told him. "That's the way it is."

He still needed the assistance of a walker or a wheelchair because the tendons in his hands and feet had shortened and drawn in. Mom said she used to pray for him to walk again, but now she prayed for him to get his voice back, a voice that others could understand.

Between classes, Jason asked Matt to wheel him into the hallway where Jason could wave to the people he knew. Many stopped to high-five him or say hello.

Every now and then, he laughed and reminded me of the brother he used to be, the old Jason, but he was softer and kinder to little kids now, always asking them for a hug—something he'd never done before.

When he wanted to go to the prom in the spring, Mom and Andy rented him a tux and let him go. As a sophomore, he'd gone to prom with my friend, but got caught speeding in the parking lot. The police didn't arrest him, but forbid him from going to the prom, which meant this was his first prom. His dance card was filled the entire night.

On graduation day, he used his walker and crossed the stage to reach for his diploma. He turned to the crowd, smiled, and gave everyone a thumbs-up. The audience cheered.

Afterward, he was quoted in *The Herald* as saying, "I want to go to college."

"Maybe he will," Mom said. "The doctors never thought he'd make it this far."

But I doubted he'd ever have the mental capacity to go to college or the physical ability to hold a job. He couldn't walk and could barely communicate. He couldn't even remember the dog's name in the book, *Where the Red Fern Grows*, immediately after reading it.

(Andy and Me)

Chapter Twenty-Five

On particularly rough days when I'm sure I can't possibly endure
more, I remind myself that my track record for getting through bad
days has been 100%.
And that's pretty good.
Unknown

Not long after the nurses removed my leg bag, I started having frequent accidents and didn't know why. Mom wrapped my bottom in Depends—adult diapers—that crinkled when I moved. (So much for the Victoria's Secret underwear!)

Mom took me to Riley's Children's Hospital in Indianapolis for medical tests. The doctors found that I had a large bladder stone that required outpatient surgery. While we were there, I met Dr. Rink, a urologist who specialized in a different kind of surgery.

Mom and I sat in his office as he explained. "Your spinal cord injury has given you a neurogenic bladder, which causes spasms and leakage. One problem with this kind of bladder is that it will store urine at a high pressure (due to the spasms.) This can lead to renal failure and subsequently death. There's a surgery that was developed to prevent the high pressure storage," Dr. Rink said.

Death? My stomach fisted. "A surgery can prevent this?"

He pointed to a diagram on the wall and continued. "I open the top of your bladder and sew a piece of intestine (usually ileum, the lower part of the small intestine) on to the dome (top). This is a bladder augmentation. I make a channel out of the bowel to make it easier to drain your bladder. Having a larger bladder prevents the high pressure storage."

He was speaking another language. I wanted to understand how it functioned, but it sounded complicated, and I wasn't sure how it would work on an everyday basis. "How will I urinate then?"

"There'll be a tunnel made out of the intestines from your bladder to right here." He pointed to a spot next to my navel. "To extract the urine, your mom, nurse, brother, or anyone, for that matter, would only have to insert the tube near your abdomen to withdraw the urine. The top part of your underwear would cover the entrance to the tunnel."

"They wouldn't have to put me on the bed, pull down my pants, and insert a catheter?"

"No," he said. "They'd insert the catheter tube into the channel below your waist. The other end of the tube would drain into a bag where the urine would be deposited. Your freedom would greatly improve. Others who have had the surgery said it's life changing."

"Do you do these all the time?" Mom asked.

The nurse in the room said, "People fly their children in from all over to see him for this procedure."

Dr. Rink shifted his weight from one foot to the other and smiled at his nurse. "I have one of the largest volumes of patients who come to me to perform this procedure." He reached into a folder bin hanging on the wall and pulled out a pamphlet. "Here's an article that I co-authored about the procedure."

Mom took the brochure and read.

Wearing underwear again made me smile. Never having to lie

naked on the ground to be catheterized made me smile bigger. Having fewer infections made me ecstatic. The surgery sounded too good to be true. My bladder was such a pain that some days I wished I had bladder control rather than the ability to walk. "Let's do it," I said.

Two years after the accident, in the summer of 2001, Andy drove me to the hospital. We arrived two days before the surgery to begin the prep work. Every couple of hours I drank a thick, sickly sweet gunk called GoLytely, to empty my bowels. It made me gag. The intestines had to be empty since the procedure involved taking a part of the bowel. Drinking the GoLytely cocktail wasn't an option. It was mandatory.

Unfortunately, I couldn't sit on a toilet. The nurses transferred me to a bed lined with chucks, flat liquid-absorbing blue paper-liners. Every time my bowels moved, they changed the pads and wiped my bottom.

My stomach gurgled and revolted at the taste, but Andy calmly coached me to stay with the program. "You can do it. Drink, drink, drink." He never left my side except to go to the gift shop to buy me bubble gum. I chewed until the flavor filled my mouth, and then drank the solution again.

It was terrible to put Andy through two days of hell, but he never complained. When I didn't want to drink anymore and when the stench in the room became unbearable, his voice remained steady and caring.

Many times he'd been my hero, the sunshine on my darkest day.

As a child, I walked in my sleep. One night there was a tornado warning, so my brothers and I slept with him and Mom. While everyone slept, I walked in my sleep out the front door and around the house to the back patio, unaware. Thunder boomed and woke me. How had I gotten outside? Terrified, I yanked the sliding door that led to Mom's bedroom, but it was locked.

I banged and banged.

Lightning flashed, throwing a spotlight on Andy who stood on the other side of the sliding door in his tighty whities, staring at me.

I screamed.

He opened the door, comforted me, and talked to me softly while he led me back to where the others were sleeping.

Today, he spoke to me in the same soothing tones, guiding me through one of the worst ordeals I ever had to endure. It was the most disgusting and degrading procedure that I'd ever gone through.

The morning of my surgery, I woke in the hospital room with Andy still beside me. I could barely hold my head up. It was like I'd had the stomach flu for days. The sour taste in my mouth reminded me of the GoLytely and my stomach lurched.

Andy unwrapped another piece of gum and plopped it into my mouth.

Mom arrived to relieve Andy. It was his turn to take care of my younger brothers, so when he turned to say goodbye, a lump clogged my throat. I wanted to cry. My courage was leaving with him. I swallowed hard.

He squeezed my shoulder and studied me. "You okay?"

I nodded, not trusting my voice, the tears on the brim of spilling over. "Thanks," I blurted.

"The worst is over." He chuckled in a teasing way, and I was sure he was referring to the rancid smell in the room.

Before I could find my voice to say anything more, a tech entered the room. The casters of her pulmonary function machine rattled and clanked.

Andy turned to go.

The tech moved to the side of the bed and introduced herself. "I'm here to measure the air in your lungs. It's a normal procedure before surgery." She explained how her machine worked. "When I say blow, I need you to blow as much air into this tube as you can." She showed me a long flexible white tube. "Are you ready?"

I nodded.

She held the plastic tube near my mouth. "Take a deep breath."

I inhaled, but couldn't suck more air into my lungs.

She covered my mouth with the tube. "Blow, blow, blow," she ordered. "Harder. Faster. Go, go, go," she cheered.

The air hissed out of my chest deflating my thin lungs. My chest sagged until I had no more energy or air to expend.

The technician read the screen, evaluated the results on the tape, and frowned. "Can you do it again?"

"I did the best I could," I said, still breathless.

A doctor in blue scrubs entered the room and introduced himself as the anesthesiologist. He examined the results of the breathing test. "Hmm," he said, scratching his chin. "Unfortunately, with your lung capacity, I can't recommend that you go through with the surgery. The surgery can take three hours, and I don't know if your body will be able to handle it."

"I can't have the surgery?" Instant tears pricked my eyes.

"No, it means that there are no guarantees that if you have the surgery you'll be able to breathe on your own afterward. You could need the assistance of a ventilator—a machine that helps you breathe."

"For how long?" Mom asked, her shoulders sagging.

"For the rest of her life."

My stomach plummeted. I turned to Mom. "Now what?" All those doctor appointments, all those hours of drinking crap, and no one ever told me this could happen. Damn the drunk driver. Did this mean I'd have to endure more accidents? And maybe death?

Mom looked at me with tears in her eyes, too.

The doctor said, "I don't know if that's what will happen, but it's my job to inform you of anything that could happen. In the end, having the surgery is your decision."

How was I supposed to decide? This decision could complicate my life even more. Maybe I wasn't supposed to have the surgery. What should I do? Yes, waiting for someone to catheterize me six times a day drove me crazy, but if I couldn't breathe on my own then how would I continue my public speaking? How would I teach? What was left if I lost those abilities, too?

Minutes lapsed. Voices on the intercom and in the hallway floated into my room. The doctor looked over my chart and my vitals. Mom and I continued to sit silently stunned. Mom's lips moved as if in silent prayer.

The urologist strolled in the room with a blue puffy scrub hat and blue footies. "You ready?" He smiled and rubbed his hands together.

The anesthesiologist told him the bad news.

My surgeon nodded. "He has to tell you that, Kelly. Yes, it's a risk, but...given your age, your health, and your ability to breath on your own now, I'm confident you'll be okay."

"If this was your daughter would you let her have the surgery?" I asked.

"Even if you were my daughter I couldn't make any promises or guarantees."

Both doctors left the room to give us time to talk about what to do.

I shut my eyes, then opened them and saw a sign. "Do you see that?"

Mom followed my line of vision and stared at the door, where I was looking. "What?"

"The cross on the door. It's in the middle. There. Don't you see it?"

She got up from her chair and pointed to the middle of the door where the smooth part of the wood separated from the mitered part. "Here?"

"Yes. It's a cross. See it in the wood grain?"

Mom nodded.

Finding the cross was like looking at a cloud in the sky and recognizing a shape. If you stared long enough you could see a different object within the fluff.

"It's a sign, Kelly. God is giving us a sign. You'll be okay. You should have the surgery."

The operating room staff waited. The clock on the wall ticked. A patient's heels clicked on the tile in the hallway, and my stomach gurgled.

The doctor was the best surgeon for my surgery. Even though I was scared, I trusted him, but I decided to trust God more. "Okay, let's do it. I'm ready."

I woke in the recovery room long enough to survey the room and see the ventilator in the corner, not connected to me. I was breathing on my own. *Thank you, God.*

A cotton fog enveloped my head. The room's surroundings and the sensations twirled inside me reminiscent of the accident, the trauma room, and Eric's abandonment. Memories clung to the walls of my mind like a slimy black leech, and sadness threatened to press its hand over my heart. *No.* I refused to let them consume me. I focused only on my ability to breathe on my own, and took a deep breath.

"Kelly, are you okay?" a nurse said.

"Yes," I whispered.

"You're doing great. The surgery is over. You're in recovery. How is your pain? On a scale of one to ten with ten being the worst, how do you feel?"

"An eight."

"I'll put a little more morphine in your IV. It'll probably make you sleepy. Try to rest."

In a few minutes, warmth spread through my body and nothing mattered. God held my hand. He was there beside me. Tears of abandonment vanished and peace cloaked me. Andy and Mom came into the room as I drifted to sleep.

I stayed in the hospital for six days to regain my strength and learn how to function with my new bladder. Medical staff educated me on how to care for the abdominal port while I educated them on how to care for me, showing them what my limitations were. Each time a new shift came on, I retrained them. Although their careers dealt with patients every day—not too many had cared for quads.

After I returned home and taught my nurses and family how to do my bathroom, I was instantly freer.

But it didn't last.

Just when I thought I could finally wear girlie underwear I started having bowel problems, diarrhea.

It began over the weekend. Mom and Andy cleaned the mess, but then it continued at school. Right in the middle of class my bottom dampened and I smelled the fumes filling my Depends. I prayed that no one could smell me, but how could they not? There was nothing I could do but wait until class was over. Then I wheeled to the nurse for help. The bad part was that I had to wait for Jenna to pick me up at our designated time, which wasn't right away.

The pediatrician said I had a bacterial infection called clostridium difficile (C. diff) and prescribed medicine. When I wasn't any better after three weeks, she referred me to a gastro-intestinal specialist in Evansville who finally diagnosed the problem. My urologist had prescribed one antibiotic and my pediatrician had prescribed another one, and they were counteractive, negating their effectiveness. In thirty seconds, the specialist figured out what had been giving me fits for over a month.

I'd rarely been to a doctor's office before the accident, but now managing my health care was a part-time job.

Once the medications were changed, my problems stopped. And finally, I was able to wear Victoria's Secret underwear. It was a day to celebrate.

The surgery was indeed life changing.

Chapter Twenty-Six

If you can't stop thinking about it, don't stop working for it.
Unknown

Shawn

In May 2001, Shawn graduated with a master's degree in accounting. In July, his sister's fiancé, Tim, died from cancer. He'd been like a brother. Shawn struggled to understand why he'd been spared after his accident years ago, but Tim hadn't.

Why had Shannon lost the love of her life when they were just getting started? How would she pick up the pieces? Why did something terrible have to happen to a young and caring man?

Once again Shawn thought of Kelly, the girl he couldn't forget, especially when his faith teetered. He took out his cell phone and dialed 411.

"City and state please?" the operator asked.

"Jasper, Indiana."

"Name?"

"Kelly Craig."

There was a brief pause. "I'm sorry, sir, there isn't a listing with that name."

"Can you tell me how many listings there are with Craig as the last name?"

The operator paused again. "There are a total of ten, sir."

"Wow, okay. How many can you give me at one time?" Shawn asked.

"Only one. You'll have to call back for the others."

"Okay, give me the first name on your list, please."

The operator paused again before Shawn received an automated response with the first name and number. He jotted the number, hung up, and dialed 411 again. He did this ten times until he retrieved all the names and numbers, logging them on a sheet of paper.

Afterward, he called each one and asked the same questions. "I'm looking for Kelly Craig who lives in Jasper, Indiana. Do you know her, or are you related to her?" Each person who answered the phone said no, they didn't know her. Some were polite, but others were impatient and rudely hung up.

How was it possible for him to call them all and not find her? Perplexed, he stored the list in a drawer and moved on to his Saturday chores. Today was laundry day.

(David Pierini/*The Herald*)

Chapter Twenty-Seven

Disability is a matter of perception.
If you can do just one thing well, you're needed by someone.
Martina Navratilova

January-May 2004

The principal of Precious Blood Catholic School asked Kathy Wolf, the third-grade teacher, if she was interested in allowing me to student teach in her classroom. The principal shared that I was a quadriplegic. Kathy accepted the challenge.

I knew many of the parishioners who attended Precious Blood Church, which was connected to the school. Many of those same families had prayed for me after the accident. They were kind, caring, and humble, which made me more comfortable.

Student teaching at Precious Blood was a dream come true. I wanted to be able to pray in the classroom and incorporate faith into my curriculum. Excited, I looked forward to meeting the students and getting on with my life. I couldn't wait to do something for others instead of waiting for someone to do something for me.

I hid my nervousness and arrived at class on time. The Doubt Devil speared his sharp fork in my mind. *Maybe the counselor who told me I'd never be able to teach in a classroom was right. Maybe I should be a professional speaker and leave teaching to others.* I flicked the red beast off my shoulder. I could do this.

Vocational rehab hired Sarah, a friend and fellow student who'd graduated the month before, to be my assistant in the classroom—to do my bathroom, make copies, write on the board, pass out and grade papers, and open my book and set it in my lap—to manage all those tasks I couldn't physically do.

After I was introduced to the students, it was time to pray. I asked them if they had something they wanted to pray for.

One student said, "Dear God, thank you for saving Miss Craig from the accident so she could be with us today."

A lump formed in my throat, but I swallowed it down.

Next, I demonstrated how my wheelchair worked. I showed them forward, backward, and how I popped wheelies. I cracked jokes and made them laugh.

I overheard one student whisper to another, "She's cool."

"Do you have any questions you want to ask me?" I asked.

They raised their hands and, one by one, asked questions like, "What's your favorite color?" "What's your favorite food?" "Do you like candy?"

I smiled a wider smile than I had in a long time. They didn't ask me questions about my injury. They saw me and not my disability. Their response moved me, and the lump returned to my throat. These children were a blessing. Teaching in a classroom would be a great environment.

In the mornings that followed my first teaching day, I woke with a smile and a new purpose. Finally, I had others who were dependent on me. *What a great feeling.* The sadness that typically started my day dissolved. While still in bed, I planned my day.

I taught at Precious Blood for eighteen weeks, observing for the first two, and then teaching one subject at a time. Each week I added a new subject until I was teaching all the subjects. Then I subtracted a different subject each day for another week. I left math until to the end, so I wouldn't have to teach it for long, since that was the most difficult subject to teach with my disabilities.

It turned out that I hardly needed my assistant. I graded my own papers using a purple marker and my left hand. Students, eager to help me, fought over who would get my book out and set it in my lap, and who would pass out papers. Children love to play teacher, and I gave them the chance. I had them go to the board and write sentences such as, "I love swimming running and biking," then asked them to insert the commas. By giving them the chance to be the teacher, it helped them retain the information. Students learned best by doing.

A teacher is more than someone who can walk, paste, cut art projects, or write on the board. A teacher is one who can teach, and I began to feel confident that teaching was something I could do well. *How blessed I was to have found the strength to get to that point in my life. Thank you, God.*

In the spring, during recess, I challenged students to race me in my wheelchair, and they lined up alongside me. Someone said, "On your mark, get set, go." And off we went, sprinting across the blacktop toward the finish line. Some days I wore sandals, and the kids asked me to wiggle my toes. They dove for a spot around my feet and watched for the little movements.

Every now and then one of my legs spasmed and shook. The kids learned what to do. They touched my leg and held it down until the spasms stopped. They weren't uncomfortable with the weirdness that came with my disability. They learned my body's idiosyncrasies and accepted them because I never made them embarrassed about asking questions. I believed that through me they learned about people with different kinds of disabilities and learned to accept and feel natural around people with disabilities.

One Monday, I gave the class a challenge. "Whoever memorizes the Apostle's Creed by Friday will get a wheelchair ride."

Their eyes got big and two out of eighteen students took the challenge.

One girl said, "I've never studied for anything harder in my life." She and another boy learned the creed and earned free rides.

When the time came to go outside, the others watched, cheered, and applauded the two winners. They took turns sitting in my lap, working my controls, and wheeling around the parking lot.

On the last day of my student teaching, the class threw me a surprise party. They set a quilt in my lap that one of the student's mothers had created. She'd sewed the back pockets of the students' jeans and pieced them together to make one large square—a keepsake that I would treasure forever. That day, I let the knot in my throat break free, and I openly cried.

I needed the students as much as they needed me. Even though they weren't my children, they'd been a constant in my life for eighteen weeks.

What would I do all summer without them? I'd miss them all.

Through my tears, I said, "Thank you. This is the first time since the accident I felt needed. I thought no one could depend on me for anything again, but you depended on me every day to give you something to do, to teach you, and I'm grateful to all of you for giving me the gift to teach you."

(David Pierini/*The Herald*)

Chapter Twenty-Eight

Planning is bringing the future into the present so that you can do something about it now.
Alan Lakein

Shawn graduated from college with a bachelor's and a master's degree in accounting, following the career path of his father and grandfather. His life was one of spreadsheets, audits, and deadlines, and he preferred to fill every single moment with a tight schedule.

He rose every morning at 6:00 and worked some nights until 8:00 or 9:00. Occasionally, he worked until midnight. If he didn't work late, he worked out at the gym before he came home. In the evenings, he cleaned, washed clothes, and read the post-it notes that he'd left scattered about for himself—on the fridge, his desk, the laundry room. He didn't want to forget anything and planned ahead, almost to a fault.

To help him stay focused, he devised a laminated card and carried it in his wallet. At the top of the card was this quote:

If you have the chance to help another and you don't, then why else are you living?

—Roberto Clemente

Shawn's 10 Dimensions for Dedicated Focus

1. **Sleep** – It's the energy source for the day ahead. Like a battery, we must recharge to function well. Sleep affects our level of patience, enthusiasm, and our attitude throughout each day.

2. **Listen** – It's how we learn. It reduces miscommunication. If we attempt to understand others' point-of-views, then we can eliminate confrontation.

3. **Routine** – We are what we repeatedly do. Good habits make good people. This includes a balance between emotional, intellectual, physical, and spiritual aspects of life.

4. **Be Humble** – Be confident in yourself, but realize that the world turns without you. Treat everyone with the same respect and kindness.

5. **Play your strengths** – We often find ourselves trying to improve our shortcomings. Instead, we should focus on our strengths. It is our talents and admirable characteristics that set us apart from others. Maximize what makes you special.

6. **See the Big Picture** – Each day will bring new obstacles and new challenges. Harness anxiety and reduce stress by keeping things in perspective. We are all here on borrowed time and will all reach the same destination, so enjoy the ride.

7. **Be Selfish** – Take time to make yourself a better person. Time to think, read, exercise, pray, and indulge in activities of interest is critical to personal growth. When we better ourselves, we are better able to help those around us.

8. **Have a Disaster Recovery Plan** – The present will soon become the past. Like a network server, we must have a plan for the unexpected. Think ahead and be prepared to take action. Be aware of the consequences that might result.

9. **Glass is Half Full** – Be a positive person. This includes expressions, words, and thoughts. Your mind is something that only you can control. A positive attitude leads to a happier life for you and those around you.

10. **Smile** – Your face is your billboard to the world. Without even saying a word, you have the power to welcome others or turn them away.

After three years of working as an accountant and living with friends, Shawn was finally moving into his own home and joining the ranks of fellow mortgage owners. As he packed his life into boxes, he scrounged through his VCR tapes, trying to decide which ones he should convert to DVDs and which ones he should pitch. He found an unmarked one and slipped it into the player.

The ESPN interview of Kelly and Eric from 2000 played on his screen. He watched it from beginning to end, once again mesmerized by Kelly's story. He wondered how she was doing. Should he keep the video or have it transferred to a DVD?

He decided to keep it in its form, ejected it from the player, and chucked it into a box. He'd have to search for her again when he had more time.

Months after he moved into his new home, many of Shawn's friends were getting married and starting families, but he hadn't found the right girl. He dated often, which helped him determine what he didn't want in a girl, but he was still no closer to finding the right woman than when he'd graduated from college.

His friends and family wanted to help and asked him what he was looking for. They asked him so often that Shawn made a list of qualities. He hoped it would help him search within himself to find what really mattered to him, what qualities were the most important.

He set up a spreadsheet to review his interests.

<u>Shawn's Personal Search for "The One"</u>

Redeeming Qualities

<u>Primary</u>
Genuinely caring and helpful to others
A doer/contributor (i.e. good teammate)

Wants to live in St. Louis area
Sociable but not overly flirtatious
Has a strong Christian faith and beliefs
Has strong inner confidence
Expresses her thoughts and emotions
Comes from a good family
Fits in well with my family
Enjoys being active
Conversational but a good listener
Is not overly materialistic
Smiles often
Believes in making one commitment
Generally conservative
Does not smoke
Does not have a sordid past
Looks good in Carolina blue
The Spark is there

Secondary
Likes to eat meat
Intellectually driven
Creative and artistic
Desires to maintain a healthy lifestyle
Likes to vacation domestically
Self-sufficient
Not attached to cats or dogs
Generally organized
Spontaneous with ideas
Not in accounting
Younger than me

He looked over his list and thought that it would at least help to serve as a compass. But was he too picky? Was there a person out there who possessed many of these characteristics? This list wasn't set in stone, nor was it something he intended to use as an evaluation criteria. If the right person came along, he'd know.

Chapter Twenty-Nine

It always seems impossible until it is done.
Nelson Mandela

March 2004

For days, I studied one of John Wooden's quotes, "Things turn out best for those who make the best out of the way things turn out."

Was I doing the best I could do given my situation? Could I do more? My speeches had broadened to include not only drinking and driving, but advocating for people with disabilities, too. But was it enough?

I remembered the disabled car salesman in Kentucky, the one who'd helped me with the van, and what he'd said about competing in the Ms. Wheelchair America pageant. I wheeled to my computer and typed the pageant name in the search bar with my mouth stick, then read the entry guidelines. Before I could enter the Ms. America pageant, I had to win at the local level. Did Indiana have a competition? I researched Google.

Yes, they did. To enter, all I had to do was complete a form. So I did.

Finding ways to feel important and things to look forward to mattered. The prospect of participating in another pageant excited me. Winning the pageant would help my public speaking platform, extend my reach, and hopefully make God proud.

When we arrived in Indianapolis for the Ms. Wheelchair Indiana competition, my immediate and extended family accompanied me. One of the third graders I student taught came with her family too. I was blessed to have one of the largest fan groups of all the contestants.

When I met the other contestants, I didn't feel any more worthy of the title. What they had achieved was no less significant than what I had accomplished. They were all heroines. Track and cheer practices were nothing compared to what these women had done and did every day.

What made me think I could be a better spokesperson than them? Maybe I wasn't.

To stay focused, I reminded myself why I was there—to build my experience and stay positive in my purpose. It wasn't to show anyone I was better than they were. I was there for the opportunity to be all that I could be and competing gave me a new challenge.

Each girl was interviewed and asked an impromptu question on stage. Mine was, "If you had to help someone through a problem what would you do?"

"Number one, I'd encourage them to pray about what to do; two, advise them to talk to friends and family who care; and three, think what was the *right* thing to do—not the easiest—but a decision you can live with."

I won the title, but the real reward was having the opportunity to meet seven other amazing women in wheelchairs who were also advocating for people with disabilities, women working as hard as me every day.

An article appeared in *The Herald* about me, people on the street congratulated me, and others wrote to me. This letter from John

Wooden stays in my scrapbook:

Dear Kelly,

A mutual friend of ours recently sent me a copy of the article concerning you that was published in The Herald. You truly are a most remarkable young lady and exemplify the words of the one who said, "God never closes one door without opening another."

We never know where our paths may lead, but must have faith in the one chosen even though we may never understand the reason why. Adversity will make us better and stronger if we accept it without bitterness. As our great president Abraham Lincoln said, "If we magnified our successes the way we magnify our disappointments, we would all be happier."

May enduring peace between all nations in this troubled world and true love for one another among all people become a reality in our time.

Sincerely,
John Wooden

On another piece of stationary, he wrote this at the top:

As I am on my way to 95 years of age.

Below it was this quote:

The years have left their imprint on my hands and on my face,
Erect no longer is my walk and slower is my pace,
But there is no fear within my heart because I'm growing old,

I only wish I had more time to better serve my Lord.
When I have gone to Him in prayer,
He has brought me inner peace,
And soon my cares and worries and other problems cease.
He has helped me in so many ways,
He has never let me down,
Why should I fear the future when soon
I could be near His crown?
Though I know down here my time is short, there is endless time up there,
And He will forgive and keep me ever in His loving care.

(David Pierini/*The Herald*)

May 2004

After school let out for the summer, it took me a few days to switch gears and move on with my empty days. I missed the students and the satisfaction I received from teaching them. To keep busy, I prepared for the Ms. Wheelchair America to get me through the emptiness. The event would take place in August.

I graduated from college on Mother's Day, a crisp spring day, a day when yellow daffodils revealed their butter color from leafy stems. Ordinarily I wouldn't have participated in the graduation ceremony, but *The Herald* was doing another article about me, and the photographer, David Pierini, who'd followed my journey since the accident, pleaded with me to attend so he could get a follow-up photo for the story.

My entire family, even Jason, accompanied me to the ceremony. After the Dean of Students handed me my diploma on stage, the audience clapped and cheered. Sarah, my student teaching assistant, received her diploma after me. As I wheeled down the steep ramp, I began to fall forward. I couldn't stop the momentum, but Sarah hurried after me and firmly placed her hand on my shoulder, stopping me from tumbling over. It was like God's hand that had guided me from the time of the accident. I breathed a long sigh of relief, thanked Sarah, and thanked God for never leaving me.

Afterward, Mom and Andy took us to dinner at a local steak house. I led the prayer before our meal and thanked God for my family, their support, and their relentless love.

Andy, through misty eyes, said. "We're proud of you, Kelly." He turned to my brothers. "Look at Kelly, you guys. She studied, worked hard, went to class, got great grades, and did it all with limitations. The pressure is on."

Ryan laughed. "Let's order, I'm hungry."

Mom smiled, but tears filled her eyes.

(David Pierini/*The Herald*)

(Me and Ms. Iowa)

Chapter Thirty

No disability or dictionary out there is capable of clearly defining who we are as a person. It's only when we step out of that labeled box, that our abilities begin to be fully recognized, giving us a better definition of who we truly are as individuals.
Robert M. Hensel

August 2004
Marriott Hotel
Richmond VA

The mission of Ms. Wheelchair America was to provide an opportunity for women in wheelchairs to advocate for the more than fifty-four million Americans living with disabilities. Unlike traditional beauty pageants, it wasn't a beauty pageant. It was a competition to select the most accomplished and articulate spokeswoman for women with disabilities. The selected representative should be able to communicate both the needs and the accomplishments of her constituency to the public, the business community, and the legislature. The winner would need to make public appearances; conduct television, radio, and print interviews to promote awareness of the needs of disabled persons; create awareness for the need to eliminate architectural and attitudinal barriers; and inform the able-bodied public of the achievements of physically disabled people across the nation.

Could I be that person? I wasn't sure.

I flew into Richmond with Mom, Andy, and Heather, my best friend from high school. We stayed at the Marriott downtown. The pageant coordinators arranged for each of the twenty-six contestants to have all the necessary amenities for their disability, which meant I had a shower chair and other supplies not typically available at hotels.

Heather accompanied me as my personal assistant, but she was also a close friend and a link to my past. We had history. Seven years prior to this event, we'd competed together in the National Cheerleading competition in Dallas. Our ten-member squad came in first in the small varsity category. Heather and I competed individually too. I took ninth; she took third place.

Had that really happened?

For a week during Ms. Wheelchair America, I was judged on personal achievements since the onset of my disability, on adjustment to my disability, on academic and vocational accomplishments, and on the personal realm of who I was. I was also evaluated on communication skills. How did I deal with the media, peers, and civic groups? Was I self-confident with motivation and initiative? How creative was I? Finally, we were all judged on our poise and appropriate attire in our presentations.

By the time of this event, I'd traveled to more than 250 schools to speak, so I'd gained confidence in many of these areas, but when I met the other contestants, my experience paled in comparison to their accomplishments.

Some had lived a lifetime with disabilities. They had arthritis and spinal muscular atrophy. Some were born with spinal meningitis, spina bifida, or arthrogryposis. One woman had suffered an injury when a tree fell on her. Several others were involved in automobile or motorcycle accidents. Although we all came from different parts of the US and had different reasons for being in a chair, we all had wheelchairs in common.

Many of the women were married and were counselors, graphic designers, stay-at-home moms, public relations managers, journalists, and teachers. I was amazed at what they'd done with their lives.

Each had a different motto. Some of my favorites were, "Turn obstacles into opportunities," "Life is 10 percent what happens to you and 90 percent how you react to it," and "Great things happen when inspiration silences excuses."

My friends helped me decide on my motto: "It's okay to be different." As a contestant, I was required to inform the community of my plans to compete. People wanted to support me. To help fund my entry, we designed pink T-shirts with a stick figure girl in a wheelchair on the front and the words, "It's okay to be different," typed beneath the girl. We sold 250 shirts.

When Ms. Wheelchair Texas, Angela Wrigglesworth, introduced herself as a teacher, I was instantly drawn to her. She'd been a teacher for four years, but had limited abilities like me. Her motto was a quote from John Wooden, "Things turn out best for those who make the best of the way things turn out."

The quote was similar to the one Mr. Wooden had sent me. After the introduction, I went to Angela and introduced myself. She asked me what I did for a living. I explained that I'd recently graduated with an elementary education degree, but was a public speaker.

"Don't rule out teaching, Kelly. Think hard about it. There's nothing you can't do. If that's where your heart is, don't ignore it."

I knew she was right, but hearing her say the words had a stronger effect and made me stop and listen. If she could teach, why couldn't I? But questions loomed in my mind. Would I disappoint God if I stopped speaking to pursue teaching? Wasn't I doing what He wanted me to do? I didn't know the answer, but maybe I needed to consider teaching again.

Each day we attended workshops on personal enhancement, self-defense, and disability laws. It was an opportunity to see into the lives of the other women and share mine.

One workshop was on relationships. The other girls were open about their experiences with guys. I was stunned at how many went on dates. The speaker warned us about the dangers in dating and getting ourselves into frightening situations. A guy could take advantage of us and there would be nothing we could do.

One girl said her date became angry when she wouldn't sleep with him and he abandoned her in a bed, put her chair outside, and took off. She didn't have a phone or a way to get to her chair. I gasped and vowed I'd never let myself be that vulnerable.

Many of the women had husbands and shared how they'd met. It gave me hope that there were great guys out there, ones with heart. Maybe someday I would meet Mr. Right. At RIC, I'd been told that more women have heart than men, and the odds were against me. But if these women could find someone to love them, I could too.

One married contestant said, "I'm sick of people saying how lucky I am to have my husband. I want to say that he's lucky to have me. After all, I clean up his crap, prepare his meals, and put up with his snoring."

We laughed, but she was serious.

I remembered the van salesman saying that his wife was lucky to have him too. No matter if the disabled were men or women, they both wanted to feel appreciated.

Ms. Virginia turned to me and said, "Don't settle, Kelly. Don't ever settle. We are beautiful and smart. Don't fall for just anyone."

One night after dinner, a DJ arrived to entertain us with music. Surely he didn't expect us to dance. But when the music started, the women wheeled out onto the dance floor and twirled their chairs, bobbed their heads, and swayed the limbs that could move. I was the only one who slunk back along the wall.

When it was my time to interview with the judges my first question was, "What would you like to see changed with the ADA law?"

My heart sank. I had no idea how to answer the question. I hadn't researched the ADA laws to speak intelligently. I stumbled through my answer. Never had I felt so unprepared for an interview.

"When has your integrity been questioned?"

Once again I tripped over my words, my answer sounding weak. I made something up and bombed the interview. I'd have to nail the speech or I'd never make the top five.

On the big day, my grandparents, aunts, uncles, cousins, and brothers attended the event miles from their homes. The US Navy escorted us up the ramp and held the microphone for those contestants who couldn't. When it was my turn, I wheeled in front of the microphone, looked out at my audience and the judges, and gave the speech I'd prepared. The judges wanted to hear about my platform, and observe my presentation delivery. I had to prove that I had the ability to represent disabled people throughout the country.

My speech:

"Do you sleep in your wheelchair? Where do you live? In a nursing home?"

After hearing these questions from children, I realized that our youth needed to be educated about the misconceptions of people in wheelchairs.

Currently, there are forty-nine million Americans who have a disability. That means that there are over 250 million Americans who aren't sure how to approach us or how to relate to us. This leads to discrimination that severely limits our participation and progress in society. In other words, these stereotypes further disable us.

Stereotypes are formed at a young age. By educating children while they are young and receptive, we have the opportunity to eliminate those stereotypes before they are created.

In order to educate them, I will go to schools to involve students in group discussions, activities, and reading children's literature—which will enlighten them about disabilities. In our group discussions, I will emphasize that people come in all different shapes, sizes, and colors, and that no one wants to be judged solely by their outward appearance.

Another powerful way for children to gain a deeper understanding is to have them temporarily experience the sensation of living with a disability. I will give them that firsthand experience through activities such as a wheelchair obstacle course and a sign language spelling bee. These activities will really open their eyes...giving them a way to truly relate to people with disabilities.

To reinforce the group discussion and activities, I will acquaint them with books that deal directly with disabilities—stories written specifically for kids, like The Berenstain Bears and the Wheelchair Commando. Stories like this act as an excellent vehicle for communicating with children, enabling them to look past disabilities, and to see that it's okay to be different, and to have people who are different in your life.

The fact is...children are our future. By working with them now, I hope to create a society where people with disabilities are treated as equals. My goal is to make this a better world, one child at a time."

The audience clapped and cheered, and I wheeled away feeling that I delivered a decent speech. But when the emcee was about to announce the top five contestants, I cringed and prayed I wouldn't be chosen. In the final round, each contestant would have to answer an impromptu question in front of the live audience, and after listening to all the other speeches, I wasn't prepared in the same way the other contestants were. My earlier interview was evidence of that.

Juliette Rizzo, Ms. Wheelchair Maryland, won the pageant. She was the Director of Communication & Media for the office of Special Education and Rehabilitative Services, in the US Department of

Education. Her knowledge of disability law was broad and her public speaking voice rocked. She was someone to look up to.

They played "We Are the Champions," by the rock band, Queen, as they crowned her and draped the banner across her body. She said, "The crown is not a destination; it's an adventure that's just about to begin. I thank you for letting me find my courage and my vision. I'm ready to change the world."

I left the conference feeling lucky that I had more abilities than some contestants and thankful for what I had. It was okay that I didn't win or make the top five because I knew the others were better advocates and knew more about disability laws. I'd only been in a chair for five years. Many had been there longer.

I rolled away empowered by the other women, and by what they'd taught me—I didn't have to let the wheelchair define me or control what I did with my life. I could make the chair a big deal if I wanted to, but it didn't have to be me. The others were far more comfortable with who they were. I needed to feel the same. If I couldn't embrace myself, how would I attract someone to love me?

You have to love yourself, Kelly, before anyone else will love you.

Chapter Thirty-One

It doesn't matter where you go. He's always there beside you.
Kelly Craig

I met Blayr Kramer at my brother Tyler's football game. Blayr's husband, Ryan, was Tyler's coach. Blayr and I were close in age and became instant friends. She asked me to go to a camp in New York for a week as a leader for Young Life, an organization for adolescents that shares the Good News of Jesus and His love for them. We'd accompany sixty students from Jasper High School.

I didn't want to go. How would I go to the bathroom, and how could I go a whole week without a shower? Plus, the trip was Blayr's vacation. Her husband, Ryan, was going too, but accompanying the boys. I didn't want her to spend her spare time taking care of me instead of with Ryan.

"Camp with sixty kids isn't my idea of a vacation, Kelly." She laughed. "I'll do your bathroom and braid your hair if it looks dirty. I don't mind helping. Really. Don't worry."

But I did worry. Staying home with my family and having my own nurse was my security blanket. I couldn't tuck that in my suitcase, and I didn't want to leave it behind.

"There'll be horseback riding, zip-lining, tug-o-wars, and mountain climbing," Blayr said.

All those things I can't do. I'll hate sitting on the sidelines.

"Pray about it and see what happens," Blayr said.

I prayed and the next Sunday at Mass our priest said, "Pick up your cross and bear it. Go forward with your life." God was talking to me, telling me that He was counting on me to go with the kids and lead them. This would be a great chance to influence the lives of teens by helping them to see that their lives had great worth and purpose.

Kids approached me at church. "We heard you might be going with us to camp. We can't wait."

I decided to go.

I tried to act nonchalant as Blayr transferred me from my chair onto the bottom bunk of our cabin. I instructed her on how to lift me—where to plant her feet, how to cradle my head, and where to put my hands so they wouldn't dangle behind me. Blayr and I had become great friends, but she hadn't put me to bed often.

Anxiety slinked in and took root. I typically didn't worry or freak out about a new adventure. Until now.

These teens were counting on me to lead them, but my insides quivered. I couldn't relax. They stared at me like I was different. I was used to the gawking but not in the privacy of my bedroom where I was never judged, where I could let myself go.

Once everyone said goodnight and settled into their bunks, the night air hovered like a heavy cloud. The slow and shallow breaths of the teens indicated they were already sleeping. Everyone slept but me. My mind raced. Visions played behind my closed lids. Visions of random people and strange places.

I don't want to be here. This was a mistake, a bad idea. I need to go home. I couldn't ask Blayr to take me home, but I wanted to. We all came together on the bus, and we needed to return as one group. I couldn't ask everyone to abandon the trip. That would be selfish.

What am I going to do? I inhaled a series of short breaths to gain control, but it didn't work. The blanket seared my skin. Someone needed to turn me.

Minutes, then hours, passed. I closed my eyes and prayed for sleep. *Get a grip, Kelly.*

But I couldn't calm down. I was trapped in my body, stuck in a strange place without the ability to do anything about it. Tears dripped down my cheeks and onto my pillow. I prayed.

Dear God, please help me get through this night.

Hours later, the morning light spilled into the cabin, chasing away my chance to feel sleep's warm embrace. With dawn's hello came a numbness that settled in from exhaustion. There was nothing I could do but keep going and trust God to get me through the rest of the trip.

During that week, the music empowered me the most, helping me to forget my exhaustion and breathe through my anxiety. The speakers' messages infiltrated my faith. "It's all about having a relationship with God," one said. Others spoke about how often we have a need for something more in life, and how materialistic things don't fill that need. They introduced Christ as a man who wants to know you, to fill that void in your life. He's the one who created you and made you perfect. We needed to let Him into our lives, to talk to him, establish a relationship with him. The speakers talked about how sin entered the world and how Christ had died for our sins so we could have a happily ever after. God sacrificed for me. I shouldn't complain about my life. I wanted to fill my life with Him.

I finally slept the third night. By that time, I'd relaxed enough to participate in the discussions with the eight girls in my cabin. Each evening we discussed the motivational speaker's message. My job was to lead the discussion after each one. We returned to our cabin and broke into groups.

"What did you get out of the speaker's message tonight?" I asked.

One by one, they shared their opinions and asked questions, but often their questions had nothing to do with the speakers.

One teen asked, "Why do bad things happen to good people?"

"Who determines who is good?" I said. "We are all sinners. A sin is a sin. Romans 8:28 says that God causes all things to work together for good. My accident might not be a blessing, but it brings about blessings. God never promised that bad things wouldn't happen to us, but He did say He would never leave or forsake us. Look up 1 Corinthians 10:13 and He will tell you Himself."

"How do you know that Jesus exists?" another teen asked.

I wasn't a priest, and didn't want to act like I had all the answers or get too preachy, but I wanted them to trust me, trust that they could ask me anything, and I wouldn't judge them. I answered their questions the way I felt led, the way I'd pushed past my own doubts. "Ask Him. Be real with Him and tell Him you're struggling with this concept. Keep seeking answers with a loving heart, and He will respond in ways you could never imagine."

"How can being a Christian fit into my life? I'm young and want to have fun."

"You can have both God and fun. He gave you twenty-four hours in a day. Spend a little time in those hours to talk to him. What can you give back to him?" I asked.

"Where do I start?"

"You're here, and that's a start. No one made you come. God doesn't expect you to completely change overnight. He rejoices in the baby steps that you take to become closer to him. God wants to know you."

One teen said, "If I make God a priority I won't be cool. My friends will call me a freak."

I remembered thinking the same thing when I was a sixteen-year-old. How should I answer this and say the right thing without a lecture? "Talk to Him about your feelings. If you do, everything will fall into place. In the end, who are we ultimately trying to impress? If you read 1 Timothy 4:12 you'll find encouragement."

Campers wrote the verses down in their notebooks.

"What does having a relationship with Jesus look like?"

"A relationship with Him is a gift that leads to eternal happiness. Imagine when someone gives you a gift, and how you can't wait to open it. Open that gift. Talk to Him one word at a time."

I did my best to answer the rest of their questions by using my life as an example. Had it worked? Had I ignited change? Maybe. But at least I'd planted a seed with those who were struggling with their walk with Christ. Maybe that seed would blossom. Maybe it would never bud. Either way, the seed was planted, and it was up to the students to continue to nourish it.

When the girls from the other cabin rushed down the hill to the community center to listen to the bands play or the speaker speak, the girls from my cabin stayed back with me, spreading towels on the grass and observing from the top of the hill near our cabin. I couldn't navigate the steps that led to the bandstand, and they didn't want to leave me behind. I found this endearing.

One day during free time, we had the opportunity to tube behind boats with the campers. The girls in our cabin begged me to try it. Why not? Didn't I want them to treat me the same?

"I'll go with you," one girl said.

"I will too," another girl said.

The tube was a three-seater, but they all wanted to go. To be fair, Blayr broke matchsticks into different lengths and had each girl draw one. The two who had the longest sticks took their turn first.

I was nervous and excited at the same time, like the first time I rode the rollercoaster at Holiday World. Two girls draped me in a life vest and placed a red helmet on my head, which was camp policy, and carried me into the water to the tube. They set me in the middle slot until I was snug. One girl sat on each side of me in her own slot.

"If we flip over who will dive in after me? I can't move to swim so promise me you'll bring my head to the surface," I said.

The girls cried out in unison, "I will!"

The driver of the boat nodded. "I won't go fast enough for you to flip, but if that happens we'll dive in after you."

"Don't baby me," I said to the driver. "Go your usual speed."

He nodded and took off.

I squinted in the sun and bounced and careened across the sparkling water. Waves splashed warm water across my arms, misted my cheeks, and dampened my long braided hair. I hadn't felt this free since before the accident, ready to take on the world and leave my imprint in the lives of the teens surrounding me.

I tubed three times so other girls could take a turn next to me. Other camp members gathered around at the water's edge to watch. I doubted they ever saw a girl like me tubing before.

The next day was the tug-o-war, and, of course, the girls wanted me to participate in this event too.

"You can be at the end of our line, Kelly," one girl said. "We'll tie the rope to your chair. How much does it weight?"

I laughed. "Three hundred pounds."

"Wow, our team will be the strongest," another girl said. She tied the end of the rope to the back of my chair. We lined up—their team against ours—with me and my chair at the end of our line, facing out.

On *go*, I was supposed to roll forward.

"On your mark, get set, go!"

Each team tugged. I threw my chair into forward drive, but within seconds, it jarred backwards and toppled over. My head and the handles of the chair hit the ground and dragged in the sand. There wasn't anything I could do but lie there and laugh.

At first, no one seemed to notice me in the dirt.

The other team dragged our team until someone on the sidelines shouted. "Stop! Wheelchair down!"

Everyone stopped pulling and turned to me. One girl covered her gaping mouth with her hand. Quickly the girls huddled around me and righted me and my chair.

"Are you okay?" they asked.

I nodded and laughed.

When they saw me laughing and realized I wasn't hurt, they laughed, too.

On the way home, the trip leader asked me, "Well, what did you think of your experience?"

"I loved it." And I meant it. It was as if the speakers had spoken only to me. Even though I had gone to be there for the girls, the experience had improved my attitude and deepened my faith. It wouldn't have happened if I hadn't wheeled out of my comfort zone.

"Will you go with us again?" the leader asked.

"I'd love to," I said without hesitation.

The song, "The Great I Am," by Phillips, Craig & Dean, became my favorite song. Whenever I hear it, I remember my first of many Young Life trips, and how I tubed and played tug-o-war with teens in New York.

Thank you, God, for taking me out of my cushy comfort zone to make a greater impact in my life, to show others how great you are, and to deepen my faith in you.

Chapter Thirty-Two

For I know the plans I have for you," declares the LORD, "plans to prosper you and not to harm you, plans to give you hope and a future.
Jeremiah 29:11 NIV

After the camping trip and the pageant, I focused on public speaking for a year instead of teaching. I traveled to Purdue, ISU, Terre Haute, IU, and the University of Evansville speaking from the platform against drinking and driving. But I missed the kids in the classroom, and when I heard a rumor that there might be a fifth-grade teacher opening at Precious Blood School, I called the principal, Chad Schneiders. Making the call was not easy for me, but obtaining a job at Precious Blood was high on my list. I practiced what I'd say, took the leap, and dialed his number.

"Could I schedule a time to meet with you?" I asked him. He hadn't been the principal when I student taught at the school, and didn't know me, but his wife was a senior in high school when I was a freshman and we ran track together.

"Absolutely," he said with no hesitation. "I'd appreciate the opportunity to meet you."

He used to teach fifth grade in the Jasper public school system before he took the principal position. I'd heard about the many positive things he was doing at the school, and looked forward to meeting him.

When I arrived, he greeted me with a smile and took me to his office. He was only twenty-nine, not much older than I was. He wore a tie and a collared shirt and carried a little notebook and pen in his shirt pocket.

He closed his office door and we talked about the students at Precious Blood and which classroom I'd student taught the previous year.

Within minutes, I relaxed, remembering my experience and how I enjoyed working at the school. "I wanted to talk to you about things that are unique to me that my resume can't answer, and give you an opportunity to ask me questions."

"You don't need to explain what you can and can't do in the classroom because of your disability. I'm confident that you're capable," he said.

"This is the only school I'm interested in teaching at. If you have an opening next year will you consider me?"

"I promise you'll have an equal opportunity to interview for a job if it becomes available."

Relief washed over me as I left his office. Not because my chances were better than another candidates, but because I took the initiative to meet with him—something that I had to push myself to do—and it had gone well. I was proud of myself and confident that if an opening surfaced I'd get the chance to interview.

In April, the rumors came to fruition. There was a fifth-grade opening. I submitted my resume, the recommendation letter from Mrs. Wolf—the teacher I student taught with the previous year, and a letter from a USI professor to Mr. Schneiders.

A week later, he called. "We'd like you to interview for the fifth grade teaching position."

"Really?" Excitement bubbled from the tip of my toes to the top of my head. I began preparing for the interview immediately. For days, my friends and family quizzed me on possible questions Mr. Schneiders might ask. I became obsessed with possible scenarios, so by the time the day came to interview I was ready. I told myself to relax, that one of my gifts was the ability to think on my feet, (which sounded funny since I couldn't stand), but I was still nervous.

Two people were in the room for the interview—Mr. Schneiders and another teacher who'd worked in a different school system for ten years but transferred to Precious Blood the year before.

"Tell us a little about yourself," she said.

I told them about the accident, where I went to school, and how I had a public speaking platform, but that I missed the kids. "When people ask me how I teach, I say, "With magic." I understand kids. I know the way they think and how to relate to them. I've taught kids to swim and cheer, but more importantly, I want to be with them, to make a difference in their lives."

Mr. Schneiders asked, "If I went into your classroom what would it look like?"

"I've toured many different schools while I traveled, and what I loved the most were *themed* classrooms. My room would look like a camping site with the words to my favorite Bible verses spelled out with twigs. I'd have a reading corner with a couple of camping chairs. The desks would be arranged in a way that I could weave in and out. My classroom would be a place conducive for learning, but for having fun too."

"Why teach at a Catholic school versus a public school?" the teacher asked.

"After going through what I've been through, the best thing about teaching at a Catholic school is having the privilege to teach about faith. Students will ultimately forget what the capital of Vermont is or how to write an inverted sentence, but their faith is a life vest for them to hold on to forever. When they suffer from life's struggles, faith will be what holds them up. To work at a school that encourages faith is a blessing."

Mr. Schneiders smiled. "What can you offer that other teachers can't?"

"Any teacher can teach, but isn't teaching more than what's in the books? My disability in this situation is not a disadvantage but an advantage. It'll teach students compassion, empathy, forgiveness, and overcoming adversity. It'll also teach them the effects of bad decisions, and the importance of never giving up."

"What is one unique thing that you would introduce into your curriculum?" the other teacher asked.

"I'd introduce literature circles resembling a book club for kids. After each reading session, students would have a 'job' assigned to them. Students would be vocal hunters, summarizers, illustrators, predictors, discussion directors, and so on. These jobs cover several language arts standards. This would be a fun way to get kids to enjoy reading, which is something I always struggled with when I was a child."

The teacher exchanged glances with Mr. Schneiders.

"Is there anything else you want to add?" he asked.

"I hope and pray that my name is placed on your heart for this position." I wheeled away from the interview feeling confident that I'd answered each question in a prepared fashion. That was the best I could do. Now, I'd have to wait.

Jenna applied for the same job, but she was also applying to other schools. If I were hired, she wouldn't be upset because she had other options. Precious Blood was the only school for me—it was close to my home and my heart.

A week later, Mr. Schneiders called. "This is one of those phone calls I enjoy making. We would love for you to take the fifth grade teaching position."

I could almost see him smiling.

"Oh, my gosh. Jesus loves me." I was giddy like a teenager, but then my mind flipped into an organizing mode. "What do I do now? Can I come and get the keys to my room?" I was designing the room in my mind already.

"You'll need to fill out forms first. The secretary will call you in the next few weeks to come in. We'll get you a key then."

With goose bumps crawling along my arms, I called Mom. "I got the job."

"You did? I'm so proud of you, Kelly. This is all you. You did this all by yourself."

Yes, I had.

News spread all around Jasper that day. Friends and family rejoiced for me. This was a dream come true, something I'd worked hard at, something I'd accomplished all on my own.

I never looked back.

Jenna was happy for me. She landed a job teaching at St. Mary's in Ireland, a small neighboring town, where she taught preschool for two years.

People sent me encouraging letters.

> Dear Kelly –
> I'm a friend of one of your friends. I've prayed for you
> for almost six years. I saw this quote and thought of you.
> Good luck with teaching. They are lucky to have you.
> > "Everyone has disabilities. It's what we do with
> > our abilities that matter."

The Message, a paper published by the Evansville diocese and distributed to all the parishioners within the diocese, interviewed me for an article. Before school started, Mary Ann Hughes published the article and this announcement:

> When Kelly Craig wheels herself into her classroom at
> Precious Blood School this year, she will bring incredible
> lessons of forgiveness and generosity with her, lessons
> probably unparalleled in her young students' lives.
>
> She's the new fifth grade teacher at the Jasper Catholic
> school, and at the tender age of twenty-five, she knows a
> lot about forgiveness.

The Herald interviewed me for another article:

> Kelly's optimistic about beginning her teaching career,
> noting, "The key with me will be to stay well-organized."
>
> She said she's eager to be in a Catholic school setting. "I
> love the parent involvement. I love that you can relate
> everything back to your faith, and that you can pray in
> your classroom."
>
> She believes that faith is the only path to overcoming
> adversity. "Without faith, the paralysis would have beaten

---

me. I'm a living example of how to overcome adversity.

"Six years ago, I was told, 'You can't do this, you can't do that.' Each time, I rose to the occasion. Anything is possible if you never give up. Although I'm in a wheelchair, my drive and will have not subsided."

Kelly has been inspired by Joni Eareckson Tada, a well-known Christian writer and radio personality also confined to a wheelchair, who once said, "I'd rather be in this chair knowing God, than on my feet without him. There are more important things in life than walking."

Kelly knows that "without the accident, my faith would not be evident in my life." She's learned that through negative experiences, "There are positive outcomes." Sometimes, that means seeing what's really important in life.

(David Pierini/*The Herald*)

Chapter Thirty-Three

In every job that must be done, there is an element of fun.
Mary Poppins

The first day of school, I sat in the doorway observing the classroom, my room, the one my Young Life teens helped me decorate. We spent all summer traveling to and from Walmart searching for camping theme supplies. The room smelled of glue and crayons. A paper beetle fluttered on the window blind.

Everything was in place—bees, bugs, beetles, and trees. The words *kindness, goodness, patience, peace,* and *joy,* spelled out with twigs and glued on green construction paper, were taped to the blinds. Bibles were lined on a bookshelf. My desk sat to the side with my raised computer keyboard in the center. Outside the window was a view of the church entrance and a large oak tree.

Eighteen student desks were in a circle, arranged so I could weave in and out with easy access to each student.

At the top of the chalkboard was this Scripture, "I can do all things through Christ who strengthens me (Philippians 4:13 NLT)." And on the classroom door was the quote, "Be the reflection of Christ," surrounded by small, scattered mirrors.

Across the room, a bulletin board designed to showcase student work had this quote at the top, "To the world you are one person, but to one person—Jesus Christ—you are the world."

Blayr, who'd volunteered to help me in the classroom, entered with her hand on her hips, observing. "It looks amazing."

"Thanks. The teens really helped," I said. They'd been my hands during the whole project.

"They said they had fun. You really have a creative eye."

"I want my students to have a great year."

Blayr placed her hand on my shoulder. "They will. They're lucky to have you."

The students arrived with backpacks stuffed with pencils, markers, gym shoes, and other supplies. In five minutes, the room went from silence to mayhem.

"Set your backpacks and supplies against the wall," I instructed. "We're going to do an activity before we get started."

After they put their backpacks down, they turned to me, and I invited them to sit on the floor in front of me. "The janitor informed me that we're running out of toilet paper and we only have this roll for the day." I nodded to a roll of toilet paper in my lap. "Take as many sheets as you think you'll need today."

Their eyes widened. Hesitatingly, one-by-one they lined up and tore off sheets of paper.

"Count your squares," I said.

They counted their sheets, their brows wrinkled with puzzlement.

"If you have three sheets you need to tell the class three things about yourself. If you have five, you'll need to tell us five things."

Their jaws dropped. A girl giggled.

"You mean, we won't really use this… for… the bathroom?" a boy asked.

"No," I said. "I made that up to get your attention."

They laughed and I did too.

After they shared information about themselves, I talked about the golden rule. "If everybody follows the golden rule then all the other rules will be obsolete."

I spoke about my disability and what I could and could not do. I demonstrated what the chair controls did, let them gape at the scar on my neck, and told them the plates beneath the scar were what kept my head up. I gave them permission to ask me anything they wanted to ask me.

One advantage to being in the chair was that fifth graders were forced to address me at eye level. Stretching the truth was a lot more difficult for them to do when I stared openly at them, mere inches from their face.

"There will be times when I need someone to write on the board and pass out papers. Could you help me with those tasks?"

Students raised their hands and shook them high in the air. "I will, I will."

They competed to be my helper, to retrieve a dropped item, to pass out papers, to push the elevator button, to bring me a hot lunch from the cafeteria. Kids wanted to help; they fought for the opportunity. They all wanted a turn to go to the board.

Throughout the year, Principal Schneiders conducted my performance reviews, but I never knew when he'd show up in my classroom. One day he came during science class. The lesson was about the anatomy of a cell. Students gathered around me on the floor in a circle with their books open.

One student passed out oatmeal cream cookies to everyone. Another student passed out a red Hot Tamale candy, a green jellybean, a caramel, and sprinkles.

"Don't eat anything," I said.

Once they each had their ingredients, I began the lesson.

Mr. Schneiders sat in the corner observing.

"Your cookie represents a cell membrane," I began. "When the cell divides it breaks apart in two separate pieces. Go ahead and split yours in half."

The students broke their cookies. "The mitochondria are the powerhouses of the cell. They convert nutrients to energy. Let's make those the red Hot Tamale. Go ahead and add that to your cookie." I paused. "The green jelly bean will be the vacuoles. They hold the food, water, and the waste. The caramel is the nucleus, which provides the "brains" for the whole operation. And finally, the icing is the cytoplasm, the fluid that fills the cell."

They followed along in their books and studied the diagrams. While the students added the ingredients to their cookies, I explained what each one did and how it was instrumental in the production of cells.

"And now for the best part," I said. "You may return to your seats and eat your cell and discuss which part tastes the best."

The students laughed, picked up their books and the cell ingredients, and returned to their seats. One student gave her cookie to Mr. Schnieders.

When we started a unit on the four types of writing—persuasive, descriptive, narrative, and informative, I asked the students to write a descriptive paragraph about the first day of school. One of my students wrote this on the erase board:

Miss Craig—
The students silently awaited her arrival. She rolled into the room full of students whose spiritually Christlike lives were about to change. When she rolled through our doorway, there was an unmistakable difference about her. But, we didn't glance at the wheelchair. Instead, we glanced at a young woman who definitely had Christ rolling alongside her. We couldn't wait to begin our journey with Christ.

One warm day in the fall, I took our science class outside and talked about insects and the food chain. "How many of you think insects are a part of the food chain?"

Most all of the students raised their hands.

"Birds eat insects. Some animals eat insects. Raise your hand if you've eaten an insect."

"Yuck." several students cried out. No one raised a hand.

"None of you have ever eaten a chocolate-covered cricket?"

Students laughed and most of them shouted, "Ew!"

"Raise your hand if you want to try one."

Almost every student raised a hand and I only had five crickets, so I had them draw sticks. The four students with the longest stick got to eat one. "Let's ask Principal Schneiders to eat one, too," one student said. The other kids cheered along.

On our way back into the school, we passed the front desk and the principal's office. He waved and the students motioned for him to come out into the lobby area. When he approached I said, "Would you like to try some of our candy?"

"Sure," he said.

Students giggled, leaning in as if anticipating his reaction. We showed him the candy and explained what it was.

"A cricket?" he said. "You want me to eat a cricket?"

Students cheered. "Do it."

"Four other students are ready to eat theirs when you do," I said and winked.

He studied the students with a smile. "I can't let you eat alone then, can I?"

"No!" they shouted in unison.

He smiled, reached into the box, and pinched a chocolate between his fingers. "You ready?"

"One. Two. Three!" the kids counted.

The four students and Mr. Schneiders glanced at each other and simultaneously popped the whole crickets into their mouths, chewed, and swallowed.

Students shouted and clapped.

Mr. Schneiders acted as if he ate insects every day. "You kids have a teacher who really knows how to make education fun."

They turned to me and clapped, but he was definitely the hero that day.

I enjoyed teaching some subjects more than others, but teaching moments in all the subjects caused me to laugh and cry.

For one assignment, one of my students drew a picture of me *standing* next to her, my wheelchair nowhere in sight. The vision caught an emotion I hadn't realized was close to the surface, it snagged a tear from deep down, and I had to swallow the lump before I could comment on how much I loved her drawing. It was the first of many pictures drawn similarly.

Another subject I was required to teach in fifth grade was sex education. It was one of my favorites to teach because society blasts children with an idea of what sex is about, but they're not sure what to believe. They like hearing the truth from a source other than their parents. We encouraged parents to talk to their kids first, but in fifth grade it was my job educate them further.

This is how I started: "Before I teach you about puberty and how babies are made, we need to get all the giggles out because you're going to say certain words that might make you feel funny. I want to make you feel comfortable about saying these words and asking questions. But first, we'll act immature; it'll be your chance to get out all the giddiness. After that, your maturity hats go back on, and we'll begin our lesson. Are you ready?"

They nodded.

"You will hear me say sex, penis, and vagina."

Kids snickered.

"I will keep saying those words, and I want you laugh."

They were laughing hard already.

"Here it goes: Sex, penis, vagina. Sex, penis, vagina." I repeated this over and over. Students' faces turned red. Some covered their faces with their hands. Others laughed.

"Now it's your turn to say them. One. Two. Three. Go."

No one said anything. They gave each other a sideways glance and giggled, but they were waiting to see who would go first.

"Go ahead," I prodded.

Several kids called out in unison: "Sex, penis, vagina, sex, penis, vagina." Some blurted the words, while others whispered them.

After five minutes, they were all uninhibited and the volume in the room had turned up a notch.

"Okay," I said, "we're done. No more immaturity. Now I'm going to teach this lesson, and I don't want any more giggling."

And the lesson began. No one laughed. No one snickered.

When I was done, I opened the discussion for questions. Some of the questions I received were, "Should we put in a tampon now and wait for it to start?" "Does pubic hair hurt when it grows in?" "Should we be scared of this change?" "Does it happen overnight?"

One student approached my desk after the lesson, lowering his voice. "I know about this… stuff. Can I talk to you about it outside?"

"Okay," I said. I gave the class an assignment and wheeled out into the hallway with the boy.

"Don't tell anyone," he said, "because my parents don't know, but I watched James Bond movies. I saw them doing that kissing stuff. Am I in trouble?"

"No." I wanted my students to feel comfortable talking to me. I'd opened the doors of communication, and already one boy walked in. He thought he'd witnessed a sex act, even though he hadn't. But at least he was able to talk to me about his feelings.

He placed his hand on his abdomen. "My stomach hurts. Can I go to the office?"

I nodded for him to go. The office nurse gave him a drink, let him lie down, and a half an hour later he returned to class without a problem.

The last lesson each day, and another favorite subject, was religion. One student helped set up the projector with the song lyrics to "How Great is Our God," by Chris Tomlin. Another student put a CD in my player and together we sang.

While the students belted out the words with animation and without reserve, they stood next to one another, their arms locked around each other, and swayed. I reflected on my life and all the power and strength it took me to get to that moment, to where I was sitting, among a classroom of children in a community that believed in me, in a country that allowed me to be all that I could be, and with a God who made it all possible.

I joined them in singing, feeling the words and agreeing with their meaning. I was exactly where I was supposed to be. *Our God is great.*

Chapter Thirty-Four

Some things are destined to be, but it takes a while to get there.
J. R. Ward, *Lover Mine*

May 2006

Shawn and his best friend and cousin, Andrew, met up with college buddies for the Kentucky Derby in Louisville, Kentucky. It was their first time to see Churchill Downs and experience the "greatest two minutes in sports." After a day of thoroughbred races, mint juleps, slot machines, and hanging with friends, they headed back to St. Louis to sleep in their own beds before work on Monday. Even though it was two o'clock in the morning, they knew they could be home in less than five hours.

The previous night they'd slept on the floor for a meager three hours before the bright lights and the chanting, "It's Derby Day," filled the apartment, and they didn't want to endure another sleepless night. Maybe Shawn was getting too old to party.

On the way, while on the Interstate, Shawn saw a sign for Jasper, Indiana, which jarred his memories of Kelly. He was surprised at how close Jasper was to the same expressway that led to St. Louis.

"Hey, isn't Jasper the city where that girl lives?" Andrew asked.

"Yes, Kelly. Good memory."

"You never did find her, did you?" Andrew asked.

"No. I tried though. Maybe I'll take a ride through that city one day." As he continued down the road, he promised to look her up again and maybe visit Jasper, but not now. He was too tired and too focused on getting home.

(Blayr and Me)

Chapter Thirty-Five

May your days be many and your troubles be few.
May all God's blessings descend upon you.
May peace be within you may your heart be strong.
May you find what you're seeking wherever you roam.
Irish Blessings

March 2007

Three teens from my Young Life group, Blayr, and I watched a video in Blayr's living room. It was our weekly Bible study meeting. The movie showed a child kicking and screaming because his father wouldn't buy him a new Transformer toy.

"It won't make you happy," the child's father said. "In one week it'll be forgotten in the corner on the floor."

The child cried. "But you said you loved me."

The analogy was that our Father knows the big picture in our life. He knows what's going to happen and what is best for us, and sometimes we can't see the reasons for why things happen (Matthew 7:9-11).

As Blayr led the discussion, I thought of my situation. I wanted to walk more than anything else.

"You might think that this one thing can make you the happiest," Blayr said, "but God may have something else in store for you, and it might be something different, something you never thought of."

What could I possibly want more than to walk again?

The teens talked about what "toy" they were waiting for, and then it was my turn.

"I want to meet someone to share my life with, but no one is going to find me in this condition." Tears filled my eyes. God loved me like the little boy in the movie, but it was tough not to feel the same way as the child. "I've been in three weddings in the last four months." I paused to suck in a breath. "What about me? When will it be my turn? If I could walk, I could find a boyfriend, a man whom I could marry, which would lead to having a family. All my life I've wanted children. If I can't walk, I'll never find a man or have a family." Talking about my unspoken feelings unleashed buried emotions and tears fell and dampened my shirt.

Blayr reached over and touched my arm.

"I mean, really, who would…put up…with a life with me?"

"Some lucky guy, that's who," Blayr said.

I didn't believe her. No one would love me the way I was, but I appreciated her compliment.

That night when Andy transferred me to bed, I prayed harder than I ever had before. "God, I know you love me, and I'm supposed to wait for you to decide what is best for me, but it's been seven years since the accident. Will you at least give me a sign that you hear my prayers?"

A Week Prior to My Prayer.

In St. Louis, Missouri, the Thursday before Easter Sunday, Shawn received a call from his manager.

"I need you to go to Indianapolis next week to meet with a client."

Indiana? That's where Kelly lives. I wonder how far Jasper is from Indianapolis.

"I'll e-mail you the client contact and engagement information. Contact travel to set up the arrangements."

"Okay."

When Shawn got home that night he Googled Jasper, Indiana, and studied a map. Jasper was about a three-hour trip from Indy. *Maybe I'll stop there on my way back and see if I can find her. Someone from Jasper has to know where she lives.*

He mentioned his idea to Shannon, his sister, who'd heard Shawn talk about Kelly.

"You don't even know for sure if she lives there."

"I know it sounds crazy, but it's not that far out of my way. I can't get this girl out of my mind. Things happen in my life, and I think about her. I want to get her address, and I don't know any other way to get it besides going there. All I want is to deliver the letter."

Shawn left St. Louis on April 9, 2007 for Greenwood, Indiana, where the audit was to take place. After his two-day assignment, he made the three-hour detour to Jasper. The red skies of dusk towered over the rolling hills on 231 South. He combed the area for a bluff. One of the articles on the Internet said Kelly lived in a house overlooking the city, but he didn't see any houses on a bluff.

He pulled his rented Camry into a Walgreens parking lot, went in, and asked the store clerk if she knew Kelly Craig. "She was the girl who was hit by a drunk driver and broke her neck."

The clerk gave him a blank stare and handed him a phone book. "Why don't you try to find her in here? If you need to copy a page you can take the book to Staples across the street."

Shawn took the book. "Thank you." He stepped away from the checkout counter and opened the book to the page where the Craig's were listed. There was a half a page filled with the last name Craig, but no Kelly Craig. Most looked familiar, probably because he'd called them before.

He drove to Staples to make a copy of the list and approached the lady at the copy center. "Can I make a copy of this page?"

The lady nodded and showed him how to use the machine.

"Um," he said, "Do you know a girl by the name of Kelly Craig?" She tilted her head.

"She was involved in a car accident years ago and was hit by a drunk driver."

"Oh, yeah, I've heard of her," the lady said. "Let me ask my coworker. I think she knows Kelly."

"Really?" Shawn's heartbeat quickened. Finally. Maybe this was the break he needed.

Another lady approached. "Can I help you?" *Kelly* was spelled out on her nametag.

That's a crazy coincidence. Shawn explained how he had seen Kelly on TV and wanted to meet her, bring her a card. "Her mom's name is Brenda. Do you know where she lives?"

The lady crossed her arms. "I-I-I do, but I'm not sure—"

"I know, this sounds really weird, but I've been trying to find her for years and drove a few hours out of my way to find her and give her a card." *Okay, that sounded even crazier.*

The lady's eyes shifted. She laughed nervously and glanced at the cashier.

The cashier shrugged, like maybe it was okay if she gave Shawn the address.

"She was on ESPN years ago," Shawn said. "They said she lived in Jasper, but every time I looked in the phone book under "Craig" I couldn't find a "Kelly." I'll go out to my car and get the letter I've written if you don't believe me. I'll be right back."

The lady nodded.

After Shawn retrieved the card and returned to the clerk, he handed her the envelope. "Here it is."

"Okay," the clerk said, handing him back the card. "I don't need to read it. I believe you." She drew a map on how to get to Kelly's house from where they were.

He followed the directions and five minutes later pulled in front of the house, a beautiful two-story home with a wood-shingled roof, a circular drive, and a large mailbox at the bottom of the driveway. And sure enough, the house sat on a little bluff overlooking the small town. *Maybe I should put the card in the mailbox. I can't knock at the door. What will I say? They'll think I've lost my mind.*

He drove up to the mailbox, opened it, and placed the card inside, then quickly drove off. He called his cousin, Andrew. "I found her."

"Kelly?" Andrew asked.

"Yes, but I chickened out and left the card in her mailbox."

"Are you crazy? You drove all that way and you're not going to knock at the door?"

"Yeah, sounds stupid, doesn't it?" Shawn asked.

"Totally. Since when do you do anything halfway?"

"Should I go back?"

"Hell, yes. Hang up, and call me back after you meet her," Andrew said.

That's all Shawn needed to hear. He turned his car around, pulled up to the end of the driveway, and reached for the plastic egg with the jellybeans sitting on the passenger seat. He retrieved his letter from the mailbox, praying that no one was watching him, and walked to the front door. His fingers trembled when he rang the bell.

Voices sounded through the door. He waited. Silence grew tight with tension.

He knocked again and swallowed hard.

Footsteps sounded. A woman opened the door. She had long strawberry blond hair, and Shawn recognized her from the ESPN video as Kelly's mother.

"I thought I heard someone knocking." She laughed.

"Are you Kelly Craig's mother?" Shawn blurted.

"Yes...?"

"My name is Shawn Schaefer, and I saw your daughter on TV years ago on ESPN, and I've thought about her... I wanted to send her a card. W-w-well, I couldn't find a Kelly Craig in the phone book. I...was...driving through this city...and I thought I'd try to find her."

"Really?"

"I was impressed with her when I saw her on TV and," Shawn wasn't sure how to sound well intended. "Look, I'm not a stalker." He handed Brenda the letter. "Would you give this to your daughter?" He handed her the Easter egg. "And this. It's symbolic of my *hunt* for her."

Kelly's mom laughed. "Sure, I'd invite you in but she's exfoliating her face right now. Her face is green," she laughed again, "and I doubt she wants anyone to see her."

"No, problem. I understand," Shawn said, not really certain why Kelly's face was green, but grateful that he could stop his stuttering.

"Thank you, wow, I'll give both of them to her," Brenda said.

Mom ran into my bathroom where I was hiding.

"Who was that?" I said, barely able to move my lips, the mask tight across my face.

She placed an envelope and a green plastic egg in my lap. "You won't believe this. A guy dressed in business clothes, very professional looking, asked if he could meet you. He asked me to give you this letter and the egg." She explained how long he'd been searching for me and the reason for the egg, but Mom's words came out jumbled.

"What?" I turned the envelope over. She wasn't making sense. "That's weird. Who was he?"

"His name is Shawn." Mom told me he'd said something about seeing me on ESPN years ago.

"Will you open it for me?" I asked her.

"Kelly, he was nervous. And cute." Mom laughed, tore open the letter, and handed it to me.

I read the note.

Kelly,

I am trying to locate the Kelly Craig from Jasper, Indiana who was severely injured in a devastating auto accident during the summer of 1999. I have read several articles and watched a segment on ESPN on this story. What I saw was a girl who displayed incredible courage, resolve, and had a good heart. At various points over the last seven years, I've had a variety of thoughts ranging from…

- She might be overwhelmed with thousands of people attempting to contact her
- Wondering how to contact someone I'd never met and not have them be weirded out
- Searching for your contact information through 411 and the internet and never having success
- Thinking through how it might be feasible to meet with her

All of this leads to my own version of an Easter egg hunt this year, which is to make one last attempt to meet this kind-hearted and soft-spoken young lady from a small town who saw her life turned upside down and showed the determination to move forward.

Why does this have any meaning to me? Well, around the same time in my life, I watched my sister's fiancé pass away from lymphoma cancer at the age of twenty-five. I have seen the impact of tragic events and the way they change lives in an instant.

You may have read this and been completely confused if you are a different Kelly Craig. If this is the case, I apologize for any inconvenience. However, if you are the Kelly Craig whose life story includes this chapter, I would appreciate the opportunity to have a short conversation with you.

Please respond whenever you have a chance.

All the best,
Shawn Schaefer

"He left his phone number. I'm not calling him. This is too weird."
"What does the note say?"
I read the note to her.
"He drove all this way to see you. You should call him." Mom said. "Call him before he leaves town. Maybe he'll come back."
How strange. Definitely not something that happened every day. "I don't know." I often received letters from people who admired my courage, and I'd never called one of them. This person was no different.
"He looked professional, Kelly. You should call him," Mom coaxed.
She helped rinse the mask off and badgered me again. "Andy and I are home. It's not like he can hurt you while we're here.
Okay, already. I'll call him. I dialed and he answered. "This is Kelly. I read your letter."
"I'm sure it sounded crazy, didn't it?"
"It's not the sort of thing that happens every day, that's for sure. Are you still in Jasper?"
"Yes, I stopped to get gas," he said.
"Do you have time to come back?"
"I won't be imposing?"
"No, you should come," I said.
He agreed and we hung up.
I turned to Mom who stood in the doorway. "He's coming over." She smiled.
Even though I hadn't met this man yet, this was the first time I felt like God was listening to my prayers and answering them.
Or maybe it was the first time I'd taken the time to hear His reply.

Chapter Thirty-Six

God knows what your silent heart wants. Even if you don't include it in your prayers. He hears what your heart whispers. He may not give it to you now but someday, when you least expect it, things will happen in the best possible way.
Unknown

Before Shawn returned to Kelly's house there was something he had to do. He returned the yellow page directory to Walgreens, and while he was in the store, he bought a candle and two boxes of chocolates. Afterward, he drove across the street to Staples and found the store clerk named Kelly.

She smiled when she saw him coming toward her.

"I found her." He handed her a box of chocolates. "I couldn't have done it without you."

She took the box. "You didn't have to do that."

"I know, but you didn't have to help me either."

Years later, the store clerk would tell Shawn that helping him find Kelly was one of the best things she ever did in her life.

Still standing in my bathroom, Mom reached into my makeup bag, took a hold of my blush brush, and moved toward my face, perched to color my cheeks.

"Let me do that." I took the brush from her hand. After Ryan had pushed me to learn how to apply my own makeup, I'd taught myself how to apply it, one-handedly.

Mom tidied up my bathroom, and I applied a little blush to my cheeks while we waited for Shawn to return. I couldn't believe that someone had watched the video of me seven years ago and was still looking for me now. It sounded creepy.

When Shawn arrived, I was sitting in my room off the foyer.

Mom greeted him and led him to me.

He was carrying a candle and a box of chocolates. He had dark spikey hair and a trim frame, and was of medium height—not too tall and not too short. I wondered if he was a runner, but his smile is what caught my attention. It showed intelligence and radiated a sincerity I didn't often see, and it caused my heart to skip a beat. My stomach fluttered too, a sensation I hadn't experienced in a long time.

"I brought you a vanilla-scented candle. Do you like candles?" The warmth of his smile echoed in his voice.

"Thanks, I do." I lied.

He entered my room, hesitating, his eyes searching for a place to leave the gifts.

"You can set them on my desk over there. Thanks."

He crossed the room and placed the gifts on my desk, then turned to me.

"Have a seat," I motioned to a chair in the corner of my room. "Can we get you something to drink?"

"No, I'm okay. I don't want to impose," he said.

For the next two hours, we talked about football, basketball, and cheerleading. We talked about family and siblings and where we worked. We talked like two young able-bodied adults getting to know each other. My chair was invisible. He never asked about the accident or my limitations.

Andy came in to meet him and shook his hand. Shawn stood and spoke to Andy with respect, retelling the story of how he'd searched for me. "I never thought Brenda might have a different last name. That never crossed my mind. No wonder I couldn't find Kelly."

Then Ted and Tyler came to meet him.

Shawn interacted with them like he'd known them all his life—asking them age-appropriate questions about the Colts and other sports teams.

When he spoke to me, it was as if I was the only one who mattered, that he was listening to every word and really hearing what I had to say. He spoke slowly as if careful about saying the right words.

Before he left, we exchanged phone numbers and e-mail addresses and hope sprouted. Maybe I'd see him again. After he left, I thanked God for bringing someone new into my life. Even if I never saw Shawn again, I'd cherish his visit forever.

But I couldn't deny the tingling sensation in the pit of my stomach.

As Shawn began his three-hour trek back to St. Louis, his spirits soared. It was the most excited he'd been in a long time. It was as if he'd won the prize, he'd conquered the tallest mountain. Not only did he get to deliver the card, but he got to meet Kelly too.

Her voice was pure softness, fragile yet strong, confident yet not cocky.

He called Andrew.

"Well? It's about time. I've been waiting forever for you to call me back."

"I didn't want to leave her house. She's beautiful—inside and out."

"Did she think you were pyscho?"

"Probably at first, but she understands. At least, I hope she does."

For the next half an hour Shawn told him what had happened, then he called his sister and rehashed the whole sequence of events with her, too.

"Do you want to see her again?" she asked.

"I do. At first, all I wanted to do was deliver the card, but once I met her, well, I want to see her again if she wants to see me again."

Chapter Thirty-Seven

One day I caught myself smiling for no reason, then I realized I was thinking of you.
Unknown

"You'll never believe what happened," I said to Blayr at school the next day, excitedly telling her everything.

"That's insane. It sounds creepy. We'll have to Google him later. What are you doing after school?"

"Nothing. Come over."

She agreed to come to my house a little after four.

Each time I had a break in teaching, I scanned e-mails and chided myself for looking, but I didn't have the willpower to stop. Part of me wanted to guard my heart. After all, just because he went out of his way to meet me didn't mean he wanted to see me again. Plus, I'd been burned by a guy before. I didn't want to feel that way again.

But just after 3:00 p.m., my computer made the dinging sound I was waiting for. In the subject line was, "Well worth the hunt." Chills ran along my arm.

I read his note:

Kelly -

Hello there. Thanks for taking time last night to chat for a while. You and your family were incredibly welcoming, and I'm glad I finally got the chance to meet you. I was happy to finally be able to deliver my letter—so to be able to talk with you was icing on the cake.

I was quite impressed that you were willing to open up and share your feelings with someone that you just met. I can tell that you are very honest and candid, which makes it easy to talk to you. If I have one regret, it was that I didn't hold the hug longer. :)

I hope you weren't too tired this morning. My drive back was uneventful in a good way. If you have the desire, give me a call any time.

Take care,
Shawn

Would he call me? Or did he want me to call him instead? I reread the letter. His only regret was not holding the hug longer? I liked that. I liked that a lot.

After school, Blayr came over, and I shared his e-mail with her.

"Are you going to write him back?"

"What do you think?"

"Let's check him out first, make sure he's legit." She sat in front of my computer ready to click away at the keys, typing in the Google search bar. "How do you spell his last name? Where does he live?"

I gave her the information and looked over her shoulder while she typed. We found his house on Google Earth and took a virtual tour. The house was on a street of well-kept homes. His was a dark brick ranch with mature trees and landscaped shrubs. "Not bad," Blayr said.

I agreed.

She clicked around a little more and confirmed where he worked and his hometown.

The more I learned, the more he seemed to be telling the truth.

"Look at you," Blayr said. "You're glowing."

"I am not."

"Do you want me to help you write him back?" she asked.

"Sure." Together we laughed as I composed my response.

She typed.

It took us an hour before I was comfortable with my response. I wanted to get it right.

Shawn,

Hi There, Glad you made it home safely last night. I felt badly that you had a three-hour drive ahead of you when you left. You are quite the persistent "egg hunter," which I appreciate. As I replayed the events that led you to my doorstep, I realized that you really went above and beyond to locate me, and I'm truly grateful and...flattered.

What could have been a seemingly awkward situation last night between two strangers turned out to be an enjoyable time spent with a guy whom I was completely comfortable talking with. My family felt the same way. You are always welcome and feel free to knock louder next time.

I will give you a call sometime this weekend. Again...it was a pleasure to meet you. Thanks again for the effort.

I have to admit that I share the same regret as you.
Kelly

Shawn read the e-mail once, then read it again. She wished he'd hugged her longer? Was she trying to be polite, or did she really want to see him again? She sounded sincere. His heart skipped a beat, and he looked forward to hearing from her. Typically, he liked to be the one to call the girl, but in this case, he didn't want to push himself on her.

For several weeks, Shawn and I continued to correspond through e-mails and phone calls. When he realized May fifteenth was my twenty-seventh birthday, he said, "Do you have plans?"

"Not really. Birthdays aren't that big of a deal around here. We celebrate them, but not with anything formal. Do you want to come to Jasper?"

"I wouldn't be imposing with your family plans?"

"No."

"Okay then. I'll plan on leaving Saturday morning and arriving around 11:00. Would that work?"

"Sure," I said.

I couldn't believe I was actually going on a date with a decent guy. I told myself it didn't mean anything. He was coming to visit, nothing more, but the reality was that he was driving three hours one way and three hours back to see me. Who does that if they're not a little interested? I tried to tame my heart, to squelch my excitement, but my emotions seemed to have a mind of their own. I couldn't lie to myself. I wanted to get to know him better.

When teachers and friends heard he was spending part of the weekend with me they asked, "What do you know about this guy? He's a stranger."

"Blayr and I Googled him, and everything he'd told me checked out." I said. They hadn't met him to know his kind heart. I understood why they were skeptical, but a part of their doubt hurt, like they didn't believe a guy would be interested in me. Besides, he hadn't asked me to marry him. He asked me out on a date. That was all.

"I'd hate for you to get hurt," one teacher said.

"I won't get hurt." But inside I worried too. Why was Shawn pursuing me? If he was pursuing me. If I gave away my heart, would I be sorry? Would this end up in disappointment? Usually, I was a good judge of character, and my gut told me that he was genuine. But I'd only spent one evening with him. How did I really know?

My thoughts teetered back and forth for days, but in the end, only time would tell.

Shawn hung up from the phone call excited that she'd agreed to see him again. *She must have some kind of feelings for me if she wants to spend her birthday with me.*

Blayr showed up an hour before Shawn was supposed to arrive to help me get ready. My nurse had gotten me up and showered me, but Blayr wanted to help apply my makeup and tidy my room.

"Can you hide the wipes, gloves, and catheters?" I asked. "I don't want anything handicap-related to be visible."

She gathered everything wheelchair-related and stored them out of sight.

"If I could hide my wheelchair I would."

She laughed. "I've never seen you this nervous."

"It feels good to be nervous about a guy for a change," I admitted.

When we heard Shawn pull up in the driveway and his car door shut, my stomach somersaulted.

"He's prompt," Mom said, approaching the front door.

He said hello to Mom and entered the foyer holding a cluster of multi-colored balloons. They floated and bobbed in the air.

"Wow," Mom said and laughed.

I wheeled to greet him, nerves jittering.

He looked more handsome than I remembered. He wore jeans, a pale blue long-sleeved shirt, and a jacket. His dark hair swept and waved across his forehead.

"Happy twenty-seventh Birthday," he said, handing the balloon collection to me.

Mom draped the strings around my wrist.

"Thanks. I've never received this many balloons in my life." I felt as excited as a little kid, but awkward at all the attention.

"You look nice," he said.

If I were the blushing type, I would have blushed. "Thank you." I introduced him to Blayr.

He smiled and shook her hand. "Kelly told me a lot about you. I'm glad to meet you."

Mom held up a camera. "Let me take a photo of you guys."

"Great idea," Blayr said, crossing to my side.

Shawn bent to my level and stood next to me, and together we posed for the camera.

Afterward, Blayr said she'd be right back and went into the kitchen with Mom, as planned.

Shawn and I migrated to my room where I turned the balloons loose and they floated to the ceiling. "Do you mind if Blayr goes to lunch with us?"

"Not at all. I'd like to get to know her better, too," he said.

We made small talk and Andy and my brothers came in to say hello.

When it was time to head to the cafe downtown, I turned to Shawn. "You'll have to drive my van, since Blayr is following us in her car. Are you okay with that?"

"No problem. Tell me what to do and where to go."

This was the part I dreaded, the part that accentuated my

differences. He would see how I traveled. I wanted the day to go seamlessly without drawing attention to my disability, but this couldn't be avoided. We went out the side door that led to the garage, and I instructed him on how to lower the access ramp from the van, hoping I could traverse quickly and smoothly.

He pressed the button to activate the ramp and watched it lower.

I wheeled into the van, and my chair locked in place. Never had I been more self-conscious.

"Wow, that was easy," he said, climbing into the driver's side.

"Now you press the button again." I nodded toward the button. "And it'll tuck the ramp inside."

The ramp clanked and folded into place.

"Cool." He turned the ignition key and adjusted the mirrors. "It's not every day I get to drive a van."

"Yeah, it's not your typical twenty-something way to travel." I laughed. Thank God, he seemed unaffected by the whole process.

"You're a good teacher," he said.

"Thanks." I wanted to blush again.

Blayr followed us. She and I had it all planned—she would stay with me as long as I wanted her to. If I gave her the signal that it was okay for her to leave, she would give a planned excuse and take off, but if something seemed off, she would stay with me until we could get rid of him.

In the diner, we talked about jobs, college, and what Blayr and I did with Young Life. It didn't take Blayr or me long to realize that Shawn seemed harmless, a total gentlemen insisting on paying for both of our meals. Blayr smiled, turned to go, and winked with approval.

From there, Shawn drove to the Riverwalk along Patoka River where we strolled along the two miles of paved trails that snaked through the edge of our city. People jogged by. Some waved. We stopped at a bench in the shade and Shawn sat across from me, his eyes level with mine, our knees almost touching, close enough that I could smell his clean, fresh cologne.

A warm breeze made me shiver.

"Are you cold?" Shawn asked, his brown eyes squinting from the glare of the sun behind me.

"No, I'm good." I lied.

He brushed his fingertips across my arm as if checking, and sent a different kind of chill through me. He left his warm hand there, triggering my nerves. The subtle gesture warmed my heart. He wasn't intimidated about touching my atrophied arm. That said a lot.

We talked about Jasper and the people who lived there, and he told me about his family.

"If you could walk, what would be the first thing you'd do?" he asked.

"I'd climb the stairs, take a shower in my own room, and sleep in my old bed."

"That's all?"

"I guess it's the simple things I miss the most. You take them for granted."

He nodded, but I doubted he understood.

Later, he took me to dinner at the country club. During our meal, he talked about his family again. "I'd love for you to come to St. Louis and meet them. You could come for the weekend."

I looked away.

"You don't want to come?"

I laughed. "No, it's not that. I'd love to meet them, but I don't wake up this way." I waved my hand over my body. "Someone has to put me to bed, get me up in the morning, and…"

"Whatever I have to do, tell me and I'll help. It doesn't matter how it's done. But if you'd rather wait, I understand."

"I'll think about it."

He reached across the table and squeezed my hand. "Let me know when you're ready."

"Thanks. Do you want to see my classroom?"

"We can do that?"

I nodded. "I have a key, and the school is connected to the church so it's open."

When we arrived, Mass had already let out.

"Precious Blood," he said. "It's a Catholic Church?"

"Yes, church and school. Why?"

"No reason really, only that I'm Catholic," he said.

"Really?" I smiled. One more thing we had in common.

When we got to the classroom and turned on the lights, I waited to see how long it would take him to discover the surprise.

He glanced at the quote above the chalkboard. *I can do all things in Christ who strengthens me.* "How appropriate. Your camping theme is creative, too."

A bookcase made of an upright, painted canoe with shelves stood in the corner. A wire bin that held papers had a covered top that resembled a tent. On the backside of my desk was the phrase, *this is How I Roll.*

"Check out the chalkboard," I said.

He turned to face the board, his arms folded behind his back, and read. "Wow, are all those notes for me?"

"Every single one," I said.

When my students heard I was going on a date with Shawn they asked if they could meet him, but I said, no. Instead, I told them they could write notes to him on the chalkboard.

Almost every student left him a personal message.

> Dear Shawn, Miss Craig is a great person. Hopefully you realize how lucky you are to have met her. I hope to hear of you from Miss Craig. Have fun today. P.S. Miss Craig rocks.

Another one:

> Shawn, Miss Craig is an awesome teacher and has an amazing personality. Have a great day with her.

One student drew a squirrel with a nut. "This is one student's analogy of you finding me."

Shawn laughed.

Several wrote that they wanted him to come to school. They wanted to meet him.

"They're protective of you," Shawn said. "That's really sweet."

"Yeah, they're amazing."

It was time for Shawn to return to St. Louis. He sat in Kelly's driveway, ready to say goodbye and begin the long trek home. The night had turned dark, but the spring air was light and full of promise. The stars glittered and twinkled.

He squatted down to Kelly's level, facing her, his hands touching her legs, squeezing them. He thought he felt her shudder. "What are you thinking?"

"About what?"

"About this, you and me."

"What do you think?" she asked.

Shawn liked that she wasn't forward. Many girls were, but she waited to take his lead. "I want to see if our relationship could turn into something more. I enjoy spending time with you, but traveling the long distance, well, I don't mind doing it, but I don't want to do it if you aren't interested, if you don't feel the same."

She smiled deep enough that Shawn saw the dimple in her chin.

"I feel the same," she said. "I want to see you again."

He leaned in closer, inches from her mouth. She smelled like the roses in his neighbor's garden. Maybe it was her shampoo. He drew closer to her lips until he felt her warm breath on his cheek. It smelled like fresh bread from the oven, a scent he wanted to memorize. His heart knocked in his chest, like a schoolboy who'd never kissed a girl before. He closed his eyes and pressed his open lips to hers, eager to taste her. Too eager. Her lips were closed. He pulled away, but it was too late.

He'd slobbered on her like he was trying to eat her face. She'd think he was the worse kisser. Ever. He hugged her and waved, thanking her again for a great day, eager to leave and erase the embarrassment of his awkward kiss from his mind.

He'd wanted it to be a passionate kiss, one that she would never forget. She'd never forget, all right. It would be memorable for all the wrong reasons.

I watched him drive off and waved, his kiss still lingering and tingling on my lips. Seven years. That's how long it had been since I'd been kissed. *Did he realize how nervous I was?* I turned to go inside. Mom would be waiting to put me to bed.

Law and Order played on the TV screen.

"Well?" Mom said and turned to me. "Look at your face. You're flushed." She and Andy were sitting on the sofa. "How did it go?"

"He's a great guy," I said.

"Will you see him again?" Andy asked.

"I hope so. He wants me to meet his family."

After Andy lifted me into bed, I said a silent prayer of thanks and planned what I'd write to Shawn tomorrow. I should have said more than I had.

The next day, Shawn received an e-mail from Kelly.

Shawn,

I can't thank you enough for making the trip to "J-Town." I had a great time, and I'm happy it all worked out. After you left, I collected my thoughts, and I wanted to say more than I did. Sometimes I have trouble expressing myself, but I wanted to write to reiterate my gratitude.

1. Knowing that you took a day off to visit makes me smile.
2. The balloons were a big hit. I love them.
3. I know I said thank you for lunch and dinner, but I don't

think I said it enough. I don't expect that treatment every time—got it?

4. At the Riverwalk you made me feel totally comfortable with whom I am, and that is priceless to me.

5. I was in awe watching how kind and open you were with my friends, brothers, and parents. They all love you by the way. You're great at making everyone feel important. I've never met a guy like you. Although I've only known you for a short time, I can tell that you are a sweet, generous, considerate, and respectful guy. The whole day was truly a reflection of who you are as a person.

With much appreciation,
Kelly

Shawn smiled. Maybe the kiss wasn't as bad as he thought. It looked like he'd get another chance.

The rest of the day breezed by and in between numbers, spreadsheets, and balancing budgets, he thought about Kelly and spending more time with her.

Chapter Thirty-Eight

*It's more than just the dates, holding hands and kissing. It's about
accepting each other's weirdness and flaws. It's about being you and
finding happiness together. It's about seeing an imperfect person
perfectly.*
Unknown

I had two dates a few years ago, but neither guy had interested me
like Shawn. One guy was an elementary ed major I met at USI and one
was studying to be a doctor, but those dates had been awkward,
whereas my time with Shawn was effortless.

We talked on the phone almost every night, thirsty for knowledge
about each other, hungry for affirmations and for discovering the ways
we blended. We talked about sports and school, family and God. Time
flew.

"I'm not pushing you," he said, "but I want you to come to St. Louis
and meet my family."

I knew it was my turn to go to there, because he'd been to my house three times, but I was hesitant.

"You're still apprehensive, aren't you?" he asked. "I promise, my family isn't that scary."

"No, it's not that. I want to meet your family, it's..." I paused. "I need to tell you what to expect first. There's a lot about my care you don't know." I gulped. *This is when he'll run.*

"Wait," he said. "Before you start, there's something you need to know. Anything you tell me about how you're different from other people is *insignificant* to me."

The way he emphasized insignificant struck a melodious chord in my mind and lodged a stone in my throat. I tried to thank him for his kind words, but emotion filled me. I sighed and regained my composure. I needed to finish. "First of all," I said, "I don't even know if I can get into your house. My portable ramp can only go up two to three steps."

"We made a ramp for you," he said.

"You did? Who?" I couldn't believe it.

"My friend James and me."

My heart melted. I couldn't believe they built me a ramp. "Okay, then. Blayr said she will go with me and can show you how to transfer me and how to do my bladder bathroom."

"Perfect."

Having Blayr would dispel the anxiety about leaving myself vulnerable. The memories from the Ms. Wheelchair America contestants of men leaving women alone without their chairs or their phones scared me. Even though I didn't think Shawn was the type to harm me, the stories from the other contestants swam in my mind, and having Blayr with me offered me comfort.

The next Saturday morning in June, Blayr helped me pack the van and dress in something cute, and we began our three-hour trek to St. Louis. We listened to the radio and sang songs along the way, which helped squelch my unease about meeting his family. "Thanks for going with me."

"Are you kidding? I wouldn't miss it. Plus, I still don't really know this guy."

"But I'm intruding on your time with Ryan."

She waved a hand. "He wants me to go with you. He loves you, too, Kelly."

Since I met Ryan and Blayr, I'd tagged along with them to so many outings Ryan kidded that he had two wives—Blayr and me.

When we pulled into the Texas Road House parking lot, our planned meeting place, Shawn and his family were waiting. Blayr parked in a spot next to them, released my ramp, and I rolled down, cringing at my *non* red carpet arrival. Would they be shocked at how disabled I was? Would his mother fear that my relationship with her son might lead to marriage? I doubted they'd ever pictured him with someone like me. Thank goodness I'd remembered to take two Baclofen to keep my legs still. A spasm would make things even more awkward.

Shawn introduced everyone and we went inside. I sat next to Blayr and Shannon, Shawn's sister.

"What did your parents think when Shawn arrived at your door that first day?" his mother asked.

"It was definitely out of the ordinary, but my mom wanted me to call him back. He made a good first impression."

Shawn smiled at me from across the table.

His family was normal. More than normal. Shannon was a nurse and understood the aspects of my injury, and Shawn's other sister, Kelly, was an elementary education major. We had a lot in common. Our conversations went smoothly and without tension.

After dinner, we ate ice cream at a local creamery. I could see why Shawn was so close to his family. Meeting them helped me see why he was such a great guy.

Later that night, Blayr, Shawn, and I watched a movie at Shawn's house. Blayr taught Shawn how to transfer me to the couch. I locked my chair and Shawn scooped his steady arms under mine, lifted me, and pivoted me to the couch. He smelled of hair gel and deodorant.

He took my hand and sat next to me, then adjusted the pillows at the end of the couch and pulled me toward him, to the pillows. "I want to snuggle with you." He glanced at Blayr and motioned for her to help him.

Together the two of them adjusted my legs. I nestled next to Shawn, half of me on his side and half on the sofa. Could he hear my heart beating? It seemed like it would jump out of my chest.

I couldn't believe I was nuzzled so close to him. I couldn't remember the last time I was safe in such caring arms. Next time Blayr could stay home.

I was in love. Reality was finally better than my dreams.

In the morning, Blayr showed Shawn how to insert the sterile tube into my abdomen to extract my urine. Shawn listened and handled every minute detail. "That was easy," he said, and kissed my forehead.

After the weekend, I was sure his family had questions about me—how does she go to the bathroom, how would we handle a long distance relationship since I couldn't drive—but no matter, I was all in. There was no turning back.

The next weekend, Shawn arrived in Jasper late on Friday evening. Whenever he visited Kelly, he stayed overnight and slept in Jason's old room upstairs. When it was time for bed, he transferred Kelly from the chair, emptied her bladder, and left to change into his gym shorts and T-shirt. "I'll be right back," he promised.

The rest of her family slept while he snuck down and crawled into bed next to her. In a twin bed. He tucked his body next to hers, face-to-face, and held her, their lips almost touching, and stared intently into her eyes. "I love you, Kelly Craig."

"I love you too, Shawn Schaefer."

She loved him.

Her gaze drifted to his lips and he saw a flash of desire in her eyes. She wanted him to kiss her.

His heart must have grown three sizes; it jolted and pulsed against his chest wall. He was overcome with an urgency to kiss her. He met her lips softly at first, but when hers parted for more, he drew every inch of her closer, inhaling her, wanting her. He wanted her to know what she meant to him.

She withdrew from the kiss. "There's something you need to know."

"Am I making you uncomfortable?" Maybe he'd been too forward.

"No, I'm very comfortable, and I love kissing you, but since the accident I've developed a relationship with God. Sex isn't something.. . I've made a commitment to Him—"

He set his finger on her lips. "Say no more. I respect your virtue and agree. Anything of value is worth waiting for."

"Thank you."

He kissed her again, long enough to feel the spark ignite and know that they'd never have a problem finding passion.

After they said goodnight, he climbed the stairs to his bedroom, went to the bathroom, and took a cold shower.

Each time I saw him the draw was stronger, more magnetic, and I couldn't forget his kisses or the way he held me without inhibitions, the way he took my breath away, and how warm he was inside and out. I wanted more.

The weeks without him dragged and the weekends with him went too fast. We spoke on the phone, each time more passionately, but it was never enough. I wanted more of him in my life. To help the weekdays go faster, I started a *Shawn* project. I ordered a personalized eight-inch by ten-inch puzzle of him through Shutterfly and wrote his personality characteristics on the back. On Valentine's Day, I wrote him a letter and gave him the framed puzzle. It was in a clear frame so he could see the front and back.

"Shawn, I once told you that with each visit and phone conversation I gain more pieces for my 'Shawn Puzzle.' Well, after ten months of getting to know your family and friends and learning about your likes and dislikes, listening to your hopes and dreams, and falling in love with your characteristics, all of the pieces of my puzzle have been collected, and I'm in awe of the image. All of the pieces fit together perfectly, and I couldn't be happier with the outcome. It's a breathtaking sight.

"You've changed me from being a spectator, a girl watching everyone else's happiness, to a girl experiencing her own happiness. My job, my friends, and my family are all forms of happiness, but I'm happy because I have you. You are that person in my life, and nothing can compare to the smile that you bring to my face. When you tell me that I'm beautiful or when you hold me tight, I can't imagine a better feeling. You continually show me in your actions and express in your words your love for me, and for that, I'm truly grateful. You have given me true and complete happiness."

Shawn told me the puzzle was the work of a creative genius and flattering, a treasure he would keep forever.

In their first year of dating, Kelly and Shawn went to Louisville's Churchill Downs, a Cardinals game, the Ozarks, Kelly's cousin's wedding, a few family reunions, Rascal Flatts' concert, holiday get-togethers, the zoo, New Year's Eve parties, IU basketball games, and Body World at the Science Museum in St. Louis. Then on her birthday, a year after they met, Shawn took her to Chicago.

While touring the city, they laughed and enjoyed the sights, but the best part of their time was visiting Kelly's doctor at RIC. It was time for her annual check-up, and Shawn wanted clarity on their future together. He wanted to ask specific questions and learn everything there was to know about Kelly's limitations.

They spent two hours with the doctor's physician assistant.

"You aren't the first guy to date a girl in a wheelchair," the assistant said. "And you won't be the last. People in wheelchairs get married all the time and some have children."

Shawn squeezed my hand.

The PA continued. "The odds for you to have a healthy marriage are in your favor because you met after the injury. You're going into this relationship with your eyes open."

Shawn asked about Kelly's health. "Is it safe to assume that she'll live a long life?"

"Her system has been compromised, but if she eats right, exercises, and has annual check-ups with her primary physician, urologist, and GI doctors, she can live a long time."

On the drive home, Shawn asked Kelly if she would mind if he called Mike Bondi. Kelly had met Renée Bondi at a speaking engagement and they'd become acquaintances. Like Kelly, Renée was a quadriplegic and speaker, but Renée was an award-winning songwriter and vocalist too. She'd been married for over twenty years to Mike. Renée told Kelly that Mike would talk to Shawn anytime he had a question.

When Shawn returned to St. Louis, he called Mike and asked him "husband-type" questions. Mike was patient and open and spoke to Shawn for over an hour. He gave Shawn traveling, marital, and parenting tips, and didn't sugarcoat anything.

"Why do you think your marriage has been successful?" Shawn asked.

Mike chuckled. "It's not always easy. But seriously, after I work long hours, help with the meals, and with our son's homework, I'm exhausted. But I look at all the single-parent families. They're doing it. We had to find different ways of doing things. And you will, too."

He continued. "Able-bodied couples don't *have* to spend time together. Renée relies on me to help her to bed every night. It gives us personal and intimate time together. Even if we've had a busy day, or we're mad at each other, we have to come together in the evening. It gives us time to talk and share our days."

Shawn never thought of that, but it made sense.

"The disability actually enhances communication," Mike added. "My love for Renée is stronger today than when we got married."

Impressive. Shawn hoped for the same. "Do quadriplegics struggle more with depression?" RIC mentioned that sometimes depression could be a problem.

"Not any more than other people. Renée has good days and bad days."

"You have to think ahead for vacations because it's logistically different," Mike said. "Boarding a plane, carrying the luggage, and adjusting the wheelchair at the gate after it's been stowed is exhausting. There were times when her chair wouldn't function properly.

"You can't rent any car either. Some major cities have more availability for the disabled, but you have to call ahead and make sure you're covered. And not every city has cabs for the disabled either.

"Another thing I'd recommend you put in place—," Mike said.

"What's that?"

"Get comfortable accepting help. We have a Rolodex filled with names of people who want to help, but when we call them we explain that they shouldn't feel guilty about saying no if they can't because we have a long list of people to call. That's really helped. You don't want friends and family to cringe every time you call."

Next, Shawn asked specific questions about intimacy that only another man would understand, and was glad he asked. Shawn's ignorance transformed into knowledge, which reassured him about his future with Kelly. There wasn't anything about her limitations he couldn't handle, or that scared him. Mike's affirmations allowed Shawn to follow his heart without hesitation.

Now, he needed to take the next step.

Chapter Thirty-Nine

Someone who really loves you sees what a mess you can be, how moody you can get, how hard you are to handle, but still wants you in their life.
Unknown

August 31, 2008

Shawn woke in Jason's old bedroom, listened to the sounds in the house, and waited for his alarm clock to beep. He should get up. It was almost 6:30 and there was no way he could sleep. He threw on his jeans and a sweatshirt and tiptoed downstairs, working to keep his footfalls from creaking on the wood floor. If he woke Kelly now his plan would fall apart. He passed her closed bedroom door and went to the kitchen. It was empty.

Brenda and Andy were supposed to golf in a scramble at 7:30. Shawn went to his car in the driveway, opened it, and climbed in, waiting for them to leave for the outing. That was the only way he'd get them alone without Kelly hearing his conversation.

Cardinals chirped, car doors slammed, cars whizzed by, and bacon wafted from somewhere nearby, but he couldn't think of food. He'd never done this before, and it was difficult to keep his excitement in check. Time slowed. Minutes dragged before Andy finally came outside. He walked toward the mailbox.

Shawn opened his car door and headed toward Andy.

Andy jumped. "Hey, Shawn. What are you doing out here?"

"Sorry to startle you. I wanted to talk to you and Brenda without Kelly listening."

"Oh? What about?"

"I'm in love with your daughter," he paused and sighed deeply and placed his hand on Andy's arm. "She's been your daughter for years, and you've been a father to her for... more than two decades, and I'm asking you to give her up, to let her spend the rest of her life with me. It's a huge thing. It would be a privilege to call her my wife, if I have your blessing."

"Yes, you have my... blessing." Andy's voice cracked. He embraced Shawn and locked his arms around him. There's no better guy for Kelly. I'm happy for you," Andy said.

"Would you ask Brenda to come out? I want to talk to her too."

"She's going to freak out." Andy turned to go, but the handicapped door whirred open in the garage and Brenda walked out.

"What's going on?" she asked, approaching.

Shawn swallowed hard. "I know that Kelly is your only daughter, and everything you've been through, but..." he swallowed again, "it would be a privilege to ask her to be my wife—."

Brenda's hands went up to cover her mouth and she broke out in sudden tears.

This woman who rarely cried, who was the epitome of strength, stood before him so choked up she couldn't speak. Was she happy or sad? Shawn couldn't tell. She'd been Kelly's hands, legs, and faith leader for almost ten years. Maybe this was too much for her to give up.

"I love Kelly," Shawn continued. "I'll love her with my whole heart, but before I ask her to marry me, I want your blessing."

He must have looked worried for suddenly Brenda drew him into a hug. "I'm...happy for...both of you." She wiped her cheeks with her fingertips. "Yes, you have... my blessing." Brenda grinned. "She's going to be surprised."

Shawn hoped so. He'd waited until the last minute to ask her parents for their blessing, hoping to keep the proposal a secret, vowing to make the moment extra special for Kelly. He wanted to take her breath away. He'd planned every detail—from the ring to the setting, and what he would say. He was overcome with the jitters, not nervous from cold feet, but from the excitement and the anticipation of experiencing one of the most important moments in his life.

Fallen leaves rushed by in swirls as Shawn and I strolled through Jasper's Riverwalk along Patoka River. The river's peaceful flow accompanied our rendezvous and we soaked up the beauty of nature and her colors surrounding us. Shawn said he had to go back to St. Louis soon, but first he wanted to go for a walk. I doubted we'd get too far because he seemed distracted. He played with the zipper on his nylon jacket, pulling it up and down. We stopped at the wooden gazebo to gaze at the river flowing along the edge.

People raced by in jogging shorts and on their mountain bikes, squinting in the sun. Some of my students and friends stopped to say hello.

Shawn sat on a bench facing me.

"Is something on your mind?" I asked him. "You're acting strange."

But before he could answer, a young boy came over and sat next to him.

"Hi," the boy said. He told us about his sister, his family, and rambled on about bees and geocaching with the Cub Scouts.

Shawn seemed impatient, and I was anxious to know what was on his mind, but minutes passed and the boy continued to chat.

Finally, a woman called from across the park and waved. "It's time to eat," she said. A large group of people sat beside her at a long table. It looked like they were having a family reunion.

"Bye," the boy said, and ran off.

Shawn sighed and took my hands. "I thought he'd never leave."

"What's wrong?"

"I've been thinking." He paused. "It's time we stopped dating."

My stomach dropped. He was breaking up with me? What had gone wrong? Eric's break-up hurtled back to me. Shawn had decided he wanted someone who could walk, fix him dinner, and push a baby in a stroller. I was too much to take care of. That's what it was.

The park spun. *Relax. Breathe. You'll get through this.* How stupid I'd been for falling again. I was Cinderella waiting for Prince Charming. That only happens in fairy tales.

But after so many days of being with Shawn, I thought we were different. Weren't we the real thing? Had I been too buried in hope that I hadn't seen what was really happening?

Shawn was saying something. What? He stood and peeled off his jacket as if suddenly warm and stuffed it in the bag on the back of my chair, then returned to the bench in front of me. He wrapped his arms around my legs, furrowed his brows, and exhaled loudly. "I think we need to talk about where our relationship is going."

What was I supposed to say? I didn't trust my voice.

He held a small box in his hand. Where had that come from?

A gust of wind carried strands of hair across my face, trapping a few in my mouth.

He reached over, collected them, brushed them to the side, and gave me one of those stares that said this was the most difficult thing he'd ever done. He was looking for me to reassure him that he was doing the right thing.

I turned my head away, but he took a hold of my chin. "You know how I think things through over and over again? It's me; it's what I do. I've asked you hundreds of questions. I've analyzed our relationship forever. I've talked to your doctors. I know you really well and you know me. We've been together long enough now that," he paused. "We need a change."

A change? Maybe the doctors or Mike Bondi scared him. They told him what it'd be like living with me.

"I've changed since I've met you. I don't want to spend another day without you. I want us to grow old together. I love you." He knelt on one knee and opened the box to reveal a large round diamond ring. "Kelly Ann Craig, will you marry me?"

"What?" I was stunned. My stomach flipped. He wasn't leaving me?

Shawn nodded and smiled, but gazed at me intensely. "Choosing my lifelong teammate is the most important decision in my life, but for me, this decision is made with confidence. I got it right. Your positivity is infectious, your beauty is breathtaking, and your heart is as big as they come."

"Is this really happening?" The diamond glistened from the tears pooling in my eyes.

"It's your time, Kelly, your turn, it's happening. I don't want us to be boyfriend and girlfriend anymore."

I closed my eyes and tears fell. All my life I'd waited for this moment—the fairytale proposal, the prince and the princess. And it was really happening. My doctors hadn't scared him away. He really did love me.

He was waiting for my answer, but where would we live? If I moved to St. Louis, I wouldn't know anyone. I'd have to hire a new nurse. Karla knew every freckle on my body, and how to take care of me. I trusted her. How could I replace her?

And who would hire me to teach? I wanted to be able to stay home and fix his meals, paint the kitchen, pay the bills, have his children, and be the wife he deserved. If I said yes, I'd never be able to give him the things I wanted him to have. Did I love him enough to set him free to marry someone who could give him what I couldn't?

No, even though I couldn't give him those things, I would find others to be my hands, to show him the love I wanted to give him. I loved him. I wanted a life with him. Somehow we'd make it work. I'd dreamt of our life together for months. "Yes, I will marry you."

He slid the diamond on my slender finger, but the ring was too big. We laughed.

"I didn't want to ruin the surprise by getting your exact measurement," he confessed. "I'll get it sized this week."

Tears fell down my cheeks, tickling my chin. "Put it on my pointer finger."

He transferred the ring to my other finger.

"This will work for now." I held out my hand and admired the perfect round diamond, simple and sweet, a symbol of his love. He bent over and scooped me out of my chair and hugged me in his lap. He put his lips over mine, and I let my salty tears fall openly into the mouth of his sweet kiss.

For today, and maybe for a few months, I wanted to enjoy the moment and share my excitement to be engaged to an amazing man. I pushed away all the fears of my unanswered questions. I twirled in my head faster than the leaves chasing on the ground, more excited than any princess who ever lived.

Shawn held her in his lap, openly pressing his lips to hers, kissing her, tasting the promises of tomorrow, basking in the glow of the sun and soaking up the moment, pretending they were the only two in the park. He couldn't believe that this beautiful girl had committed to spending the rest of her life by his side.

When they finished professing their love to each other, they strolled over to the pavilion to find the little boy. Shawn waved to him.

The boy raced over, crumbs still on his face.

"Would you take a few pictures for us? I asked Kelly to marry me."

The boy seemed unimpressed with the proposal and more interested in learning about the camera and directing a photo shoot.

After several photos, Kelly urged Shawn to take her back to her parent's house.

When they arrived, Brenda and Andy sat poolside lounging on the back patio.

Glowing, Kelly wheeled over to them, showed off the ring, and shared the details of the proposal.

Brenda and Andy hugged them both and congratulated them.

Afterward, Shawn and Kelly sped away in the van as if they were heading to paradise. He'd made dinner reservations at the West Baden Resort in French Lick, a half hour away.

"I thought you had to go back to St. Louis," Kelly said.

He reached for her hand. "I wanted to throw you off. Leaving was never my plan."

She smiled.

During dinner, they reminisced about their sixteen months of dating, the proposal, and the excitement of planning their future. Shawn called his parents to share the news, and when his head hit the pillow that night, he felt like he'd won the lottery—the one that granted him a lifetime as the husband of Kelly Ann Craig.

When Shawn reflected back on his proposal, he remembered the three quotes he tried to live by and how they related to Kelly.

1.) *Make it happen.* If he hadn't traveled to meet Kelly, he never would have met her.

2.) *There's a time and place for everything.* God's time for Shawn to meet Kelly wasn't until seven years after her accident, a time when they were both ready.

3.) *You are what you repeatedly do,* Will Durant. Shawn and Kelly both believed in this quote. They strived to do better. Excellence wasn't an act, but a habit. It came from making the right choices every day.

He wanted to marry someone who made him want to be better, and in turn, he wanted to be the person who helped make Kelly better.

They couldn't be more suited for one another.

Chapter Forty

You don't need someone to complete you;
you only need someone to accept you completely.
Unknown

Difficult decisions had to be made. Not only did Shawn and I have to plan the wedding, we had to decide where we'd live and who would move. One of us would have to bend more than the other.

For weeks, we talked about the pros and cons of one of us moving. How could we find an equal compromise? If I moved to St. Louis, we'd be close to Shawn's family and closer to a larger metropolitan community that had more cultural opportunities. But, I wouldn't have the support system I had in Jasper, and I'd have to hire a new nurse. On the other hand, Jasper had less traffic and was a smaller community—a great place to raise a family.

We decided to both apply for jobs in the opposite communities and see what happened first, that we'd consider the first sensible opportunity. I applied for teaching jobs in Shawn's hometown, Belleville, Illinois, and he applied for accounting jobs in Jasper. The economy was depressed and jobs were scarce, but in ten months Shawn ended up with two interview opportunities and I had one.

I interviewed for a position as a religion teacher at Althoff Catholic High School, Shawn's high school and his mother's employer. She was a guidance counselor there. They offered the job to a woman who had a theology degree.

The best option became available for Shawn at Masterbrand Cabinets in their finance department. It was a step backward for him from a career equity standpoint because it didn't require a CPA license or a master's degree, both which he had, but he swallowed his pride.

His sacrifice was the greatest gift. I could stay in Jasper, keep my job, my nurse, and live close to my family.

"I get to wake up to a kiss from my best friend—my lifetime love," he said. It's totally worth it," he reassured me.

The night Shawn proposed, he sat at his computer and showed Kelly an Excel spreadsheet for the wedding plans. There were tabs for the budget, honeymoon, order of events, and a list of fifteen groomsmen and bridesmaids. He wanted to be intimately involved in the wedding planning because it was symbolic of starting his life with her. He looked forward to spending time together and growing together through the planning experience.

Shawn scrolled his files and stumbled on his "The One" list, clicked it, and chuckled. He hadn't looked at the list since before he met Kelly, but he knew she possessed every single trait.

She glanced over his shoulder. "What's that?"

He told her about the list.

"I can't believe you did that."

"People were asking me about what kind of girl I was looking for, so I made a list. But look, you have all of these qualities."

"Let me see." She read it over his shoulder. "Not the 'enjoys being active part.' "

"Before the accident you were active. You couldn't sit still."

"True."

He kissed her. "I knew without that list that you were the right one."

She smiled.

Shawn opened a new file and together they compiled a new list, their guest list. An hour later, they had included close to six hundred people.

With her input and extensive discussion, Shawn kept the wedding budget current and tracked expenses. He set up appointments to meet with three priests, the disc jockey, bus driver, hotel reception wedding planner, and wedding musicians. Father Jack from Shawn's hometown parish, Father Gary from Precious Blood, and Father Ted Tempel, the retired priest who'd married Brenda and Andy, would all be at the wedding.

Kelly and Shawn met with Father Ted for the required pre-marriage counseling. Spending time with Father Ted was one of the best parts of the wedding planning. "Most people spend more time planning the wedding than planning their marriage," Father said. "Your main goal is to help each other get to heaven. We can't depend on each other for happiness. That comes from within."

Kelly nodded.

"Have you decided who's going to do which chores?" Father asked.

Shawn exchanged glances with Kelly. "She'll do the shopping, and I'll do the dishes."

Father nodded. "That's a great start."

"I have a high school helper who assists me with grocery shopping, wrapping presents, and putting away laundry. She works as my hands. Plus, my great Aunt Martha Jane will prepare two home-cooked meals for us each week."

"Excellent," Father said.

"And we'll hire a house cleaner," Shawn added.

They talked about money management and Father suggested they keep their money together because it would force them to communicate.

For a man who'd never been married, Father knew a lot about marriages and how to make them work.

When they had time, Shawn and Kelly met with their selected wedding attendants in person—all fifteen guys and girls—to ask them to participate in the wedding. At the rehearsal dinner, Shawn and Kelly shared a written passage about what made each person special to them. Since Kelly had done this for her students each year—wrote them personalized cards and highlighted what she liked about them—she saw how powerful her words could be.

After mutually agreeing to go to Maui for their honeymoon, Shawn made arrangements.

(David Pierini, Photographer)

Chapter Forty-One

And just like that, he picked her up and dusted her off. Without even trying. That's how their love was. When she was at her worst, he saw her at her best.
Author Unknown

September 6, 2009
Jasper, Indiana
Our Wedding Day

The morning of the ceremony, Shawn's sister, Kelly, woke at my house to get ready with the rest of the girls. "I have something for you," she said. "It's from Shawn. I need to pop it in the DVD player."

I showed her to my bedroom and nodded toward the player. Shawn's sister turned on the television, inserted the disk, and placed a necklace box in my lap.

Shawn appeared on the screen. "I wanted to do something different and send you a video instead of writing you a card." He proceeded to list all the things he was thankful for that led him to me. "You are my one and only, Kelly, and after today you and I will become one. As a symbol of that oneness I'm presenting you with this necklace."

His sister opened the necklace case to reveal a thin silver chain with a single pearl pendant at the end.

"Wow, it's beautiful." My eyes filled with tears.

"Do you want me to put it around your neck?"

"Yes, could you?"

She fastened the necklace at the nape of my neck and held up a mirror.

"Thank you. It's perfect."

Shawn ended the video singing Van Halen's song, "Not Enough." He was a self-proclaimed bad singer, but the words were sweet. He was the cutest bad singer I knew.

Before the ceremony began, Shawn waited in the groom's room off to the side of the altar at Precious Blood Church with Andrew and Luke, his co-best men. Blayr's husband, Ryan, entered the side door and handed Shawn a letter from Kelly. Shawn opened it.

Dear Shawn,

I dreamt of you when I was a little girl, a teen, and then an adult. Today that dream will come true, an answered prayer. From the moment I met you, you captured my heart, and I have complete confidence that it's in good hands. I've never felt more protected or loved. I love your hugs, your friendly hellos, our quality conversations, your family, and how you make me a better me. I'm in awe that God placed you in my life. I promise not only to love you in good times and in bad, and in sickness and in health, but in so much more.

I promise…
Not to freak out every time I hear you chew loudly or clank your spoon against the bowl
To politely ask you to roll over when you're snoring
Not to shop until we're broke
To be your best friend
To always put your interests before mine
To enjoy watching UNC play at least half as much as you do
To be a continual learner
To remember we are a team
To make for sure you get a spot in our garage
To recall how I felt about you on this day through the bumpy patches of our marriage
To never buy you black shirts
To always remember the sacrifice you made for us by moving
To be half as organized as you
To encourage and inspire you
To be there for you in laughter and in tears
To honor your goals and dreams
To love you in the only way I know how…completely and forever.
This day and every day, I take you as my husband. I want to have and hold you from this day forward.

Love always and forever,

Kelly

Shawn's heart swelled with excitement and anticipation of the ceremony. Tears filled his eyes. He touched the watch that she'd given him the night before. She'd said, "This is a symbol of our lifetime together." He hoped the symbol would stand the test of time.

He was the most blessed man alive. He tucked the letter into his pants pocket.

Ryan set his hand on Shawn's shoulder, bowed his head, and prayed. "Dear Heavenly Father, bless this man and this marriage. Keep Shawn and Kelly close to you. May they flourish and prosper in their lives together. Amen."

The song, "You Raise Me Up" sounded in the distance, the *mothers'* song, Shawn's signal. His heart knocked. It was time to meet Kelly at the altar. He thanked Ryan, wiped his tears, and took a deep breath, but his heart skittered. The church would be filled.

A knock sounded at the door and the wedding planner entered. She waved for him, Andrew, and Luke to stand at the front of the church. He lifted his shoulders and adjusted his tie and the three of them followed her out the door and lined up at the altar facing the congregation. Almost every seat was taken.

One by one, the bridesmaids strutted down the aisle in an apple green gown and a small crystal drop necklace. Each girl was accompanied by a groomsman and held a bouquet of miniature pink roses, green chrysanthemums, and white and green larger roses. They lined up on the opposite side of the altar and the guys lined up next to Shawn.

And then he saw her. His bride. His stunning bride. No one else mattered. There was only her. Tears trickled down his face. The congregation stood and faced the rear of the church.

Andy walked beside her, but all Shawn saw was Kelly and how radiant she looked. When she joined him at the altar, he took her hand and gave it a light squeeze, then turned to face Father Ted.

When I entered the church and the congregation turned to watch me, I couldn't believe how many people were there, people who'd been there for me since I moved to Jasper, family, old and new friends. Every person mattered.

Father Ted began the Mass. He thanked everyone for coming. "I know that God works in mysterious ways, but I never knew he worked through ESPN."

Everyone laughed. Shawn and I sat side-by-side holding hands at the candle-lit altar and waited for the ceremony to continue. I wanted to slow it down, to remember every detail, to hear every word and feel every emotion.

Father Ted paused to swallow, like he had a wad of tears threatening to block his next words. He'd known me since I was a little girl. He looked out into the congregation and into the eyes of our many friends and family. "The greatest expression of love is to lay down your life for another."

His gaze turned to Shawn and me. "You two have demonstrated that you are people of faith and know that God will always be there for you. With Christ at the center of your marriage, you will have an unshakable bond."

When it was time for us to light the unity candle, the Rascal Flatts' song, "Bless the Broken Road," played, but I couldn't concentrate on the lyrics, only on keeping my hand steady. Then Shawn knelt beside me and we prayed during the song.

Next, we recited our memorized vows. Father made it easy, encouraging us, but he said, "I'm not getting married to you. You're marrying each other, so you need to memorize your vows." Thankfully, Shawn and I didn't stumble over the words.

Blayr's husband, Ryan, gave the reading from the NLT, Proverbs 3:5-6. It was his favorite verse. Today, his eyes shifted from the Bible to Shawn and me, as if we were the only ones in the room. His eyes shone brightly with deep conviction and his sincerity reflected in the way he enunciated the words, "Trust in the Lord with all your heart, do not depend on your own understanding. Seek His will in all you do, and He will show you which path to take." In the years I'd known Ryan, he'd given me sound advice backed with Scripture. This was the best advice he'd ever given me. It was like God was speaking directly to me.

In another part of the Mass, my students sang, "All That We Have," a song we often sang during school Masses. The choir consisted of at least five students from each of the four classes I'd taught. Their little voices rang out without reservation, and I sat a little taller, prouder than a parent. They played a huge role in my life, so having them in our wedding seemed natural and a blessing.

When they got to the line, *love isn't just for a day*, I smiled. I'd talked about this phrase in class, how friends came and went in our lives, but it was those people who stuck around during the good times, and especially the bad, that exemplified love, like the people in the church. Real love was unconditional with no beginning or end. The way God loves us is a love we should aspire to give, and He loves us every day, not only when we ask for it, or when we're at our best.

Hearing my students sing the words now I wondered if they understood their meaning, if they felt my love and God's never-ending love for them. I doubted they understood the magnitude of that line, but at least I'd planted the seed and made them more aware of the words.

At the closing of the Mass, Father Ted raised his hands. "Please welcome Mr. and Mrs. Shawn Schaefer."

The congregation applauded, and Shawn did something amazing, something he'd practiced, something that surprised our friends. He lifted me from my chair, held me in his arms, and kissed me in front of everyone, and then carried me down the altar steps toward our new life together, my chair empty at the altar.

For months, Shawn had lifted weights and panted through push-ups and cardio exercises so he could dance with me in his arms at the reception. We'd practiced at home. He had to lift and hold me a certain way that would allow me to wrap my left arm around his neck. Otherwise, the hold wouldn't work. Today, he held me to his chest in an effortless and natural manner.

(David Pierini, Photographer)

After the ceremony, Jarrad Odle, a former IU basketball player said, "Kelly, you're the only person who's made me cry twice in my life— once after the accident and today at the ceremony."

It was hard to believe that I'd made a man cry twice and that his reasons for crying were totally different.

The wedding reception was held at the French Lick Resort, the perfect destination for my fairytale wedding where guests could spend the night and receive top-notch attention, where they could visit a resort they might not have had the opportunity to experience, and I could be a princess for a day. The hotel was decorated with First Century European elegance, the rooms plush with expensive carpets, linens, and granite countertops.

The dining hall was set up for 542 people. Each chair and table was covered in white linen. Some tables had white tablecloths with little green polka dots. I loved polka dots. They were speckled throughout many of the wedding details. There were green dots on the groomsmen's ties, the ribbons on the bridesmaid's bouquets, and the menu cards.

In another section of the large room was a round table decorated with jars, bowls, and curved vases of red, blue, green, and yellow wrapped candies. My mother-in-law had purchased Skittles, Laffy Taffy, Tootsie Rolls, Hershey Kisses, Tootsie Pops, Starburst, and Jolly Ranchers. (There were no Lemon Heads.) Aunt Shari Krempp arranged the table with the original and bright candy wrappers, and set a sign out that said, *"Thank you for coming and being so sweet. Please fill a bag of our favorite treats. Love, Shawn and Kelly."*

Aunt Melinda had designed and drawn pictures in a spiral bound coloring book, based on a fairytale I'd written about Shawn and me. The books were stacked on part of the table along with bin of crayons. Kids were encouraged to take a book and color the pictures. Many took them as souvenirs.

An artist sat in a corner of the room drawing caricatures of guests who wanted their picture drawn as a memento.

Before dinner, Blayr gave a toast. "When I first heard of Shawn, I thought he was a stalker, but within minutes of talking to him, I realized he was a genuine guy with a huge heart." She raised her glass to toast. "Here's to my best friend on the very best day of her life."

She was right. This was the best day of my life, and it included my wheelchair. I wished the night could go on forever.

Our highly-coveted DJ, Jack Wier, set up his electronics at the front of the wooden dance floor. The Black Eyed Peas song, "I Gotta Feeling" kicked off the reception. People sang along about the up-beat promise to a great night. People danced. Even Jason danced with his walker, his caretaker looking on.

When the song, "Here," by Rascal Flatts, began, Shawn bent in front of me on the edge of the dance floor, his eyes gleaming. "You ready?"

A crackle of energy sparked between us, warm and fresh. I nodded and smiled. This was our song, my time to get lost in the moment.

Friends and family parted and gathered around the perimeter of the wooden floor. Cameras flashed. Time stood still.

Shawn scooped his strong, competent hands beneath me, his fingertips leaving a trail along the wrinkles of my dress. He held me to his chest, his eyes smoldering with adoration. I was his princess, mesmerized. We were the only two in the room. He twirled me in rhythm to the music, paused, swayed, and turned.

The song's lyrics mirrored our path, the road that led him to me. He sang to me, his eyes never leaving mine. Of the millions of paths he could have taken, he took the path that led to me.

"I never thought I'd find you, or feel your love," he said. "I had to go through all those broken hearts to get to you, Kelly, but I found you, and I'd do it all again."

I couldn't take my eyes off him. He was mine. "Thank you for searching. I'm glad you found me." *Thank you God for showing him the way to my heart.*

The room spun not only because of the way Shawn moved with me, but because I was dizzy from his love and the love of our friends and family celebrating with us. I caught a glimpse of them in the fringe of my vision, wet tissues in their palms. *Thank you for these wonderful people too.*

I didn't want the night to end. The song faded. Shawn dipped me and pressed his lips to mine before gently returning me to my chair.

"I can't believe the song is over already," I said.

"We'll have more dances," he said. "This is the first of many."

Our guests applauded and wiped their eyes.

(David Pierini, Photographer)

Father Ted joked that we could've eloped and made a down payment on a house for what the wedding cost, but Andy said the memory was worth every penny, especially when he got to dance with me. He lifted me from my chair like Shawn had, his arms strong too, circling me and holding me with tenderness. The DJ played "Cinderella," by Steven Curtis Chapman.

Perspiration lined Andy's brow as he twirled me. He was the first prince in my life, my hero, and the man who showed me what true love meant. In his love for Mom, he revealed the way a man should treat a woman. He made me a priority, my care and comfort important, and he listened. He listened when others didn't or wouldn't.

The dance was a celebration, something I'd never forget—not only because Andy made me feel special, but because the moment with Andy was symbolic, the way he protected me, listened to me, held me close, and showed me Christ's love. He hadn't dropped me in life or the dance.

The next day, we opened gifts at my parent's house with Shawn's family. We were tired, but it was nice to open the gifts together. When Shawn and I registered, we chose practical and easy appliances, items my high school helper needed or a cleaning lady could use. We were all about keeping household chores simple. After the gift opening, we headed to St. Louis where we'd depart the next morning for our honeymoon.

We honeymooned in Hawaii for eight days and brought Karla, my nurse, and her husband. Karla took care of my showers and bathroom routine. Each day, Shawn and I ate brunch by the poolside, relaxed in the sun, and in the afternoon Karla showered me and dressed me for the evening. I wanted to look beautiful every night for dinner. It was an unforgettable time together in paradise.

Two months after the wedding, our house was ready to move into—a house that fit all my needs. It had an open shower, an automatic door donated by Andy's friend (the one who gave us my first one—I was more appreciative this time), and a sidewalk that led from the front of the house to the back porch, where I loved sitting in the sun. There were many things I didn't like about being an adult, but living on our own was not one of them.

Shawn carried me across the threshold and the first piece of artwork he hung was one of my framed pineapple drawings.

"Where should I put it?" he asked.

I searched for the perfect place. "Over the kitchen sink, where everyone who enters can see." I cocked my head. "It'll be a reminder from God that I should welcome what He gives me because I don't know where it will lead. It could be sweeter than I imagined."

And it was.

Chapter Forty-Two

Nobody said life would be easy; they just said it would be worth it.
Unknown

Our first fight was about nuts.

Shawn and I were in the grocery store, filling our cart with extra groceries for company. Ten of his family members were coming into town for Shawn's birthday and his mother's birthday. We were a little on edge. He wanted everything to be perfect.

In the snack aisle, he reached for a large can of cocktail peanuts.

"We already have nuts," I said. "We don't need more."

He tilted his head and furrowed his brows. "You don't get it. We're having a party for a lot of people, and they might like peanuts, not *mixed* nuts like those at home." His voice was forced and louder than usual.

I turned to wheel away, my face heated.

"We can't expect them to pick out the nuts they don't like, can we?" he called after me.

I paused and turned to him. "Think about how silly you sound." Embarrassed that he might raise his voice another notch, I said, "I'll meet you at the checkout."

We drove home in silence.

Hours later, he apologized.

Days later, we laughed about how dumb it was to fight over nuts, but weren't most marital disagreements over silly things?

One thing we never disagreed about was having a family; we both wanted one, and I knew he'd make the best dad. My whole life I wanted to be a stay-at-home mom with five children. That didn't change after I married Shawn. I wanted to look at my child's face and see Shawn's doe eyes and his mannerisms—the way he smiled, the curve of his chin, his crooked toes—all of him. And yes, I wanted to see me too—the girl I once was, the girl I wanted to be, the one I missed, to live vicariously through my child.

But the more I researched the possibility of conceiving a child, the more frightened I became. Yes, scientifically, I could get pregnant. I had all the female parts and cycles. The doctors we consulted gave us a green light. Family and friends threw concerns at us, and I wanted to prove them all wrong. I'd show them.

But this wasn't only about my life.

If I conceived, then what? Could I carry the baby to term, and if the child was born and had severe disabilities, how would Shawn cope? There were too many risks—risks to me and the baby, risks to Shawn. I couldn't jeopardize that.

I cried. I grieved for what might have been. I cursed the drunk driver and how far his deed continued to reach into my life. I cried in Shawn's arms. He held me, smoothed the back of my head, and tears filled his eyes too.

When our tears dried, I lifted my cross again, but this time I had help, Shawn's help. He showed me the adoption route and how great the need was in our country and other countries for parents.

I put my desires aside to do what Jesus would do.

When we researched international adoptions, we were drawn to the Congo.

It's been named the worst place on earth to be a woman. There are an estimated five million orphans in the Democratic Republic of the Congo (DRC). (The population of Missouri is six million.) The average yearly income of a Congolese citizen is one hundred twenty US dollars.

Life expectancy is fifty-one years. Twenty percent of their population doesn't live past five years old—one in five people die in childhood. Almost half of the children don't have access to school or a means to obtain an education. War and conflict have led to the death of 5.4 million people since 1998, the deadliest war since World War II.

The statistics broke our hearts and the decision was made. We pursued a Congolese adoption. We also liked that, unlike other countries, we both didn't have to travel; we could hire an escort to get the children, adopt two at a time, and the process would only take ten to twelve months.

After months of paper work, home studies, medical evaluations, counseling sessions with adoption agencies, and appointments with an adoption attorney, in July of 2012, two children were referred to us.

Sam was three months old and Emmy was six weeks old. We were ecstatic.

We bought cribs and bedding, tiny shoes and onesies, decorated their rooms, and framed and hung their pictures above their beds. We organized a fundraiser for their village to tell our friends and family about the adoption and make people aware of the needs in Africa.

Mudlove, a bracelet company in Warsaw, Indiana, that donates proceeds from their sales for food and water to Africa, designed two hundred bracelets with an adjustable elastic band and the word *Africa* across the front. They cost us $3.00 each, and we sold them for $5.00. With the proceeds, we bought Lifestraws and sent them to the village where Sam and Emmy live. Lifestraws are used to purify water in lakes and rivers and can purify mud.

Since our referral, the country's laws have changed and are out of our control. Our children have grown in Africa and no longer need cribs. Through prayer, we wait, determined to act upon our call to adopt. There are times when our three-year wait has gotten the best of us, but we trust God's timing. He's bigger than the Congolese government who has placed an indefinite suspension on adoption. We can't give up because we're frustrated.

There are twin beds in their rooms now, with updated photos above their beds. This marathon called adoption has been the longest gestational period a woman could ever have, but we're hopeful. I've learned, through Shawn and the good things he's brought to my life, that patience is rewarded.

Shawn remains hopeful that Sam and Emmy will come home soon too. He says, "The transition will be crazy for all of us. In the blink of their little eyes, their world will look, sound, taste, and feel different. They'll experience a loss that we may never comprehend.

"There will be months and maybe years of adjustments, challenges, and hardships that we can't possibly understand at this point. Yet, we're ready to open our arms, let our world turn upside down with the chaos.

"No matter how God delivers a child to be entrusted in our care, we'll do the best we can do. Like Father Ted says, 'If God has brought you to it, then He will see you through it.'"

I have confidence and faith that God will hold my hand through more good times and bad.

A few years after Shawn took the job with the cabinet company, he decided to go back to school to get his teaching degree. He wanted to do more good in the world. Sitting behind an accounting desk wouldn't accomplish that. Now, he teaches high school math, a subject most teachers shrink from. He wanted to influence the lives of children, and he is. His students respect him and so do I.

I don't know how my story will end, but my wish is to grow old with Shawn.

It used to be that my greatest fear was never walking again. Now, my greatest fear is losing Shawn. I'd miss his compassion and his heart. He's the only one who gets me, the only one I can ask to do something for me and he never argues or seems annoyed, and many times he anticipates my needs before I ask. He just knows. He gets me breakfast every morning and once a week brings me a special treat like a donut from the local bakery. He places my blanket in the dryer every night before he transfers me to bed.

He says, "You didn't ask for this situation, Kelly, but I knew what I was getting into before I married you."

I love my life!

A Note from Kelly

Miracles come in many obscure moments. I've spent most of my life awaiting my big break.

I expected my miracle to be in the form of a pill, injection, or surgery, which would enable my spine to heal and give me the mobile freedom I've been praying for. But that didn't happen. Jenna sent me an engagement congratulations card with a verse from Kristen Jongen, someone I didn't know, but I loved her words: *My miracle came unannounced and in an odd package. It looked different than what I imagined—untimely, unexpected, unpretentious—yet it fit perfectly. Divinely constructed solely for me.* It was like she'd written the words especially for me.

Thank you for reading my story. If my book inspired you, and you know of someone whose life has been *fractured* and could benefit from reading my memoir, will you recommend my book to them?

We all go through scene changes in our lives that leave us feeling lost and distraught, but our Heavenly Director says, *the show must go on.* He will take your fractured pieces and fill in the cracks with what *you* need to feel complete, so you can play the role you were meant to play. The role might not be glamorous or easy, but your role is essential to the show.

Many people think that I play the part God picked for me really well. Most days that's true while other days I am merely a great actress hiding my feelings. The truth is...I still mourn for the old me every day.

As if being punched in the gut, I'm hit daily with inescapable reminders of what I miss about being able-bodied. Frequently, my breath is taken away and tears fill my eyes when I write my weekly checks to those who help me. Some go to Karla, my nurse, my after school helper, and the teacher who helps me with my bathroom at school. When I have to ask others to drive me places, when I order my medical supplies that most thirty-five-year-olds aren't ordering, and when I see a mess and can't clean it up, I'm reminded of my loss. I'm reminded of how physically, emotionally, and financially uncomplicated my life used to be when I'm in pain and it consumes me, when I take a vacation and my injury comes with me, and when my favorite song plays and I can't dance. I want to rub Shawn's back when it hurts, tie a child's shoes when she asks, and participate in a sport when all I can do is watch.

Then I remember what Renée Bondi said. "Look heavenward when your thoughts go to those negative places. You have Jesus and that's all that matters. His kingdom is where the real prize lies."

Each day, I try to look upward and am challenged to listen to Him and what He expects of me. I know that I'm not the only one who suffers from pain, frustration, and disappointment. It's a daily battle for many people to cope with challenges. Isn't that life? Everyone has something they struggle from.

Some days you feel like you can overcome anything, and other days you're consumed with your shortcomings. Am I right?

Personally, I don't believe that anyone ever reaches a point where they've made it with no more tears, pain, sadness, or struggle. That is part of being human.

One of my favorite parts of the Bible is where Jesus shows his human side. Even when He was about to perform his greatest act of dying for our salvation, He turned heavenward and asked God to take his suffering away, *but only if* it was God's Will. So therefore, I will pray for a miracle for God to take my ailments away, but if this is God's way to use me best, who am I to argue? I must play the role I was meant to play.

My prayer is that you too will embrace your role and shine brightly.

Thank you for reading,
Kelly Schaefer

THE END

Follow me at my Facebook page, Kelly Craig Schaefer. (https://www.facebook.com/KellyCraigSchaefer) I look forward to hearing from you.

If you'd like to watch the You Tube video of our wedding, please visit this link: http://tinyurl.com/KellyShawnWedding or scan the QR code below.

Letters and Notes

If you live to be 100, I hope I live to be 100 minus one day, so I never have to live a day without you.
Winnie the Pooh

March 2015
Love Letters

Dear Shawn,

I love the way you eat your least favorite food first, saving the best for last; the way you set aside time to watch *The Bachelor* with me; the way you bite your knuckle when you're working at your desk, your eyes pasted to the computer screen, your brain deep in thought; the way you eat a bowl of cereal and drink chocolate milk in a frosted glass in the evenings; the way you cope quietly, alone with the grind of your thoughts; the way you stock the refrigerator with Mountain Dew, 100% Cran-Grape juice, Propel and Arnold Palmer drinks; the way you love to read self-help books but rarely finish them; the way you transform your hair from limp and dull, to trendy and exciting; the way you plan so far in advance that our Christmas cards have to be ordered by Halloween; the way you talk slowly and carefully trying not to say the words *um* or *like*. I love your laugh, your little butt, and your soft lips.

But most of all Shawn, I love the way that God formed your heart. You choose the right path despite its difficulties, you choose to be kind, and choose others over yourself. Along with Christ, you are my moral compass. What would Shawn do? You challenge me daily to be the best Kelly I can be. Thank you for continually loving me, even when I'm not loving.

When July 10 arrives each summer, I'm not sad because that was the day that led me to you. I will mourn for John and Jason, and for my loss, but I'm in awe of the gain. I would have never met you if it hadn't been for the accident.

You're the best thing that happened to me. Thank you for being you and for choosing me to be yours.

Love you,
Kelly Ann

My Dearest Kelly,

You are my beautiful wife, my teammate, my little jub-jub, my groundhog, and my lifetime love. Like these different names, you fulfill many meanings in my life.

I love our simple time together—going to sleep and waking next to you, holding you close each night, sharing prayers with you, receiving kisses from you, and sharing your life journey. I wouldn't trade my front row seat in your life for anything.

I love how we complement one another as we shine in different areas and help each other become a better person. I love your positive energy and how you make light of your daily challenges.

I love how supportive you are of the things that matter to me. The way you sprinkle your creativity throughout our home and make it an inviting place.

I love how children are drawn to you and change for the better from your influence. I love that this is the beginning of more.

I love that you are mine.

Our paths wouldn't have crossed if not for that horrific accident. I'm sorry for the daily hardships you and your brother face because of the drunk driver. I would like to take the cross from you and carry it, but since that isn't possible, I will help you lift it the best way I know how.

I don't understand why this was God's plan for you, but I also can't imagine my life without you. For this reason, I selfishly pray that God calls me home before you because I'm not sure I'm strong enough to carry on without you.

It's not healthy to live one's life consumed with proving doubters wrong—it's not a meaningful purpose—but it's satisfying to see that you have continually beat the odds, especially when they were stacked against you. Maybe it's your competitive nature, or maybe it's the strength you gain from an unwavering belief in God and yourself, but you consistently rise above, and I love that about you.

Doubters questioned whether you'd go back to college. You did. They questioned whether you'd graduate. You did. They questioned whether you'd teach in a classroom. You are. You're a show-stopping, life-changing, and inspiring teacher.

Then they questioned whether you could handle a marriage if it knocked on your door. Now, six years later, you've shown them you are the best wife any husband could ask for. If doubters are uncertain if you have what it takes to be a mother, they don't know you well. When Sam and Emmy come home, others will see what I've known a long time—you're the best mother a child could ask for!

I've admired you on the ESPN video, when we first met, when we exchanged vows, and all the times in between. I hope my actions reflect how I cherish you. There is no greater honor than to be called your husband. You have my biggest gift—my heart.

Everything you are and everything you do is extraordinary. Your outer beauty is second to none, but the inner beauty is the magical part. It's the kind of magic that can't be touched but continually leaves me in wonder and awe.

Our love is a miracle. That's the only way I can explain it. God sent you to me to change my life, and to show me that love, real love, makes all the difference. You are God's greatest miracle in my life. They say that "love can move mountains," but before I met you, I didn't know what that meant. Now, I would say that's an understatement... perhaps it should be "mountain ranges."

It's your love that helped me grow stronger in my love for Jesus Christ. And it is the love found in our marriage with Christ at the center that makes each day a new gift to be unwrapped. It is an intimate, devoted, enduring, and everlasting love. And for those reasons, it is true that love conquers all. I find myself falling more in love with you each day. And I can't wait to love you more.

Love Always ~
Shaun-Patrick

A Note from Ted

Ted, my youngest brother, was six at the time of my accident. Today, he's a senior at Indiana University in the Kelley School of Business.

Kelly,

Our lawn mower has been through rough times in our family. Tyler got it stuck in our pool area where it never should have been; Mom rammed it into a parked car and when she backed away, she had it in drive instead of reverse, and hit the parked car again. I had the tractor on cruise control when I accidentally ran over Dad's newly planted apple tree, gashing the limb.

Dad did what he could to save the tree. He sealed the wound with black paint, but I didn't think it would survive.

Beyond all odds, the tree survived and a couple years later, it was the first of four trees to produce an apple.

Kelly, you're like that tree. Although that apple tree was cut and near dead, it came back from its injuries and surprised everyone with producing the first fruit. Like the tree, you were wounded, but your resilience and strength gave you the ability to power through all odds, to deliver the sweetest fruit by becoming a teacher and mentor to children.

Your examples of strength, resilience, and a never-give-up attitude are characteristics I've tried to apply to my life when faced with challenges that aren't nearly half as demanding as yours.

Your determination to suppress your doubts about your abilities and to know your strengths and weaknesses maximized your potential and made an impact in my life.

I used to wonder, how is she going to go to college? How is she going to be a teacher? How is she going to get hired? How is she going to open a book to the right page for her students?

Yet, you did it. You were able to fulfill your dreams and squelch my questions. Now, years later when you talk about adopting two children from Congo, I don't doubt that you have the ability, the strength, and the resilience to be the best mother you can be.

I won't doubt you again.

Ted

Jason Update

Jason continues to need 24-hour care, unable to carry out the simplest tasks such as eating with a fork or writing with a pen. He's embarrassed when people stare at him and when they assume he doesn't understand everything around him, but he does understand. If they knew what he's been through, and how far he's come, those stares would be handshakes and smiles rather than stares.

He lives in an apartment in Bloomington near Indiana University because there are more opportunities for entertainment, and he likes to feel like he's a part of a college experience by living near a college campus. Because he suffered a brain injury, Medicaid pays for help from an organization that's based out of Bloomington. Jason's caretaker drives him to a gym almost every day where he lifts weights.

He wants to be like everyone else—to feel normal, live independently, and have a family. In addition, he wants to contribute to society, to work and have purpose, but his limitations—short-term memory loss, slow dialogue, inability to move quickly, and lack of fine motor skills—don't allow him to function in a job.

Please pray for him to find reasons to smile and for ways he can achieve his simple goals.

(Robert McCarty Photography)

Kelly Craig Schaefer
Speaker/Teacher/Author

Kelly's story was featured on ESPN and in the Rosie Magazine.

In 1998, she won awards in the National Cheerleading competitions and was a cheerleader for the Indiana University Hoosiers, but in 1999, when a drunk driver rendered her a quadriplegic, she lost all her athletic ability.

She has traveled to hundreds of Midwest schools to share her story, demonstrating how the human spirit, combined with personal faith and the support of loved ones, can overcome challenges and enable others to succeed beyond their wildest imagination.

Below are a few of the topics Kelly has spoken about, but her presentations can be geared toward the needs and demographics of your community.

- Change

- Consequences of drinking and driving
- Faith
- Recognizing the Silver Lining
- Maximizing Opportunities

While audiences differ in demographics, they all share a desire to be inspired, to learn, and to be motivated. Kelly is blessed that her story can help others. If any of the topics resonate with your organization's needs, please contact her about a speaking engagement. She will accommodate your requests as her schedule permits.

Kelly Craig Schaefer
To schedule a speaking event contact her at:
KellyandShawnSchaefer@gmail.com

Endorsements:

When Kelly came to our school to talk to us, she changed the way me and many of my friends look at drugs and alcohol. When I get up and brush my teeth or do my own makeup, I think about how she can't do that because of one drunk driver's mistake. I wouldn't want to hurt someone just because I got behind the wheel after having a couple drinks so I'll forever stay drug and alcohol free because of Kelly and her speech.
~Jessica, a middle school student

I'm thankful that Kelly has the courage to share her story with others. She has seriously touched my life. I wish she could come back every month so she could keep reminding others about her tragic story. Because I know Kelly can't realistically come back every month, she has motivated me to become an advocator and to speak out about the dangers of drunk driving.
~Sarah, a high school student

When I saw Kelly's poster advertising her speech, I knew it was something I needed to attend. I needed a wake-up call. Before Kelly's speech, I was making irresponsible decisions like driving while intoxicated. I needed a wake-up call and that is exactly what Kelly's speech did for me. After hearing her story and everything she goes through, I don't want to do that to anyone or myself. Thank you Kelly for putting my life in perspective!

~Dave, a college student

Kelly is a true hero to me. Her courage, attitude, and message are awesome. True heroism is hard to find, but Kelly proves every day that she is deserving of the title.

~Elaine Brown, Judge

Kelly's message is personal and powerful. Her life after the accident is a strong testimony that needs to be shared with people of all ages. Kelly speaks with candor infused with humor, and she really connects with her audience. I'm so glad my daughter heard firsthand how dangerous drunk driving really is.

~Karen, Parent

Acknowledgments

To Mom and Andy. You taught me how to live with strength. Thank you for always moving forward and never looking back.

To my mister. You make my story seem fictional, and each day when I wake up next to you, I can't believe you are real. I love you. Thank you for your unwavering love and support.

To my in-laws. You have raised an unbelievable man. Thank you for your continued support and loving me as one of your own.

To the Author of Life. Without you, there would be no story. Thank you for giving me a second chance and for putting all of the right people in my life to help support me.

To my students. Thank you for giving me purpose and filling me with pride.

To my first principal, Mr. Schneiders. I have been a teacher for ten years because of you. Thank you for seeing my potential.

To my brothers. You made me tough. Please continue.

To my nurse, Karla. Your presence every morning enables me to be a teacher and a wife who is looking good and feeling good. You are irreplaceable.

To my friends. Thank you for appreciating me and what I have to offer (by that, I don't mean my amazing parking spaces at the mall).

To my favorite writer who happens to be my aunt. Thank you for handling my story with great care. You have a gift, and it's been a privilege working with you.

To all those who prayed. You are too many to name, but your kindness has carried me and my family through the fiercest storm. Thank you.